JOHNNY EVERS

Johnny Evers

A Baseball Life

Dennis Snelling

McFarland & Company, Inc., Publishers
Jefferson, North Carolina

LIBRARY OF CONGRESS CATALOGUING-IN-PUBLICATION DATA

Snelling, Dennis, 1958–
    Johnny Evers : a baseball life / Dennis Snelling.
        p.   cm.
    Includes bibliographical references and index.

    ISBN 978-0-7864-7591-9 (softcover : acid free paper) ∞
    ISBN 978-1-4766-1520-2 (ebook)

    1. Evers, Johnny.   2. Baseball players—United States—Biography.
    I. Title.
    GV865.E87S64 2014
    796.357092—dc23
    [B]   2014010660

BRITISH LIBRARY CATALOGUING DATA ARE AVAILABLE

On the cover: Johnny Evers in 1909, at the height of his fame and
physical ability, just a few months after the Cubs captured their third
straight National League pennant and second consecutive World Series.
(National Baseball Hall of Fame Library—Cooperstown, New York.)

Printed in the United States of America

*McFarland & Company, Inc., Publishers
    Box 611, Jefferson, North Carolina 28640
    www.mcfarlandpub.com*

Table of Contents

When things go wrong it is my nature to kick. I may be wrong nine times out of ten, perhaps I am, but I can't stand it to see things going bad, and I have to say something about it. Personally, I try to be a human being. Perhaps I don't always succeed, but I aim to.
—Johnny Evers

You only find a man of his natural ability and brains about once in ten years.
—John McGraw, when asked about Johnny Evers in 1914

Johnny Evers cannot keep a watch going because his body is so full of electricity. This may sound ridiculous on the face of it, but it is absolutely true. Evers has been presented with several fine watches and they will not keep accurate time when he carries them because of something in his physical makeup which prevents every timepiece from doing its job properly.
—Christy Mathewson

Johnny is all right, but he is an awful crab.
—umpire Billy Evans

Evers with his brains taught me more baseball than I ever dreamed about. He was psychic. He could sense where a player was going to hit if the pitcher threw the ball where he was supposed to.
—Rabbit Maranville

I don't know what I can do with him. I don't think he is civilized.
—National League president John Tener, exasperated by Evers's repeated ejections by umpires

It's all right to say, "Be a good loser," but I'd like to see one. It's like a painted face; it don't reach very deep.
—Johnny Evers

Preface

History has rendered Joe Tinker, Johnny Evers and Frank Chance insep-
arable, forever intertwined. Rather than this being attributed to their incredible success and long tenure as an infield unit, their joint fame is most often
tied to eight lines of verse dashed off during the summer of 1910 by a prominent
New York newspaper columnist—simple doggerel that took on a life of its
own. However, the three men were very different from each other, even as
they were collectively responsible for the ascendancy of one of baseball's all-
time great franchises. It is unfortunate that Evers, a singular personality and
a unique talent, has been unable to break free from the reputation of his teammates. When he is remembered individually, it is for his legendary battles with
umpires, his playing for the "Miracle Braves," or, most often, the Merkle Play—
the ultimate example of heads-up baseball that stole a pennant from the New
York Giants in 1908.

But Johnny Evers was more than that. During the first two decades of
the 1900s, when people spoke of the best second basemen of that era, three
men were almost always mentioned; Napoleon Lajoie, Eddie Collins and
Johnny Evers. He spent a decade battling John McGraw for National League
pennants—one or the other captured every league title between 1904 and
1914, save one, and McGraw regarded Evers as a genius on the diamond who
made those around him play better, whether they wanted to or not. When it
came to the Cubs, and later the Braves, it was Evers whom McGraw feared
most.

What has been forgotten about Johnny Evers, the lifetime .270 hitter
awarded a plaque in Cooperstown, is that he changed the way second base
was played, literally writing the book on the position. He developed the snap
throw and the one-handed sweep tag when these techniques were unknown

or rarely employed. He was scientific in his approach, working out calculations to give his team an edge in every conceivable situation.

While loved by neither teammates nor opponents, he served as captain, and chief enforcer, of the best defensive team of his era, and was an energetic and exciting key player for a team that enjoyed the most successful five-year regular season run of any major league baseball team—and he was a member of the last two Chicago Cubs World Series champions, more than a century ago.

One of the toughest players of his era to strike out, he could do a little of everything with the bat, even display surprising pop on occasion. He was an excellent base stealer and bunter, and a clutch hitter. His statistics may not appear impressive at first glance, but look closer. In his time as an everyday player (all but two injury-plagued seasons between 1903 and 1915), he outhit the league average by thirty points—.283 to .253.

He won a Most Valuable Player Award in 1914, and might have captured another in 1908 had there been such a prize—battling Honus Wagner, Mike Donlin and Christy Mathewson for the honor. He definitely would have won the Rookie of the Year Award had there been one in 1903, Comeback Player of the Year in 1912, and most likely a few Gold Gloves as well—certainly in 1914 and the seasons in which he registered five hundred or more assists, and likely several more for his role in positioning the defense of the best team in baseball at the time.

Evers was a winner, a member of five regular season champions and three World Series victors; in twenty World Series games he was a lifetime .316 hitter and stole eight bases. In his final fourteen Series contests, he only lost once. During his fifteen full big league seasons, his teams never finished lower than third place.

He was famous for his run-ins with umpires—and infamous for his being quoted that the best umpire was "a dead one." He was wired for competition, with a short fuse when it came to losing. Baseball was his reason for existence.

While he courted the press and remained in the public eye all his life, Johnny Evers rarely revealed his feelings about anything besides baseball. In many ways he led a tragic and frustrated life, marred by a somewhat distant relationship with his son and a mostly off-again marriage to his wife—a rocky union that slowly disintegrated following the death of his young daughter, a fracture that widened due to his long absences and obsession with the sport that made him famous. His business failures did not help. Johnny Evers's off-the-field battles were met with the same competitive fire and conviction as his battles on the field.

You will not find within these pages a debate about whether or not Johnny Evers deserves to be in the Hall of Fame—he is in, and no amount of statistical analysis will change that. There is no one alive today who saw him play. Nor is there film of him in his prime so we could judge for ourselves.

You will find within these pages an attempt to clarify events and correct some fallacies about Evers that have been published over the years—some perpetuated by Evers himself, who in the tradition of many baseball players exaggerated the truth at times, or sometimes confused his facts. There is no contemporary evidence, for instance, that he was pulled from the stands to play his first game for Troy in the New York State League, or that the Cubs threatened to strike if he was put into the lineup when he arrived there as a rookie. Or that Frank Selee tried to get rid of him four times during his first spring training with the Cubs.

It was famously said that he read the rulebook every night before he went to sleep, but in his first public speech in 1910, he indicated exactly the opposite, admitting that most of his plays came to him instinctively. He definitely knew the rules of baseball, but nine seasons into his career had not memorized them.

Much has been written about his marriage ending shortly after his daughter's death in 1914, and about how he and his wife never spoke again. Yet Evers's wife and son accompanied him to spring training on several occasions after that, and both joined him on the Chicago White Sox trip to Europe in October 1924. Census records show them living together as late as 1925.

Many accounts of Evers's life have him missing much of the 1911 season because of an automobile accident that claimed the life of his best friend. Evers himself stated a couple of years after the accident that he was a nervous wreck after the incident and could not bring himself to play for several weeks. But the accident actually occurred in 1910 and he missed eight games. He did suffer a nervous breakdown shortly after the 1911 season began that cost him nearly three-fourths of the year.

Evers's feud with Joe Tinker has been characterized as lasting anywhere from two to thirty years depending on the source, and Evers often referred to an injury caused by Tinker that never happened as the source for his animus toward his double-play partner. The truth is that the men had a complicated relationship defined by rivalry and competition, and they later fell into a camaraderie few outside can understand, but common to those with a shared history.

There are of course other myths—that he only weighed ninety-five pounds when he arrived in Chicago as a rookie; that he could never wear watches because he had too much electricity in his system. And his versions of the Merkle incident employed increased dramatic license over the years.

This is not to say that Evers willingly obfuscated—memories are sketchy sometimes, and sometimes we all remember things the way we wish they were.

The life of Johnny Evers is a fascinating story of a fascinating individual, a talented athlete who shaped and influenced baseball in more ways than he is usually given credit for. It is also the story of an ultimate competitor—a genius on the diamond when he was second in command, but someone who could never get out of his own way when he was in charge.

Johnny Evers lived for baseball and gave back more than he received, a true ambassador for the game after he achieved his measure of fame. He was never forgotten during his time, and he remained passionate about, and in touch with, the game to the end. He was "The Crab," "The Trojan," "Jawn Evers." While not the equivalent in terms of talent, he was definitely the National League's competitive counterpart to Ty Cobb.

A book like this is never completed without help from many people. Jim Norby was always a source of encouragement and read the entire first draft of the manuscript, offering helpful suggestions along the way. Tim Wiles of the National Baseball Hall of Fame in Cooperstown, New York, shared his research on "Baseball's Sad Lexicon," the poem by Franklin P. Adams that forever joined Evers to Tinker and Chance; he also provided copies of the Evers newspaper clipping file. John Horne, also of the Baseball Hall of Fame, was always quick to respond to photo requests. George Rugg at the Hesburgh Library at the University of Notre Dame was especially helpful in navigating the small collection of Evers items housed there. Sara Weber, of the same institution, was always quick to respond to my requests.

Robert Warrington graciously provided a photo from his collection depicting Evers and Pat Moran, taken shortly after Evers joined the Philadelphia Phillies at the end of his playing career. Jeff Thomas and the staff of the San Francisco Library and San Francisco History Room were especially helpful in locating photographs of Evers. The staff at the Cleveland Public Library were quick to respond to my requests.

And as always, I have to thank my patient family, who put up with their husband and father buried in newspaper articles, trolling books of statistics, and filling wastebaskets with paper that had been sacrificed to the editing process. To them, I am eternally grateful—I could never accomplish this without their love and support.

CHAPTER ONE

The Kid from the Collar City

Thirteen old men gathered at Boston's Somerset Hotel on May 31, 1951, the eve of the National League's Diamond Jubilee, which was to be commemorated the next afternoon at Braves Field.[1] The hearty laughter and grandiose boasting quickly betrayed them as former baseball players, and further, that they enjoyed a special bond. This was not the first gathering of the surviving members of the celebrated 1914 Boston Braves; these heroes of the New England sports scene had reunited several times, most notably during the 1948 World Series when Boston represented the National League in the Fall Classic for only the second time.

As these aging comrades swapped stories, decried the lively ball, and remembered those having departed both recently and long ago, they could not help but look at each other and recognize that their time together was growing short. They marveled at eighty-four-year-old Cy Young, a recent attendee of the American League's Golden Jubilee. Between puffs on his cigar, Hank Gowdy noted the higher salaries of the modern player and good-naturedly moaned, "We were all too early," an observation with which no one in the room would disagree. Rabbit Maranville offered a toast to the memory of George Stallings, the manager who had unapologetically bullied his players to the most unlikely of championships.

A year earlier, sportswriters had formally designated the Boston Braves' championship in 1914 as the greatest sports upset during the first half of the twentieth century, and the vote was not close.[2] Fame is indeed an elusive mistress, but these men, with their thinning hair, dimming eyes, and softening physiques, had captured their measure of immortality, forever connected to one of the greatest stories in the history of team sports. They also knew that their obituaries would note above all else that they had been members of the team that had battled from last place on July 4 to win the National League pennant. The team whose mention became a rallying cry for those facing seemingly impossible odds. The team that became the object lesson for those who ever thought about giving up. The team that would forever be known as the "Miracle Braves."

Among those missing from the celebration was a man whose drive and talent played a central role in the unprecedented achievement responsible for their collective fame; a man from Troy, New York—by way of the Chicago Cubs—who was already a star by the time he joined Boston in the spring of 1914. He was the Braves' team captain that year, as well as unofficial co-manager, and even in death managed to cast a long shadow over the reunion despite his passing some four years earlier—eleven months after he had been elected to the Baseball Hall of Fame. As a teammate he had not been loved, but in later years he became more admired and respected than he had been resented. Some even became his close friends. But whether you liked him or not, you never forgot the experience of sharing a baseball diamond with Johnny Evers.

In the late 1800s, Troy, New York, sat (and of course still sits) at the base of a bluff that slopes to the east bank of the Hudson River in upstate New York, nearly equidistant from New York City (150 miles) and Boston (175 miles). The town is situated on land originally settled by Mohican Indians, a site the local tribes sold to the Dutch in the 1600s. Although the property subsequently passed into British hands, the richest and most influential family in the region remained the Van Rensselaer family, descendants of one of the founders of the Dutch East India Company. As the village flourished following the American Revolution, its citizens voted to name the town after the ancient city in Homer's *Iliad*. Today it is interconnected geographically and socially with nearby Albany and Schenectady, the three towns anchoring what is called "The Capital District." Often referred to as "The Collar City" because of its long history in shirt-making—most famously the Arrow brand of Cluett Peabody and Company—Troy was also one of the largest cities in the state of New York in the 1800s and second nationally only to Pittsburgh in steel production. Money poured into Troy, and its eclectic mix of nineteenth-century architecture—shaped in no small part by major fires that twice swept the heart of the city—remains largely preserved today.

Buoyed by its location across the Hudson from the terminus of the Erie Canal, Troy was one of the nation's most prosperous communities throughout the 1800s, boasting a high standard of living thanks to its proximity to a major waterway and a manufacturing base ready-made to serve a rapidly expanding country. It was also home to the Rensselaer Polytechnic Institute, a private research university founded in 1824 that survives as the oldest school of its kind in the English-speaking world. Founded by Stephen Van Rensselaer, who served as New York's lieutenant governor and became one of the richest men in the history of the United States, the university, which granted the country's first civil engineering degrees, remains an important institution even as it approaches its two hundredth anniversary.

While there was considerable money to be made in the Capital Region of New York, there also existed a considerable divide between the "haves" and the "have-nots," the latter often living crowded together in row houses. As a result, Troy was a union hotbed and its textile mills gave rise to the first all-woman union in the country. The city reached its peak population of more than 75,000 following the incorporation of Lansingburgh shortly after the turn of the twentieth century, and it garnered a reputation for illicit activities and a rough blue-collar mentality that sometimes manifested itself in vice and violence. In short, Troy had a little bit of everything.

Troy was also a baseball town—for several years it was a *major league* baseball town, with franchises in both the National Association and its successor, the National League. While many Americans of the time frowned upon baseball as a profession, considering it a pastime for ruffians and the uneducated, the Irish and Germans who flocked to the factory towns in the United States, such as Troy, embraced the game and excelled at it.

The area's first serious baseball club was formed in Lansingburgh in 1860, and by the end of the decade the Haymakers, as they were called, were competing against some of the top nines in the country, including the Brooklyn Eckfords and the New York Mutuals. The team even challenged baseball's first openly professional team, the Cincinnati Red Stockings, twice losing to the undefeated barnstorming squad in very competitive games.

The Haymakers asked for and received another shot at Cincinnati, a three-game series on the Red Stockings' home grounds in late August 1869. Ten thousand fans were on hand while another one thousand remained in Troy, awaiting play-by-play results of the action relayed via telegraph wire. The first game of the highly anticipated series was played on August 26; the Haymakers jumped out to a 6–0 lead, but Cincinnati rallied to tie the score, 17–17, after five innings. In the top of the sixth, Cincinnati's Cal McVey struck a ball into foul territory near home plate. The ball was fielded by Haymakers catcher Bill Craver, who threw to first for an apparent out under the rules of the time, but the umpire ruled McVey was not out and that the at bat was to continue. Haymakers team president James McKeon, angered by what had

One of the first openly professional baseball clubs, the Lansingburgh/Troy Haymakers played the legendary—and up to that point undefeated—Cincinnati Red Stockings to a 17–17 tie through six innings on August 26, 1869, before walking off the field following an adverse ruling by an umpire. Star catcher Bill Craver is seated at the far left of the front row, while Steve Bellan, the first Latin to play major league baseball, is standing at the far right of the back row. Seated L to R: Bill Craver, Marshall King, William "Cherokee" Fisher, Charley Bearman, Bub McAtee. Standing L to R: Mike Powers, William "Clipper" Flynn, Steve King, Steve Bellan. (National Baseball Hall of Fame Library—Cooperstown, New York.)

been in his view several questionable calls by the umpire, immediately ordered his men to pack up their bats and vacate the premises. The umpire forfeited the contest to Cincinnati, and the Red Stockings refused to play the remainder of the series against the Haymakers, who beat a hasty retreat to Troy during the night. The Red Stockings also refused to meet the Haymakers later in the year during a visit to the New York State Fair in Elmira. The aborted contest was the closest the legendary Red Stockings came to losing a game in 1869.[3]

Two years later, the Haymakers became a charter member of the National Association, representing Troy in both 1871 and 1872. The team was notable for employing the first Jewish major league player and manager, Lip Pike, and the first Latin ballplayer in major league history, Steve Bellan.[4]

Although Troy was absent from the top levels of baseball between 1873 and 1878, the town was represented by Bill Craver, who, after serving as player-manager of the Haymakers in 1871, was employed by several major league teams. Unfortunately, Craver's checkered career ended abruptly in 1877 when he was expelled for life along with three Louisville teammates who had schemed to throw games in the National League's first gambling scandal.[5]

Troy returned to the majors in 1879 when the National League expanded from six teams to eight, and while the franchise lasted only four years without enjoying a winning season, five future Hall of Famers made their big league debuts for the Collar City—pitchers Mickey Welch and Tim Keefe, infielders Roger Connor and Dan Brouthers, and catcher Buck Ewing. In addition, Hall of Famer Mike "King" Kelly—baseball's most popular player during the 1880s—was a native of Troy who spent most of his career playing for Cincinnati, Chicago and Boston. Kelly had not lived in Troy long; shortly after his father returned from the Civil War, the family, including five-year-old Michael, moved to Washington D.C.[6] Nevertheless, the city has always been proud to be identified as the birthplace of baseball's most charismatic nineteenth-century star.

Troy was asked to withdraw from the National League after the 1882 season, along with fellow tail-ender Worcester, Massachusetts, in order to add teams in New York City and Philadelphia, major cities that enabled the league to better compete with the rival American Association. Troy and Worcester were made honorary members of the National League, a designation they hold to this day.[7]

In all, sixteen sons of Troy appeared in major league uniforms during the 1800s. Among them was a left-handed second baseman named Tom Evers, whose nephew, John Joseph Evers, was born in Troy on July 21, 1881; when Johnny Evers was three years old, his uncle was playing for Washington in the Union Association.[8] Johnny's father, also named John, had played ball locally and was a respected member of the Troy community—Irish-Catholic and a staunch Democrat intimately involved in politics. Born and raised in Troy, the elder Evers began his adult working life as a molder for a couple of steel manufacturers and became influential in the union. He later clerked for the local postmaster, served as assistant clerk for the Board of Water Commissioners, and was a twelve-year member of the local school board, one year of which he served as president.[9] He and his brothers were also members of the very popular Excelsior Zouave Drum Corps.[10] Outgoing and popular, John Evers was a prominent supporter of a number of benevolent associations, one of which was named in his honor.

The younger Evers—the family name was pronounced Ee-vers within the Capital District and Eh-vers outside of it—was one of nine children and immediately took to the game of baseball. He would run off to Carroll's Hill at every opportunity, more often than not by himself, hitting a ball and then running and catching it, endlessly repeating the cycle until it was too dark to continue.[11] Sometimes there were pick-up games on the hill with other children, which usually culminated in police chasing them from the private property.[12] South Troy was a baseball hotbed within a city that was already a hotbed of baseball, and Johnny Evers never forgot the local sandlot games, so numerous on Sundays and holidays, he said, "It was not an unusual sight in some of the fields to see the outfielders of one game within a few feet of home plate and the catcher of another." But the highlight for Evers was attending games involving local professionals.

"Invariably when Young America has his mind set on going to the game," chuckled Evers years later, after he had become a major leaguer, "he gets there somehow or another, whether he has the price of admission or not. We usually had our minds set and we usually got to the game."[13] After arriving, he and his friends headed immediately to the bleachers—which Evers preferred because they afforded a vantage point from where he could best study the action.

Baseball in the late 1800s was considered a game of execution, surprise and fast thinking, even while being played by those thought to be uneducated, at least in a conventional sense. Strategy was quite different from today—the modern fan would be taken aback by runners repeatedly tagged out during seemingly foolhardy dashes around the bases.

But early players viewed offense differently, distinguishing runs that could be scored with the bat from those that could be scored with the brains and feet. The closest analogy today would be to football, where the running game is used to set up the passing attack—and running is continued even when seemingly ineffective because it forces the defense to play in a way that it is hoped opens up a pass play in a key situation.

Aggressive base running in the early days of baseball was utilized the same way—as a means to keep the defense from plugging the gaps, or to keep the gaps open longer. When Johnny Evers teamed with Chicago sportswriter Hugh Fullerton on the book *Touching Second* in 1910, he noted, "Every ball player knows there are five 'infield grooves' and four 'outfield grooves,' spaces between the fielders where any ball hit with moderate force will be 'safe' unless a marvelous stop intervenes."[14]

If an infielder had to consider whether a base runner might take off, he would position himself closer to the base, opening up the "grooves" for the hitter. In addition, it was considered an advantage every time a base runner forced a defensive player to make a throw—the more throws, the more chance for an error. Players' gloves were rudimentary and big innings were often generated from errors. Because of that, there were many specialized bunts, hit-and-run plays, delayed steals, double steals and aggressive base running. Batters bunted or took good pitches in these situations; even if unsuccessful, in the era before the home run it was considered vital to keep the defense on the defensive. Scoring runs was a team effort—hitters and runners working together. The objective was to outthink the other guy and keep him off-balance.

From the beginning, young Johnny Evers was attracted to the mental and strategic side of baseball—it was almost second nature to him.

"I would pick apart every play that was made," he remembered, "and then ponder myself whether the play was made right or whether it should have been played according to *my* ideas."[15] Evers dreamed of playing on that diamond, donning the same uniform that had been proudly worn by Dan Brouthers and Mickey Welch.

After graduating from St. Joseph's Brothers Teacher's School in 1898, Evers looked for something to occupy his off hours. He was a New York Giants fan, and baseball was his first love. But instead of joining a team—or even forming one—the teenager created an entire amateur baseball *league*, consisting of a half-dozen teams including his own, which he christened the "Cheer-Ups."

The teams played on Sundays. During the week, Evers was employed as a sign painter until he developed symptoms of lead poisoning and was forced to abandon that vocation in favor of clerking at a shirt factory, duties that involved laboring in the inspection room of the ironing department, for which he would later claim to have earned four dollars per week.[16] The Cheer-Ups were both popular and successful, catching the attention of Lou Bacon, manager of the local New York State League team. Evers was wiry and quick, and displayed a stereotypical Irish temper often sparked by his uncanny ability to take offense to slights, real or imagined, faster than anyone alive; as if to advertise that fact, his head seemed to be attached slightly off-kilter and was punctuated with a lantern jaw jutting at an angle that seemed to reflect an absolutely genuine air of defiance. Evers' face was lightly freckled, a family trait, and his fair skin, reddish hair and piercing blue eyes betrayed his ethnic origins.

A left-handed hitter and right-handed thrower, Evers was extremely quick out of the batter's box. He was of average height for the time, five-feet-nine inches tall, but skinny; some say he weighed less than 110 pounds when he played for Troy. Even Evers went along with this over time, but Joe Tinker, in an interview shortly after Evers's death, laughed at that notion and insisted that when Evers joined the Cubs he weighed around 145—which was also likely an exaggeration. The truth probably lies somewhere in between.[17]

Evers turned down Bacon's offer at first, leery of quitting his job and then not being able to make it as a ballplayer. He finally tried out for the Trojans in March of 1902.[18] Evers was so skinny it was said that the shirt of his baseball uniform looked like a balloon before it was inflated, but he was nonetheless an impressive athlete.[19] At the end of April, he played in a pair of exhibition games against the traveling Negro barnstorming team, the Cuban X Giants, when Bacon's shortstop was holding out for more pay. (Later, more romantic fiction had the Troy manager spotting Evers in the bleachers before the first game with the Cubans and convincing him to play.)

Evers played right field, collected a couple of hits, and continued with the team during the exhibition season, at the conclusion of which Bacon offered the young man sixty dollars a month to play for Troy.

Johnny Evers made his professional debut on May 9, 1902, as a shortstop in the season-opening contest against Ilion on a bracingly cold day that limited attendance to roughly three hundred hardy souls.[20] Despite his collecting only one hit in his first two games, the *Troy Northern Budget* was impressed and declared Evers to be playing so well, he had already earned a permanent spot on the team.[21] His most impressive early performance came at Albany on May 20, when he collected three hits in five at bats, including a double and a stolen base, while handling eight chances in the field without an error. The team returned home, and on May 26, Evers hit his first professional home run as Troy ran its record to a surprising 8–6.

Johnny Evers was having the time of his life. When the team was at home, he put his street clothes on over his uniform and walked from his house to the ballpark, shedding his outer garments upon reaching his destination. On warm days his father, a near-invalid in increasingly poor health, would station himself in the sunshine on a hill outside the ballpark to watch his son play.[22]

The Troy home field, rebuilt after a cyclone destroyed it in 1892, boasted neither a scoreboard nor a dedicated space for local reporters; its most unusual features included a right field fence short in both distance and height, of which the left-handed-hitting Evers took full advantage. The park's left field area allowed a player to hit a home run into a stream beyond its boundary, at least on a bounce and a roll.

The Trojans were always among the most profitable teams in the league, regardless of their position in the standings. The New York State League was in its fourth year of operation and very competitive, boasting more than three-dozen former and future major leaguers on its rosters in 1902. Ex-Cleveland star Clarence "Cupid" Childs, who had recently completed a thirteen-year major league career with a lifetime batting average of .306, played for Syracuse, while ten-year big league veteran Tommy Dowd toiled for Johnstown (also known as Amsterdam-Gloversville-Johnstown, or A-G-J, for the three towns the team represented). Future major league stars Frank Schulte and Mike Mitchell wore the uniforms of Syracuse and Schenectady.

The players took the contests seriously and Evers witnessed firsthand the cutthroat nature of the professional game. In early June, a major brawl erupted when Syracuse first baseman Cy Townsend attacked an umpire during a game at Troy. The Stars were losing for the second day in a row, and Townsend took exception when he was called out on an attempted steal of second base. Without even dusting himself off, he leaped straight up and, as the *Syracuse Evening Telegram* described it, attempted to "shake the nose from the umpire's face." Townsend's actions culminated in his slapping the umpire as players came pouring off the bench from every direction. He was finally subdued, but not before he attempted to assault the chief of police and was marched to jail, followed by an angry mob of Troy fans anxious to mete out their own brand of crude justice.[23] Townsend was briefly suspended; he was back in the lineup six days after the incident, collecting six hits in seven at bats in his first two games after serving his punishment.[24]

A month later, Troy right fielder Bill Smink and Binghamton reserve catcher John Daniels had a fistfight of such intensity that both men were placed under arrest.[25]

Shortly after the Trojans hit their high-water mark with a record of 15–14, Lou Bacon moved Evers, who was hitting .234 with three home runs, from lead-off to third in the batting order. But the Trojans' lack of pitching talent caught up with them, and they lost thirty of their next thirty-six games to drop hopelessly out of contention in a season lasting slightly more than one hundred games. Their best pitcher, Joseph "Chick" Robitaille, abandoned the team and was replaced by future New York Giants star George "Hooks" Wiltse, whose brother was a pitcher for the Philadelphia Athletics. But the twenty-two-year-old Wiltse, available because the league he was playing in had folded, was inexperienced and, despite his talent, would prove inconsistent.[26]

Although the team struggled, it remained popular, drawing so well during a July 4 double-header against Albany that fans had to be overflowed onto the field. All balls hit into the crowd were ground-rule doubles, resulting in twenty-three such two-baggers generated by the teams in the second game alone, despite the contest's being halted at the end of the seventh inning.[27]

A couple of weeks later, Troy and Utica battled for twelve innings before Evers sent the cheering crowd home with a terrific drive down the right field line that easily cleared the fence. It was his third home run in as many games and his first walk-off circuit blast.[28]

Evers's success translated into an offer from an outlaw team in Plattsburg, New York, that would have more than doubled his salary, but he turned it down largely because of his father's deteriorating health.[29] Late in the month,

Evers missed three of four games due to illness. Lou Bacon signed thirty-six-year-old former big leaguer Lou Bierbauer to fill in at second base and moved regular second baseman Ed Shortell over to Evers's position. But Bierbauer was clearly through as a ballplayer and was released after only three games, at which point Evers returned to the lineup.[30]

In early August, Evers was talking to his father about his latest game. Near the end of their conversation, the expression on the older man's face became serious and he stated in a sad but clear voice, "I guess I won't go out to the games anymore." Johnny Evers did not argue—he knew what his father was trying to tell him.[31]

Two weeks later, his father's health took a turn for the worse—as did Evers's play. On August 15 he made three errors against Binghamton and followed that with two more the next day. Evers was excused from the last game of the home stand and a short road trip so he could remain at his father's bedside. On August 21, an hour before the train carrying the Trojans returned home, John Evers, Sr., died. He was fifty-four years old. A pair of funerals was held three days later; among the pallbearers was former Troy Mayor Dennis Whelan. The Osgood Steam Ship Company was well-represented at both ceremonies, which were held at the family home and at the Catholic church.[32]

Evers returned to Troy's lineup on August 27, but still shaken by his father's death, played poorly in a loss that dropped Troy's record to 34–57. After that, he pulled himself together and helped his team establish a five-game winning streak, which proved to be the last five games Johnny Evers would play for the Trojans; shortly after his return to the team following his father's death, Lou Bacon had informed the twenty-one-year-old that he had been purchased by the Chicago Cubs, along with Canadian left-hander Alex Hardy—who would report after he made his last start for Troy later in the week.

Hardy had been the Cubs' main target, but Bacon had persuaded his old friend, Cubs manager Frank Selee, to take a look at

John J. Evers.

John J. Evers Sr. Despite failing health, the former molder, postmaster's clerk, water commission clerk and school board president watched his son play for Troy every chance he could. Unfortunately he died at age fifty-four, only a week before his son's services were sold to Chicago.

Evers as well, complete with a money-back guarantee—if he did not like Evers, he could return the $200 purchase price. In announcing the transaction, the *Chicago Tribune* simply reported, "Troy's clever shortstop, Evers, has been sold to the Chicago National League club and will report to that club on Tuesday."[33] Evers was leading the New York State League in home runs, with ten (he always credited the short right field fence at his home park for his power display, and seemed honest in his self-assessment—every one of his home runs was hit at home), and he had a batting average of .291 in eighty-four games played, including .330 in his final fifty-one games with Troy. While he had committed his share of errors, Evers also was among the league leaders in chances accepted per game, demonstrating his quickness, aggressiveness and excellent range in the field.

Following the August 31 double-header at Albany, Johnny Evers joined the other Trojans on a trolley car bound for the railroad station, at which point he and his friends would part ways. As they arrived, an anxious Evers, struck by the realization his teammates would be heading back to Troy without him, went inside the station and purchased a number of cigars. Walking back to the group, he handed one to each of his teammates, all the while wearing a nervous grin on his face.

One of the players yelled, "Good luck, Johnny!" That was quickly followed by several more shouts of encouragement, including from one teammate who cried out, "We'll all be pulling for you, John."

Evers clumsily thrust the remaining cigars into his pocket, completed a final round of handshakes, and settled into the smoking car for the long night's ride to Philadelphia, where he would join his new teammates.[34] As the train shuddered and jerked into motion, Evers glanced out of the window, gave a final wave, and then closed his eyes, thinking about his father and how he had just missed seeing this day. As the lights of Albany receded, one could picture Evers imagining his father sitting on a hill somewhere up above and settling in to watch his son's first major league game.

CHAPTER TWO

Rookie

The Chicago Cubs boast a long history—dating to 1870 as an independent team dubbed the White Stockings. The team then spent three seasons in the National Association, sandwiched around two years of inactivity following the great Chicago Fire of October 1871. White Stockings owner William Hulbert shifted his franchise to the newly formed National League in 1876 and imported several big stars, including the game's best pitcher, Boston's Albert Spalding, and one of its best position players, Marshalltown, Iowa, native Adrian Anson, a friend of Spalding's who had been playing for the powerful Athletics of Philadelphia. Other important additions included Spalding's Boston teammates Ross Barnes—who would hit the National League's first home run—Cal McVey and Deacon White. The infusion of talent resulted in Chicago's winning the National League's first pennant.

Spalding retired following the 1877 season to concentrate on his burgeoning sporting goods business—which bears his name to this day—but the White Stockings continued to enjoy success, thanks in no small measure to the man who would become the constant in Chicago baseball for two decades, "Cap" Anson. The indestructible star was a big, strapping run producer who hit .300 year in and year out. Anson never left the team; even in the face of interlopers such as the American Association, the Union Association and the Players League, he remained true to the White Stockings. Chicago captured National League pennants in 1880 (winning sixty-seven of eighty-four games for a .798 winning percentage), and 1881.

After William Hulbert died in 1882, Al Spalding took control and the team drew more than one hundred thousand people while continuing its dominance with a third straight pennant. The White Stockings were back on top again in 1885, winning eighty-seven times against only twenty-five defeats. The run of championships would end after the 1886 pennant-winners lost to the American Association St. Louis Browns in a post-season "World Series."[1]

The team slipped badly as the 1890s began. Chicago's most talented and popular player that decade was outfielder Bill Lange, a six-foot-two, two-hundred-pound Californian who despite his size was incredibly fast and an excellent outfielder and hitter—he had to be fast playing centerfield at West Side Grounds, which featured dimensions of 340 feet to left, 316 feet to right, and an incredible 560 feet to straightaway center.[2]

Lange would play seven seasons for Chicago, hitting .330 lifetime—with a best of .389—and was one of the National League's leading base stealers. But the White Stockings achieved only two winning seasons between 1892 and 1897, and Cap Anson was finally convinced to retire at age forty-five by his old friend Spalding, after twenty-seven seasons as a major league player.[3] Anson had aged to the point where he was called "Pop," and when he departed, local wags began calling the team the "Orphans."

Bill Lange then shocked Chicago baseball fans by retiring in his prime after the 1899 season to marry a woman from San Francisco and pursue real estate ventures with his new father-in-law.[4] Before taking his leave, the brash Californian was asked to take a look at a young catcher named Frank Chance at a baseball tournament in the Bay Area and agreed that Al Spalding should sign him—securing one of the building blocks for the White Stockings' next great team. But that success remained in the future as Chicago once again fell into the second division after Lange retired.

Al Spalding sold controlling interest in the franchise in 1902 to team president James Hart and moved to San Diego, California, devoting his time to promoting baseball and looking after his business interests.[5] Hart in turned hired Frank Selee, manager of the mighty Boston Red Stockings of the 1890s—another franchise that had faded as of late. The Cubs' president had no intention of interfering with his new manager—he summed up his philosophy a year later to a reporter, saying, "All I care to know is that the team is winning and that the players are behaving themselves."[6] Hart's charge to Selee was simple: return Chicago baseball to its former prominence.

Sporting a massive mustache that seemed an effort to make up for the lack of hair atop his head, forty-two-year-old Frank Selee was a quiet man with ice-cold blue eyes, a dry sense of humor, and an almost serene demeanor quite appropriate for a son of a Methodist minister. He was what one today would call a "player's manager," believing, often in spite of what should have been convincing evidence to the contrary, that treating his players with consideration would influence them to reciprocate. He was newly married to a much younger auburn-haired beauty named May, whose Irish accent betrayed her place of birth. A woman possessing a comfortable self-assurance that enabled her to acquire friends easily, she was tall—taller than her husband—and a great fan of baseball with an excellent working knowledge of the game and its players.

May Selee attended most Cubs home games and occasionally appeared unannounced on the road; her husband never objected. She was accepted by players and enjoyed their interactions, such as the time she laughingly wagered Joe Tinker one dollar that the Cubs would not take a single game during a home stand against the powerhouse Pittsburgh Pirates. When she lost the bet, she cheerfully paid up.[7]

Frank Selee had never been much of a ballplayer, but he was one of baseball's best judges of talent—the architect of a Boston juggernaut that captured five National League pennants between 1891 and 1898. But the fight had been taken out of him as the roster aged and the team wrestled with star catcher Marty Bergen's bizarre behavior—most of Bergen's teammates, and indeed Selee himself, grew frightened of him (as well they should have). Bergen's ultimate murder-suicide of his entire family in January 1900, while shocking, was even more frightening in retrospect to those who had been around him on a daily basis. The mental image of a wild-eyed Bergen chasing his two young screaming children with a bloody ax that had already taken the measure of their mother was impossible to rid from one's mind.[8]

The team Selee was taking over in Chicago had been terrible in 1901, winning only fifty-three games while losing eighty-six. Its fortunes had not been helped by the National League's war with the newly-minted American League, and courtrooms seemed jammed with various disputes involving teams and their players, who were jumping between leagues with increasing alacrity. Chicago was far from immune to the lack of respect for contracts.[9]

Selee was determined to make the team younger, but recognized the task would not be accomplished all at once; he also needed players of unquestioned loyalty. One of them was the man he chose to be his new team captain, thirty-six-year-old former Boston Red Stockings second baseman Bobby Lowe, longtime member of what was considered the best infield in baseball history to that point—a group assembled by Selee that had included first baseman Fred Tenney, shortstop Herman Long and third baseman Jimmy Collins. Born Robert Lincoln Lowe in honor of the president assassinated three months before his birth, Lowe had gained notoriety in 1894 as the first player to hit four home runs in a major league game.[10] Selee also signed twenty-eight-year-old outfielder Jimmy Slagle who, like Lowe, had played for him in Boston. Veterans aside, Selee had so many young players at spring training that one sportswriter wrote about the new manager's "Cubs." The nickname eventually stuck, replacing the "Orphans."[11] The Cubs began 1902 with Lowe at second and twenty-one-year-old rookie Joe Tinker, acquired from Portland of the Northwestern League, at short. But every other position remained unsettled, save for catcher, which was manned by Johnny Kling and Frank Chance.

Despite lineup and injury issues, the Cubs registered marked improvement in 1902, remaining within striking distance of the first division with a record of 55–55 when Johnny Evers arrived at the beginning of September. The National League championship was by then all but decided—the Pittsburgh Pirates would capture the pennant by the incredible margin of twenty-seven-and-one-half games—which allowed teams the freedom to experiment in preparation for the next season.

On the afternoon of September 1, Evers reached the train station in Philadelphia, having neither eaten nor slept all night. He was met by a Cubs representative who escorted him to the team's hotel, with only enough time to toss his satchel into his room and sprint across the street to the ballpark. After donning his uniform, Evers walked out of the centerfield clubhouse at the brick, steel and concrete Philadelphia Baseball Grounds (later known as the Baker Bowl) and was nearly overwhelmed by his first sight of a major league stadium—if one does not count the old wooden ballpark at Troy. His heart raced as he crossed the outfield, its odd hump betraying the location of a railroad tunnel running beneath the playing surface. He grew ever more excited after catching sight of six thousand people, packed into a double-decker grandstand punctuated with fanciful turrets at each end that would have been appropriate for a jousting tournament.

A decade later there were stories, related by Evers and others, that included having bats thrown at him by his new teammates when he first took batting practice with the Cubs, and being forced to ride to the ballpark on the roof of the team's carriage. These stories fit the romantic image of a feisty Evers who had to battle for everything he got. It is not clear that these events were entirely factual, but likely exaggerations aside, Evers certainly experienced the usual hazing given a rookie; after one glance at his skinny frame, the clubhouse manager handed Evers one of Bill Lange's old uniforms, which completely engulfed the youngster since it had been designed for a man five inches taller and some sixty to eighty pounds heavier.[12]

In later years, it would also be claimed that Cubs players threatened to strike if Selee put the scrawny shortstop, who was twenty-one years old but claimed to be nineteen, into the lineup. That, however, seems doubtful since

Evers was playing for the Cubs the same day he arrived, batting sixth in both games of a double-header against the Phillies. Joe Tinker was shifted to third base—Selee was still looking for answers at the hot corner and at first base—and Bobby Lowe, nursing a sore knee, remained at second.

His nervousness obvious to even the most casual observer, Evers endured a rough first day—only one hit in seven at bats against Doc White and Bill Duggleby, and three errors in fifteen chances in the field. While running the bases, he and Philadelphia third baseman Harry Wolverton collided with such force that both men remained prone for several minutes.[13] After the game, Evers avoided eye contact with his manager, certain he was going to be packed up and sent home, but Selee assured the young shortstop that he was aware of his less than restful night on the train and instructed him to get some sleep and report the next day.[14]

If Evers was initially intimidated by major league baseball, he did not remain so for long. Selee arranged for him to take extra batting practice each day and moved him to second base, where he seemed much more at home defensively.[15] Evers enjoyed an outstanding series in Boston, collecting four hits in eleven at bats and handling twenty-two chances in the field without an error.[16] He followed that up with a flawless four-game series against the New York Giants, handling nineteen chances with nary a bobble.

Evers turned his first double play in his first home game, against St. Louis, and on September 15 against Cincinnati, participated in the first "Tinker to Evers to Chance" twin killing. He was criticized for taking too long to make his throws from shortstop, and it was apparent that Evers's arm was more suited to second base; once placed there he was praised for his quickness in making the pivot on double plays.[17]

The Cubs ended 1902 in fifth place with a final record of 68–69—a decided improvement on the 1901 season.[18] Frank Selee had seen enough of Johnny Evers to decide to keep him, at least as a utility infielder. It was also clear that the youngster's future was at second base, where he did not make an error in the nineteen games he played the position, compared to seven errors in seven games at shortstop.[19] Writing for *The Sporting Life*, W.A. Phelon was favorably impressed and engaged in a little hyperbole meant to attract the reader's attention: "Young Evers leads all the second basemen in the country for the 20 games or so he has played. This lad is one of the greatest natural fielders who ever wore a Chicago uniform, and if he acquires a good batting gait will yet be one of the wonders of the age."[20]

As a hitter, Evers had improved during his first month in the majors, but fell short of his production at Troy, batting only .222 and unable to register a single extra-base hit in nearly one hundred at bats. But he had shown aggressiveness and savvy beyond his years, and Selee announced Evers as among those players signed to contracts for the 1903 season. There was no going back to Troy—at least on the diamond.

Frank Selee knew Johnny Evers was a fast learner and improving every day. Selee also knew he now could take his time developing the youngster; the player raids were over, as the National League had reached a peace agreement with the three-year-old American League in January.[21] Before the jumping ended, Selee landed thirty-three-year-old switch-hitting third baseman James "Doc" Casey, late of the Detroit Tigers, hoping the veteran would finally plug the Cubs' hole at the hot corner.[22]

Thirteen players, including Johnny Evers, gathered at the Rock Island Station on the morning of March 7, 1903, to begin a four-day cross-country train trip to Los Angeles for the Cubs' first West Coast spring training. Frank Selee was already out west, and Frank Chance, owner of a prune orchard in Fresno, would also meet his teammates there. Joe Tinker and rookie pitcher Jake Weimer would hop aboard in Kansas City. The team was to remain in Los Angeles until March 26, at which point the Cubs would barnstorm their way back through Arizona, New Mexico, Colorado and Nebraska.[23]

The players, many of them traveling to California for the first time, were enthusiastic to a man. Johnny Evers hauled a batch of newspapers and a clutch of his favorite cigars, while others readied for a long and hopefully lucrative poker game. Doc Casey brought along materials to study for his upcoming dental examination—and tools to practice his trade on his new teammates. Pitcher Jack Taylor, perhaps thinking it still possible to hunt buffalo from the window of a train out west, carried a rifle with him. Newly acquired Frank Corridon packed a violin.[24]

What the players observed upon disembarking in California had to seem like something out of a fantasy world. For Johnny Evers, it was certainly far removed from the iced-over streams and slippery mud trails that marked March in Troy. Los Angeles was not yet a motion picture capital—that remained more than a decade into the future—but the city had recently exploded to a population of more than one hundred thousand and was gaining a national reputation as a sort of Shangri-La where the sun always shone and orange groves stretched as far as the eye could see. The beaches were clean and the air was clear and pure; at the time it was possible for a person to stand on the higher hills to the northwest and take in a view encompassing the entire foothill and valley areas between Los Angeles and Santa Monica. The city was proud of its parks and promoted their year-round use. The most visited were Westlake and East Side—which were closer to the population center—Elysian Park, and finally Griffith Park, stretching more than three thousand acres to the north.

Frank Selee took advantage of the impeccable climate to rally his players onto the practice field at ten o'clock each morning for the first of two daily workout sessions.[25] He asked Bobby Lowe to take Evers under his wing and teach him the finer points of second base play and big league life.[26] During early workouts, Evers showed off an improved throwing arm and quickness around the bag that the aging Lowe lacked. He was termed the surprise of camp and, according to W.A. Phelon, was not only stellar defensively, he was also "knocking the tar out of the ball."[27]

Jim Morley, owner of the local Los Angeles entry in the newly formed Pacific Coast League, had signed big league stars including Rube Waddell, Dummy Hoy, Joe Corbett and Doc Newton in his quest to field a major league caliber team. He was impressed by Evers and asked if he could make a deal to acquire him for Los Angeles. Selee said no.[28]

As training camp neared its end, Frank Selee made final adjustments to his roster. Concerned about Frank Chance's defense and history of injuries, he signed first baseman Bill Hanlon, a weak-hitting twenty-seven-year-old California State League veteran who had played for Morley in 1902. Their practice in Los Angeles complete, the Cubs began the journey home, chugging through the desert and across the Rocky Mountains, with stops in places such as El Paso, Pueblo, Denver and Omaha. While in Colorado Springs, Selee again flatly rejected an offer for Evers. (A decade later, a story about Evers in *Baseball Magazine* claimed that Selee tried to dispose of Evers on four separate occasions during the return trip from Los Angeles, but that Evers had killed all four potential deals. Again, this makes for a nice story but does not mesh with the facts.[29])

Johnny Kling and Joe Tinker asked to be dropped off in Kansas City to spend time with family before traveling on their own to Chicago in time for an exhibition game that was to be played on April 12. But Kling and Tinker were AWOL on that day, much to Selee's displeasure. Angered that the men had taken advantage of his player-friendly nature, Selee's mood was not lightened when he discovered that the two had participated in an exhibition game in Kansas City for the rival Chicago White Sox.[30] The wayward duo finally arrived in St. Louis for the opening game of the season, somehow remaining straight-faced while declaring surprise that their appearance for Charles Comiskey's team had generated controversy.

In truth, Kling had been unhappy for months. The rifle-armed catcher had been promised a five-hundred-dollar bonus at the end of the 1902 season for carrying an extra workload behind the plate, but was handed only two hundred dollars by James Hart with the explanation that the team had lost money and could afford no more. This had angered Kling to the point that he half-seriously approached Byron McKibbon—whom he had played for in

St. Joseph, Missouri, before joining the Cubs in 1900—about jumping to a team McKibbon was managing in the Pacific Northwest League.[31]

Kling and Tinker were back, but Doc Casey was going to miss the opening series in St. Louis, with Selee's permission, so he could travel to Baltimore to take his final dental license examination. As a result, the Cubs were forced to open the 1903 season with Joe Tinker at third, Evers at short and Bobby Lowe at second.[32]

The weather was bitterly cold; the traditional parade to the grounds was canceled, so the players were asked to report to the ballpark an hour early in order for fans to get a glimpse of them before the game. Evers smacked two of Chicago's four hits, but committed an error. Even worse, Joe Tinker, looking uncomfortable at third, made two miscues and the Cubs lost, 2–1.[33] Evers committed another error the next day, although he did hit a ninth-inning triple—a ball that probably should have been handled by the Cardinals outfielder—and scored the winning run on Bobby Lowe's sacrifice fly.[34]

But if the first two days had been shaky for Evers, the third was a disaster, even though the Cubs won the game. He made three errors, including a pair on one play that allowed two runs to score, giving him five miscues in three games and a fielding average barely above .700.[35] It was clear that shortstop was not Johnny Evers's position.

The experiment with Bill Hanlon was not going well either. He was hitless in the first three games, collecting two fewer than the number managed by the pitchers batting behind him in the order. Evers played one more game at shortstop and managed to get through it without making an error—somehow he accepted no chances at all that day.[36] Doc Casey returned to the lineup on April 22 and Evers went to the bench.

On April 27, Frank Chance was inserted into the lineup at first base, batting third. A week later, back-up catcher Charlie Raub split his finger on a foul tip early in a game. Selee moved Chance behind the plate, sent Bobby Lowe over to first and placed Evers at second. Evers responded with a three-for-three day and handled seven chances without an error. James Hart attended the game and commented afterward, "That looks like a pretty good infield to me."[37] Two days later, Evers was in the lineup to stay; Chance was returned to first, and Bobby Lowe, still hampered by the knee injury he had suffered the previous September, became the team's utility infielder—the official company line was that Lowe was being given time to recover.

The Cubs began the 1903 season with a record of 8–8 and then reeled off sixteen wins in seventeen games between May 6 and May 25 to move into first place ahead of the New York Giants. After dropping a pair of contests to the Giants at the Polo Grounds and falling to second, the Cubs took the series finale behind Jack Taylor, then swept the Cardinals and took two more from

Brooklyn to regain first place with a record of 30–11. That led to a rematch against New York at the West Side Grounds.

It was a disaster. The Giants swept the series on the Cubs' home field, with Christy Mathewson easily taking the first game—he was on his way to his first of four thirty-win seasons, supposedly the result of his wife's decreeing an end to his all-night poker games. Joe McGinnity followed Mathewson by defeating Chicago twice in three days, knocking the Cubs into second place. Defending champion Pittsburgh then reeled off fifteen straight victories and the Cubs slipped to third, where, except for a few days in August, they would reside for the remainder of the 1903 season.

Following the Giants series, Selee rested Joe Tinker for a few days, putting Bobby Lowe at second and moving Evers to short; Evers made six errors in five games. In one of those contests, a 3–2 loss to the last-place Phillies, Evers and Chance committed throwing miscues on the same play that allowed Philadelphia to score the winning run.[38]

At that point, Evers was hitting a solid .291 while batting in the seventh spot and playing standout defense—when at second base. It was clear that

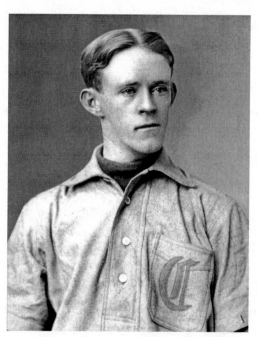

Tinker had to come back in at short and Evers needed to return to second, which meant putting Lowe back on the bench.

The Cubs traveled to Troy on June 28 for an exhibition game against the local nine, and Johnny Evers was treated as if he were a king. Before the contest he sat chewing on a cigar and swapping stories with some of his old friends. More than 3,500 attended the game, and every player on the Troy ball club lined up to shake Evers's hand. One year earlier he had played on the same field, against Schenectady, with his father sitting up on the hill watching his every move. The majors

This photograph of rookie Chicago Cubs infielder Johnny Evers was published on the front page of the September 26, 1903, issue of *The Sporting Life*. The only difference in this photograph and the copy that was published is that the Old English "C" on the shirt pocket was deleted. (Author's collection.)

had seemed a million miles away. Now Evers was returning as a coming star of a quickly improving team representing the nation's second largest city. He would not revive memories of 1902 with a home run that day, but he did bring the crowd to its feet with a roar when he smashed a double off Hooks Wiltse. The Cubs won easily, 9–1.[39]

A week and a half later it was discovered that Bobby Lowe's chronic sore knee was the result of a broken kneecap. The doctor declared the thirty-seven-year-old out for the season; in fact, the doctor indicated it was not clear that Lowe would ever play again.[40]

With Doc Casey nursing a bad finger and Frank Chance having strained his back, Frank Selee could not afford to carry Lowe—longstanding relationship or not. Evers was playing his position anyway. Professional sport has always been a callous business. Selee informed the team captain he was being released.[41] The Cubs manager gathered the team the next day for the purpose of electing a new captain. They chose Frank Chance.[42]

During a special ceremony in the clubhouse prior to a game against Brooklyn, Lowe was presented a watch locket, inset with diamonds. Selee thanked the veteran for his contributions and wished him luck in finding a managerial position.[43] "It's pretty hard to have to part with Bob in such a way," remarked Selee, "as he and I have been together fourteen years." But Lowe was not touched by the tribute—he was angry. He maintained that he only needed a growth removed from the injured knee and could have returned in a few weeks. He said he considered his release unjust, in light of his long service. But in Selee's opinion, Lowe's knee could never again be counted on in the heat of battle, and he felt it was time for him to retire as a player.[44]

The plain truth was that Johnny Evers was better.

At the end of July, the Cubs signed Johnny Evers to a contract for $2,800, one of the richest ever given to a player of his youth and inexperience.[45] Selee moved him to fifth in the batting order shortly after Lowe's release, and he remained there until sidelined for a few days with a sore arm. While recuperating, Evers was allowed to make a short visit home, near the first anniversary of his father's death.

When he returned, Evers was moved back into the seventh spot and continued to hit the ball—collecting nineteen hits in forty-one at bats, a .463 average, between September 2 and September 12, including doubles in five straight games. He was beginning to attract attention—on September 26, his photograph was featured front and center on Page One of *The Sporting Life*. W.A. Phelon continued raving about the youngster's play: "Evers is now the heaviest hitting second baseman in the game, outside of Lajoie, and is certainly one of the best fielders. His head work in all sharp plays around the bag is wonderful for so young a novice, and is fully equal to the stunts done by veterans of the game."[46]

The Cubs finished the season with a 10–3 win over Boston on September 27 that left them in third place, a game and a half behind the second-place Giants. They also took twelve of twenty games from Pittsburgh, winners of three straight National League pennants, becoming the first squad to take a season series from the Pirates in two years.

The pitching was improved; Jake Weimer, Selee's pre-season find from Kansas City, joined Jack Taylor and Bob Wicker, acquired a week into the season from St. Louis, as twenty-game winners for the Cubs. The offense was better too—every regular in the lineup, save for right fielder Dick Harley, hit better than .280. Frank Chance emerged as a star, hitting .327 and leading the major leagues in stolen bases. Chicago's team batting average had improved by twenty-five points, and Selee finally had the majority of his lineup settled— although the outfield still needed some work.

Joe Tinker was especially excited about his team's prospects, pointing out that the Cubs were young and unknown at the beginning of 1903, yet had fought hard all year. "It was a bunch of young kids chasing the pennant," said Tinker. "Watch us next season."[47]

Meanwhile, had there been a National League Rookie of the Year Award in 1903, it would have gone to Johnny Evers. He played second base like a veteran, succeeding at his uncle's old position; longtime Cubs fans compared him to Fred Pfeffer, the great White Stockings infielder of the 1880s (Pfeffer coincidentally had played his first big league season for Troy, when Johnny Evers was a year old). Evers also improved substantially as a hitter, bunting and slashing from the left side for thirty-four extra-base hits and a .293 batting average.

Tinker, Evers and Chance were in place. The Cubs had to find a way to get past Honus Wagner's Pirates and John McGraw's Giants, but they were in position to battle those two teams as legitimate contenders for the National League pennant for the foreseeable future.

CHAPTER THREE

Foraging for Wins in the Land of the Giants

At the conclusion of the 1903 season, James Hart challenged Charles Comiskey to a first-ever series of games between the Cubs and White Sox to settle the matter of baseball supremacy in the city of Chicago—and maybe make a little money. However, during the series Hart was told that pitcher Jack Taylor was not doing his best, and after Taylor's third straight loss he confronted the right-hander, accusing him of crooked play.

Taylor emphatically denied the allegation and shouted that he would never play for Chicago again.[1] Hart responded that he had absolutely no problem in fulfilling the veteran pitcher's wish, and two months later he did exactly that, sending Taylor to the St. Louis Cardinals in exchange for second-year pitcher Mordecai Brown.[2] In the end, a trade Hart made in anger would prove one of the most fortuitous in Cubs history.

Brown, whose pitching hand had been mangled in a feed chopper as a youngster, was predictably nicknamed "Three Finger" as a result of his losing battle with the farm machinery. Originally a scatter-armed infielder, his disability—combined with an intimidating side-arm delivery—made him a most formidable pitcher, causing his devastating curveball to rotate erratically, yet accurately, toward the plate from his stubby, gnarled fingers.

Brown was also a fitness fanatic. While undertaking his daily running regimen he would sometimes leap and spin and pirouette like a top—when asked what he was doing, Brown cheerfully replied, "Learning to field bunts." An excellent defensive player, Brown also included twice-a-day isometrics in his exercise routine, often conducted in concert with teammates who quickly discovered they could never keep up with him.[3]

A trade made in anger by Cubs president James Hart netted the franchise Mordecai "Three Finger" Brown—a deal that proved one of the most fortuitous in team history. Over the next nine years, Brown would win 186 games, pitch the Cubs to four National League pennants, and engage in one of the greatest pitching rivalries of all time with New York Giants star Christy Mathewson. (Library of Congress—George Grantham Bain Collection.)

Prior to spring training in 1904, James Hart sent every married man on the team an invitation to bring their wives along to California. Despite his lacking a spouse, Evers somehow received one of the letters at his home in Troy; amused by the missive and obviously relishing single life as a ballplayer in a big city, Evers wrote back that he lacked a wife, and furthermore, he "was keeping hidden in Troy lest some maiden should drag him out and claim him."[4]

When Frank Selee met Evers in California, the Cubs manager was pleased that the twenty-two-year-old had put on some weight; he was certain the added heft would aid the second baseman against bigger men barreling in to break up double plays. Selee openly predicted Evers would be the best second baseman in the league.[5]

Because fielders' gloves were small, the orthodox method of receiving a throw at second base involved using both hands. But Evers, always looking for an edge, spent the spring catching tosses one-handed, which allowed him to extend his reach while maintaining his balance, something especially advantageous in fielding inaccurate throws. Although he would be criticized by those who scoffed that his style of play was what one today would term "hot-dogging," Evers could not care less. As he had when a boy years before in the bleachers at Troy, he constantly sought ways to improve.

Another practice Evers questioned was the prevalent technique for making throws; at the time, after fielding a ground ball, second basemen set their feet and then threw overhand to first base. Evers noted, "The record for running the distance from the plate to first base, a distance of ninety feet, is three and one-fifth seconds. That means the runner is covering about twenty-eight feet per second ... you cannot afford to lose even one-tenth of a second, because even so small a loss of time will give the runner an advantage of 2.8 feet according to [this] example." His solution was the sidearm—or what he called the underhand—snap throw. Encouraged by Frank Chance, Evers would practice snap throws by the hour, beginning from a stationary position and then incorporating various scenarios while on the move until he was as accurate as he had been using the orthodox method.[6]

Evers also practiced moving off the bag with the catch, side-stepping base runners hurtling toward him from his blind side, hell-bent on destruction. This allowed him to quicken his release. He attempted to make his tag plays by catching the ball and sweeping his glove onto sliding runners in one motion. Evers *was* flashy around the bag—but his unusual style proved both crowd-pleasing and effective. It was nothing less than the birth of the modern style of playing second base.

Always the most energetic man on the field, Evers became more vocal in his second full season. He and Joe Tinker were constantly devising plays, developing signals, and discovering creative methods of getting under an opponent's skin. Evers greatly admired Johnny Kling, whose nickname "Noisy" was bestowed in recognition of the fact that he never shut up during games. He noticed Kling's ability to criticize umpires in ways that would work to his later advantage, or at least make his point without being ejected; Evers would never master the art of challenging umpires as Kling did—a relentless competitor, Evers tended to press his points aggressively, something for which he quickly became known.

Evers, Tinker and Kling made the Cubs one of great examples of "inside baseball" and probably the most combative team in the game—a characteristic that admirers referred to as "ginger." Detractors branded it as "bush" and downright annoying.

The Cubs hoped to get off to as fast a start as they had in 1903, but were handicapped by injuries to all three of their catchers—Frank Chance, Johnny Kling and Jack O'Neill. At one point, Doc Casey was pressed into service at the position when no one else was available.[7] A dozen games into the 1904 season, Chicago's record was only 5–6, plus a tie.

Things began turning around for the Cubs in their first series against the Pirates. Evers was gaining a reputation for playing his best against the better teams, and he seemed to be everywhere against Pittsburgh, almost like a shortstop playing second base. He had four putouts and eight assists in the first game of the series on April 30, and four putouts and six assists the next game. He had ten assists on May 3 as the Cubs won 15–3 despite being victimized by a triple play, and he closed the series with seven assists and two more putouts—including a running, leaping catch of a line drive in short right field—during the Cubs' fourth win in the five-game series.[8]

Not long after, outfielders Jimmy Slagle and Jack McCarthy were sidelined by injuries, necessitating the shift of battery mates Johnny Kling and Bob Wicker to the outer garden to fill the breach. Despite the patchwork lineup, the Cubs continued winning; their streak had reached seven games when the front-running New York Giants came to West Side Grounds on May 20. National League president Harry Pulliam was on hand to watch Giants star Christy Mathewson take the mound in the first game of the series against Jake Weimer.

The game entered the bottom of the ninth with the score 2–1 in favor of New York. Frank Chance was first up for the Cubs and, patient as always, he walked on four pitches. After Johnny Kling singled to left, Davy Jones followed with a perfect bunt down the third base line to load the bases. Infielders Otto Williams and Joe Tinker, coaching the bases, admonished the home crowd to rise from their seats and shout support for the home team.

Evers was up next. With photographers lining the field, flash powder exploding at every move, Evers took the first pitch for a ball. At that moment, Johnny Kling wandered a bit too far off the second base bag and Giants catcher Jack Warner, instantly measuring the distance and calculating the necessary velocity for a successful throw, knew he had him. In a flash he fired the ball past Mathewson and picked off his rival catcher. Warner then readied himself for a return throw and a possible collision—he hoped Chance would try to score from third on the play. But the Cubs captain did not take the bait.

There was nothing Kling could do but sheepishly trot back to the bench, head down, before a suddenly quieted crowd. Once Kling retired from the field, the fans turned their attention back to Evers and resumed screaming.

Evers squeezed the bat handle and stared at Mathewson, who stared right back. As the right-hander let go of the next pitch, Evers flicked the bat straight out from his body and allowed the ball to hit it, absorbing enough force that the ball bounded slowly to Mathewson's right. Evers fell away from the pitch at contact, immediately dropping the bat and sprinting from the batter's box in a mad dash for first base, dirt clods flying in his wake. Mathewson snatched at the ball with his bare hand but it glanced off his fingers and dribbled a few inches away. Chance had broken for the plate the instant Evers bunted the ball, and it was already too late to catch him; Mathewson knew his only play was to try retiring Evers at first. But Evers was far too fast and Mathewson's throw wasn't nearly in time. The crowd exploded in celebration as Chance scored the tying run. Not only that, Davy Jones had moved up to second on the play.

Jack O'Neill was the next batter and he immediately lined a pitch into right-center, scoring Jones with the winning run; the Chicago Cubs had captured their eighth win in a row and were in first place.[9]

The Cubs continued winning, capturing sixteen of eighteen as they jockeyed for the league lead with both the Giants and Cincinnati Reds. The Cubs were hitting only .238 as a team—nearly forty points off their 1903 pace—but their much-improved pitching was keeping them in the race. On June 4, Evers slapped three singles and a double in his first four times at bat, as he and Joe Tinker combined for seven hits against Philadelphia to move Chicago into first place once again.[10]

But they dropped two of three at Brooklyn before heading to the Polo Grounds on June 10 for a three-game set against the Giants in what was rapidly evolving into baseball's most heated rivalry. Christy Mathewson one-hit the Cubs in the first game of the series, as Evers saw his hitless string stretch to fourteen at bats since his big day in Philadelphia.[11] But Bob Wicker nearly matched Mathewson's feat the next afternoon, pitching a twelve-inning, two-hit shutout for an exciting 1–0 Chicago victory in front of more than twenty-eight thousand fans. Joe McGinnity took the loss, his first of the season after starting the year with twelve consecutive wins.

Wicker's victory was a true nail-biter. Evers committed a base-running blunder in the seventh inning; with two out, he doubled and then moved to third on Joe Tinker's single. When Jack Warner tossed the ball back to McGinnity, Tinker attempted a delayed steal. McGinnity wheeled and fired to Bill Dahlen, who was covering second. It was clear that Tinker was going to be out by several feet, but Dahlen dropped the ball.

Seeing this, Evers made a break for home, thinking Dahlen had forgotten him. He had not. Dahlen alertly grabbed the ball before it rolled away and fired a strike to Warner, who tagged the sliding Evers at the plate to end the inning.

Evers was able to redeem himself in the top of the twelfth. Chance led off with a single and then beat a throw to second on an attempted double play. After Chance advanced to third on a grounder, Evers came to the plate. Reaching for an outside pitch, he slapped the ball the opposite way, just beyond the reach of Giants third baseman Art Devlin, to score Chance with the lead run. Wicker struck out Devlin in the bottom of the twelfth to end the game and the pitcher was carried triumphantly from the field on the shoulders of Cubs fans who had vaulted from the stands to celebrate.[12]

The Cubs closed out the series with a 3–2 win against Mathewson as Frank Chance hit a double, a triple and a home run; Chicago was once again in the lead with a record of 29–14. New York was at 29–15 and Cincinnati 30–16.[13]

But the Cubs lost five of their next seven and never again saw first place. Evers wrenched his ankle in a loss to Boston on June 14 and missed the next game, which the Cubs also lost.[14] Chicago dropped five in a row to begin July, including defeats by scores of 10–2, 19–2 and 11–6. Jake Weimer had to be carried from the field on July 4 when a ball hit by opposing pitcher Roscoe Miller struck him on the kneecap; he was not seriously hurt, but the Cubs could not seem to shake the series of injuries and misfortunes that had nagged them since the start of the season.[15]

Flashes of frustration erupted among the players. Weimer was suspended for three days by Frank Selee for "insubordination." Frank Chance shoved an umpire in a game against Cincinnati at West Side Grounds, igniting a near-riot that earned him a three-day suspension from the league.[16] Tinker and Weimer engaged in a fistfight that left Weimer with a black eye.[17]

The Cubs were streaky all season; they won eleven of twelve in mid–July, including eight in a row—then lost five of six, including three out of four to New York at home. In August, they won six in a row, then lost three of four, won four in a row, and dropped four straight. In September, they had an eight-game winning streak, immediately followed by a six-game skid. They managed to take four of five at the end of the month against New York at the Polo Grounds, but the pennant race had long been decided by then. The Cubs finished one rung higher in the standings than in 1903, in second place, thirteen games behind the Giants, who won 106 games.

Meanwhile, Johnny Evers had established himself as one of the game's best second basemen. He also proved durable, playing in 152 games, and had gained attention for his style of play—the one-handed catch and tag, the sidearm snap throw, side-stepping of base runners on his follow-through, and the constant maneuvering and calling of defensive plays. Evers had not only become a crowd favorite, he was changing the way his position was played. Not that his technique was completely polished; Evers led National League second basemen in putouts and assists—he led all infielders (except for first basemen) in total chances. But he also led all second basemen in errors.

The Cubs had only one player, Frank Chance, hit higher than .270; the team's batting average dropped twenty-seven points from a year earlier, and that proved too much to overcome, even as Cubs pitchers allowed almost a half-run less per game than in 1903; Mordecai Brown and Jake Weimer both finished in the league's top five with earned run averages of less than two runs per game. There was work to be done if the Cubs were going to overhaul the Giants in 1905.

The Cubs made four major additions for 1905—utility man Arthur "Solly" Hofman, who had joined Chicago at the tail end of the 1904 season, outfielders Bill Maloney and Frank Schulte—the latter a former opponent of Johnny Evers in the New York State League—and Notre Dame pitcher Ed Reulbach. All of them, aside from Reulbach, who was coaching a college team and thus excused from spring training, joined twenty-one teammates in Santa Monica, California, in early March.

The trips to California were expensive, and James Hart hoped 1905 would be the year his investment would pay off. But rain wreaked havoc with the training schedule—far from what Hart had hoped. The Cubs finally left for home on March 28 with Joe Tinker nursing a bad thumb, Frank Chance a bad ankle, and the team plagued by inactivity and lackluster play due to the inclement weather.

Not only that, Frank Selee was extremely ill—he lost fifteen pounds during spring training. He was beginning to lose a battle with tuberculosis.

While Cubs players had been attempting to round into shape in California, James Hart had been making improvements at home. He added an upper deck to the bleachers at West Side Grounds and completed plans to remodel the clubhouse, featuring new lockers and a half-dozen showers.

But changes to the home field did not translate into changes in the fortunes of the team that played there. Injuries plagued the Cubs from the outset of the 1905 season. Frank Chance was out of the lineup with a sprained foot that was encased in a walking cast, and Bob Wicker was under quarantine with what was feared to be smallpox. The durable Johnny Evers was about to be bitten by the injury bug as well.

The Cubs had split their first six games of the season when they faced Cincinnati at West Side Grounds on April 22. In the top of the tenth with the score tied at 3–3, Reds rookie Cliff Blankenship reached first via error, and Johnny Kling decided to call a trick play in an effort to catch him by surprise. He signaled for Evers to sneak over and behind Blankenship and then fired the ball to first base.

Unfortunately, the throw was off target, and as Evers reached for the ball, Blankenship stumbled, slamming his shoulder squarely into Evers's midsection. The force threw the Cubs infielder onto his back. As Evers opened his eyes and stared into the sky, attempting to make sense of what had happened, he tried struggling to his feet but realized he could not. He attempted to breathe, but could only gasp to no real effect—it felt as if a cannonball had been imbedded in his midsection. Evers was finally carried off the field. The injury was not considered serious at first—he gamely insisted he would be back in the lineup the next day.[18] Then it was day to day. Ultimately he missed almost an entire month.

Frank Chance made his return from his foot injury on May 17 and Evers rejoined him in the lineup a day later. But the team still failed to hit. By mid–June the Cubs were barely batting .220 as a team, with Chance, whose average was nearly .400, the only player inflicting any damage on opposing pitchers. On June 13, Christy Mathewson no-hit Chicago in a magnificent pitchers' duel against Mordecai Brown. Only two Cubs batters reached base, both on errors. Brown carried a two-hit shutout through eight innings, but weakened after striking out Mike Donlin for the third time to lead off the ninth and surrendered four hits and the winning run. Evers made a sparkling defensive play when Art Devlin stole second in the seventh; Kling's throw was too wide and too late to retire Devlin, but Evers made a one-handed stab of the ball and slapped his glove on Devlin when he over slid the bag.[19]

Mathewson's no-hitter came during a stretch in which the Cubs were actually gaining momentum—it was their only loss in thirteen games. During that period, Chicago pitchers allowed more than two runs only twice. The Cubs also began scoring—Evers went three for three in an 18–2 shellacking of St. Louis, which was followed the next day by a 9–1 blasting of the Cardinals. Ed Reulbach was providing a big boost to the pitching staff, despite constant weariness stemming from his inability to sleep on trains. He defeated Jack

Taylor, 2–1, as both men pitched eighteen-inning complete games, Frank Schulte's triple and Billy Maloney's sacrifice fly finally clinching victory for the Cubs.[20] Reulbach later pitched a twenty-inning complete-game victory against Philadelphia, with Chance calling the pitches for the rookie from his position at first base. Reulbach lost seven pounds during the game and slept almost all of the next day.[21]

July 21 was Evers's twenty-fourth birthday—although everyone else thought it was only his twenty-second—and he celebrated in Boston by hitting his first major league home run. Leading off in the fifth inning, he smacked Chick Fraser's second pitch over the right field fence. Relishing his first homer since shortly before his father died, Evers took his time trotting slowly around the bases. He capped off the day with an eleventh-inning double that scored Frank Chance with the winning run.[22]

But the rest of July was a disaster for Evers. He committed four errors against Pittsburgh on July 5 in an 11-inning, 8–3 loss.[23] Late in the month he severely injured his thumb and missed several games. Evers tried returning to the lineup on July 29 but made two errors and was pulled from the game; he would miss another month because of his hand injury—his second extended absence of the 1905 season.[24]

⚾ ⚾ ⚾

Frank Selee was obviously not a well man. His lost weight and sunken features alarmed many, and he was not directing the team with his usual energy and passion. On July 1, Selee's doctor ordered him to bed, publicly blaming the manager's physical deterioration on intestinal problems; Frank Chance was temporarily placed in charge.[25] Then Selee developed a fever and was hospitalized for what was announced as appendicitis.[26] For a time he was unable to take solid food and grew weaker—the result of his worsening case of tuberculosis.

On July 28, Selee wrote a letter to James Hart, requesting a leave of absence: "It is with sincere regret, as it is hard for me to sever myself from the pleasant associations I have enjoyed under you." Selee went on to say that he was proud of his players and hoped to return the next spring.[27] In early August, Selee announced he was leaving for Colorado with his wife in an effort to regain his health.[28] A benefit was eventually organized in late September, with all receipts going to the Cubs manager.[29]

At the same time Selee was exiting, James Hart decided it was time to step aside after sixteen years at the helm of the Cubs and twenty-five years in the game. On July 15, he announced he was phasing out of his duties with the Cubs and selling controlling interest in the franchise to Charles W. Murphy, a former secretary of the New York Giants; Murphy was named the team's

vice-president. It was said that he would assume many of the duties tradition-
ally assigned to Hart and would eventually succeed him as president.[30]

It was clear that Murphy, who had once been employed by the *Cincinnati
Times-Star*, had a financial backer—he was not wealthy enough to purchase a
team on his own. Given his background with the Cubs' main rival, there was
concern that the Giants might be making a clandestine grab at control. However, it turned out that the man financing Murphy was Charles P. Taft, brother
of William Howard Taft, secretary of war under Theodore Roosevelt and his
eventual successor as president of the United States.[31] Taft lived in Cincinnati,
was friendly with Cincinnati Reds management, and, like his brother, was an
enormous fan of the game.

Johnny Evers finally returned to the lineup on September 3, after missing
another thirty-one games. By that time it was too late for the Cubs to make a
run at the Giants, but they did have one more series to play against them—
and like most Cubs-Giants series, it did not lack for passion.

There were so many injuries and ejections in the opening game that John
McGraw had to play left field for a couple of innings. Afterward, the pugna-
cious Giants manager nearly got into a fistfight with a Cubs fan, an altercation
prevented only by the alert intervention of a nearby policeman. The worst
was ignited in some that afternoon—fans threw pop bottles from the bleachers
at Giants right fielder George Browne as he chased down Billy Maloney's triple.
New York shortstop Bill Dahlen collided with Chicago rookie Hans Lobert
when Lobert attempted to steal a base. The two barked at each other, "warming
the atmosphere a bit." Johnny Evers smacked a pair of doubles—one of which
he unsuccessfully attempted to stretch into a triple—and committed two
errors. But he also made a great play on a looping liner in short left field that
kept the Giants from loading the bases in the eighth inning.

Evers scored the winning run the next day against Mathewson, handing
the great right-hander his first defeat since July 4. The winning tally came with
Evers at third and Jimmy Slagle at first. A slow grounder was hit to Bill Dahlen,
who raced to second in an attempt to beat a sliding Slagle to the bag for a
force out to end the inning. It was a close play, and Dahlen, in an effort to
project confidence that he had successfully retired the runner, rolled the ball
back to the pitcher's mound. The only problem was that Slagle had been called
safe. Dahlen managed to fool only Mathewson, who had headed for the bench
and was not there to pick up the ball. Seeing this, Evers dashed home without
a throw.

The series finale boasted the second largest crowd in the history of West
Side Grounds, an estimated twenty-seven thousand. One feature of the game

Joe Tinker (left) and Johnny Evers. They performed as if one person on the infield, but did not speak to each other for nearly two years after engaging in a fistfight prior to an exhibition game in Bedford, Indiana, in September 1905. (National Baseball Hall of Fame Library—Cooperstown, New York.)

was umpire Bob Emslie blacking out one pitch after being hit by a foul tip in the chest; he fainted when he looked up to watch a foul fly into the grandstand. Emslie recovered to finish the game and the Cubs won easily, thanks to a nine-run fifth inning against Joe McGinnity and Red Ames. Evers hit his third double of the series, and he and Tinker handled twenty chances between them with only one error, committed by Tinker.[32]

The Cubs ended their season with a double-header sweep of St. Louis on a beautiful autumn day in Chicago. Evers scored the winning run in the twelfth inning of the first game, having reached base after, as the *Chicago Tribune* reported, "St. Louis second baseman [Art] Hoelskoetter got the ball mixed up with some of the consonants in his name and fumbled it." Mordecai Brown won the seven-inning nightcap—his eighteenth victory of the season against twelve losses after starting the season 4–9—and even hit a home run.[33] Chicago finished in third place with a record of 92–61, somewhat disappointing for a team that had as its goal to win it all. Jake Weimer and Ed Reulbach joined Brown as eighteen-game winners, with Reulbach compiling an impressive 1.42 earned run average, second in the league behind only Christy Mathewson. Carl Lundgren and Bob Wicker added thirteen wins apiece for a pitching staff with a team earned run average of 2.04.

Johnny Evers had enjoyed another successful season, albeit an interrupted one, hitting .276 in 99 games to lead all National League second basemen in batting average for the second time in three seasons. He finished third among Cubs regulars in hitting and second in sacrifice hits, despite missing more than fifty games. More importantly, the twenty-four-year-old had combined with twenty-five-year-old Joe Tinker to form one of the best middle infields in the game.

The two men disagreed on the origin of their feud. Johnny Evers claimed it began when Joe Tinker threw a ball to him as hard as he could at extremely close range, injuring his hand and then laughing about it. For his part, Tinker traced their mutual animosity to an incident prior to an exhibition game on September 13, 1905, at Bedford, Indiana.

The Cubs were taking advantage of a break in the schedule to play a series of exhibition games. When the team arrived in Bedford, Evers agreed to arrange for a carriage to take several players, including the extremely superstitious Tinker, from the hotel to the ballpark the next day. But Evers and the carriage departed without Tinker, leaving the shortstop to make his own arrangements, contrary to his usual custom. The two men had reportedly bickered all summer, and when Tinker finally arrived at the ballpark, he was steaming.

Tinker spotted Evers in the outfield and sprinted over to where he was standing. A shouting match ensued, which soon begat punching. The fight, which attracted the rapt attention of those present, continued unabated until Bob Wicker, a native of Bedford, pulled the men apart. None of the Cubs players would talk about the incident, which occupied members of the Chicago press well past midnight as they relayed news of the altercation.[34]

Evers would later place Tinker's throwing the ball at him as occurring in

1907, but it makes sense that it would have happened about this time—perhaps shortly after he had recovered from his thumb injury, which had kept him out of the lineup until a week and a half before the Bedford exhibition. The mists of time conspire to render a murky chronology—but in the wake of these episodes, Evers and Tinker would later claim they did not speak off the field to each other for the better part of the next two years. Ironically, at the same time the two would reach the height of their success, in no small part due to one another.

CHAPTER FOUR

===============================

The Best Team in Baseball, But Not Necessarily in Chicago

On October 16, 1905, the Chicago Cubs clinched the second-ever City Series against the Chicago White Sox and, bragging rights in tow, James Hart bid an official goodbye to baseball.[1] While doing so, he could not help speaking as if he would continue having a direct hand in the Cubs' future: "We have so many players that have made good, but have not reached their prime.... With the new material we already have and a deal or two which we hope to make during the winter, I believe a team can be built up which eventually will win the pennant. It may not be next year, but it is bound to come...."[2]

There was speculation all winter about who would manage the Cubs in 1906; Frank Chance had served well in that role, but there was concern that pulling double duty would diminish his much-needed contributions as a player. Some speculated about a Frank Selee return, but he was far too ill.[3] There were rumors that Cap Anson wanted the job—but that proved nothing more than idle talk. Ned Hanlon and Cubs scout George Huff were also mentioned.[4] In the end, Charles Murphy stuck with Chance, signing him to a three-year contract.

Frank Chance was as different from Frank Selee as Charles Murphy was from James Hart. Chance was a poker player and managed like one—relying on variations of delayed and double steals. Deaf in his left ear, he had a bit of a stutter—some thought that, like his deafness, it was related to repeated blows to the head by pitched balls. Christy Mathewson recalled Chance's speaking with a slight lisp that became more pronounced as he became angry—not that anyone dared point it out.[5]

As the unquestioned boss, he gave no quarter to his men; in addition to being manager, he was the team's best player and in a position to challenge anyone on the team. He was not at all hesitant to do so. When Johnny Kling was holding out in the spring, he wrote Chance that he would report if given a raise. Chance fired back, "Won't expect you with us this year."[6] Kling reported.

When Johnny Evers showed signs of becoming more combative with umpires, Chance took him aside and sternly lectured, "If there is any kicking to be done on this team, I'll do it. If I hear any of it from you or anyone else, I'll put you out of the game myself."[7] Evers had complete respect for Chance and did as he was told.

Now that Chance was in charge, there were changes he wanted to make, the first of which was replacing thirty-six-year-old Doc Casey at third. Left-hander Jack Pfiester had been acquired from Omaha, which made Jake Weimer expendable. Chance traded the thirty-two-year-old Weimer to Cincinnati in exchange for Harry Steinfeldt—an excellent if injury-prone and luck-challenged third baseman for the Reds. Twenty-eight years old and a veteran of eight seasons with Cincinnati, Steinfeldt had only once played as many as 130 games in a major league season, but he was talented, and when not moping or obsessed about the fates being against him, he was as good as there was at the hot corner.[8]

With Steinfeldt on board, Chance unloaded Casey along with pitcher Button Briggs and outfielders Jack McCarthy and Billy Maloney to Brooklyn in exchange for outfielder Jimmy Sheckard—a solid player if a bit streaky with the bat; Chance despised hitters who habitually swung at the first pitch, which is why he exhibited little angst about parting with the speedy Maloney.[9] He also sent Jack O'Neill to Boston for Pat Moran in a swap of back-up catchers.

Johnny Evers spent the winter working in the Troy shoe store he had purchased in 1903. Evers had always wanted to branch out into the business world, and had acquired the establishment from the previous owners at the suggestion of their store manager. In exchange for arranging the deal and running the establishment on a day-to-day basis, Evers awarded the store manager half interest in the business. Evers arrived at the shop each day, which bore his name in large, gold letters above the display window; much of the time his duties consisted of talking baseball with the folks of Troy, who knew him well and addressed him as "Johnny."

In the evenings, Evers chain-smoked his beloved cigars and played pinochle with his old pals. But baseball was always on his mind—he struggled to gain weight, knowing the long season would melt away pounds he could not otherwise afford to lose. He wanted to be known as a durable player and the ninety-nine games he played in 1905 was not his idea of durability.

Evers began the 1906 season almost as if a man possessed. On Opening Day in Cincinnati he made a diving attempt on a hit up the middle by Miller Huggins, turning a complete somersault that landed him back on his feet after he failed to come up with the ball.[10] The next day he saved a run by cutting off a hot grounder with Cy Seymour on third when Seymour, who thought the ball would get past Evers, broke for the plate. Evers let his momentum carry him straight at the Reds' base runner, who vainly attempted to process the sight of this crazy infielder making a beeline for him across the diamond instead of making a throw. Seymour froze in his tracks, unable to decide what to do. Evers simply ran up to him and tagged him out.[11] Evers made another

Frank Chance demanded obedience from his players. When Evers began arguing with umpires, Chance took him aside and scolded him. "If there is any kicking to be done on this team, I'll do it," he lectured Evers. Chance remains the only manager of the Chicago Cubs in the last century to lead his team to a World Series title, accomplishing the feat twice. (Library of Congress—George Grantham Bain Collection.)

diving stop behind second in a game against St. Louis, flat out on the ground, to save a possible base hit.

The Cubs continued their annual pattern of early-season inconsistency. They hosted Pittsburgh on April 25 at West Side Grounds, after splitting the first two games of the series. The game went into the eleventh inning, at which point the Cubs unraveled defensively, beginning with pitcher Jack Pfiester's bobble of Honus Wagner's one-out grounder. Once Pfiester finally gathered possession of the ball, he threw it past Chance, who, after chasing it down, threw to second in an effort to get Wagner. Unfortunately, Wagner was the only one in the immediate vicinity, so he continued on to third.

Pfiester struck out the next batter and it appeared he would escape further damage when the next man up dribbled a grounder to Evers. However, Evers bobbled the ball, dropped it, and then picked it up only to have it squirt backward out of his hand as Wagner scored.[12] The defeat dropped the Cubs into a tie with St. Louis for sixth place.

The sloppy loss seemed to shake the team out of its lethargy; the Cubs immediately began a ten-game winning streak that moved them into first place on May 7. When asked about his team's standing, Charles Murphy admitted that he felt "pretty good." He went on to say, "The standing of the club at the present time justifies the changes made last winter at the suggestion of Capt. Chance, who is an excellent judge of players as well as a grand ballplayer. We have a good ball team and will be in the race to the finish."[13]

Chance was not yet satisfied—he coveted more pitching and arranged to acquire two-time twenty-game winner Jack Harper from Cincinnati to complete an earlier trade that had sent Hans Lobert to the Reds.

Thirty-four games into the 1906 season, the Chicago Cubs were in first place. But as always, their measuring stick was the New York Giants. John McGraw brought his hobbled two-time defending National League champions to Chicago on May 20 for a four-game series. Christy Mathewson was not at top speed—he was still recovering from a near-fatal case of diphtheria— and Mike Donlin, the Giants' best hitter, was on crutches with a broken ankle.

Twenty-five thousand fans converged on the West Side Grounds for the first game—when tickets stopped being sold at two-thirty, two thousand disappointed patrons were standing outside on the sidewalk. Another 1,500 posited themselves on rooftops outside the ballpark for a bird's-eye view of the proceedings. Additional police were summoned to control the crowd, which had pushed its way onto the playing field and erased the chalk lines; they had to be redrawn before the game could start.

The Giants, aiming to intimidate, donned the black uniforms they had worn while defeating the Philadelphia Athletics in the World Series the previous October. They struck first, stringing together four hits in the third to score three runs. The Cubs answered with two runs in the bottom of the inning, thanks to doubles by Jimmy Slagle, Jimmy Sheckard and Frank Schulte.

The Cubs tied the score in the fifth and had the bases loaded with one out and Evers at the plate. Frank Chance was on third and signaled for a squeeze play, which Evers executed perfectly. Giants catcher Frank Bowerman leaped from behind the batter's box and snatched the ball in front of home plate, but instead of throwing to first to get Evers, he reversed his path in the hope of catching Chance flying down the line. The Cubs manager slid away from a diving Bowerman, scraping his toe across the back of the plate and kicking up a cloud of dust as the umpire screamed "Safe!" Shortly after that, Evers was momentarily knocked out in a collision with Giants second baseman Larry Gardner on a tag play, but somehow maintained contact with the bag. By the time the inning ended, five runs had crossed the plate and the Cubs were in control; they won, 10–4.[14]

But the next two days proved disappointing. Both Ed Reulbach and Bob Wicker were defeated by the aggressive Giants, who had torn so many of their black uniform trousers that they had switched back to their gray road togs with shirt fronts emblazoned with the phrase "World's Champions."[15]

After rain delayed the final game of the series by a day, New York took its third in a row from Chicago. The Giants scored five runs in the third; after Carl Lundgren walked in a run with two out, George Browne hit a slow roller to Evers, who threw wildly to first—so wildly that three runs scored before Chance could track down the ball. The Cubs rallied, knocking out Christy Mathewson after three innings, and tied the score in the fifth against Hooks Wiltse. But Joe Tinker let in the winning run with his second error of the game, the ball slipping out of his hands on a throw home.[16] The Giants were in first place. After the fifth-place St. Louis Cardinals swept the Cubs in a May 30 double-header, Chance felt he needed more pitching if he wanted to overtake McGraw and the Giants; Jack Harper had been a particular disappointment, remaining unavailable due to a torn fingernail suffered in practice. There also were whispers that he was not always eager to pitch.

On the first of June, Frank Chance got the man he wanted, Cincinnati's Orval Overall. The strapping six-foot-two right-hander had been a star athlete at the University of California and in the Pacific Coast League, winning thirty-two games for the PCL champion Tacoma Tigers in 1904. Signed by the Reds to great fanfare, he threw hard but tended to be wild, and lost twenty-three games in his rookie season while pitching more than three hundred innings. So far, his second season had been even more disappointing—a record of 4–5 with forty-six walks in eighty-two innings. Chance knew Overall well; they had played against each other as amateurs in central California. In fact, Overall had witnessed Chance's first serious beaning—one that had nearly killed him.

Overall maintained that Chance's hearing and speech were permanently impaired by the blow and said that the pitcher who had hit him, Charlie Button, was so shaken by the incident he never played again.[17]

Chance was certain Overall had been misused by the Reds, who assumed that because of his size he could work endlessly. Chance knew better and was certain he could correct the pitcher's control issues. The price for the Reds' right-hander was Bob Wicker—popular opinion held the trade to be an even swap of disappointing pitchers, but Chance was sure he got the better of the deal.[18]

The New York Giants welcomed the Cubs to the Polo Grounds on June 5 for another key series. Chicago had regained the lead by a game and a half, but the teams were even in the loss column. Pittsburgh was right on the heels of both.

Focused by the desire to beat the Giants, Johnny Evers corrected his recent defensive woes; in the first game of the series he had eight assists, at least four of which smothered sure base hits. William Koelsch, covering McGraw's team for *The Sporting Life*, commented, "[L]ittle Johnny Evers simply robbed our boys of hits all afternoon."[19] Mordecai Brown shut out the Giants as the Cubs won, 6–0.

It got worse for New York. In the second contest Orval Overall pitched eight innings in relief of Jack Harper, who was finally making his Cubs debut. Harper was hit on the hand by a line drive and immediately left the game due to injury; it would be the only inning the right-hander would ever pitch for Chicago.[20] Overall did a fine job as the Cubs clubbed the Giants, 11–3. Frank Schulte collected five hits and Joe Tinker four.[21]

Then the Cubs really humiliated New York, scoring eleven runs in the first inning the next day on the way to a 19–0 rout—it was a score Cubs fans would summon to taunt the Giants for years. Christy Mathewson lasted only one-third of an inning, and Joe McGinnity, who relieved him, had to be lifted after only an inning and a third.[22] Even though the Giants took the final game of the series, they had fallen to third place. Frank Chance and his players had sent a message to John McGraw—the pecking order of the National League had changed.

The Cubs returned from their three-week road trip to an enthusiastic crowd of fourteen thousand. A teddy bear craze was sweeping America at the time—the popular stuffed toys were nicknamed in honor of President Theodore Roosevelt—and Chance was presented with one encased in glass. The dee-lighted manager instantly declared it the team's official mascot. Chicago then defeated St. Louis, 8–7, with the Cubs manager scoring the win-

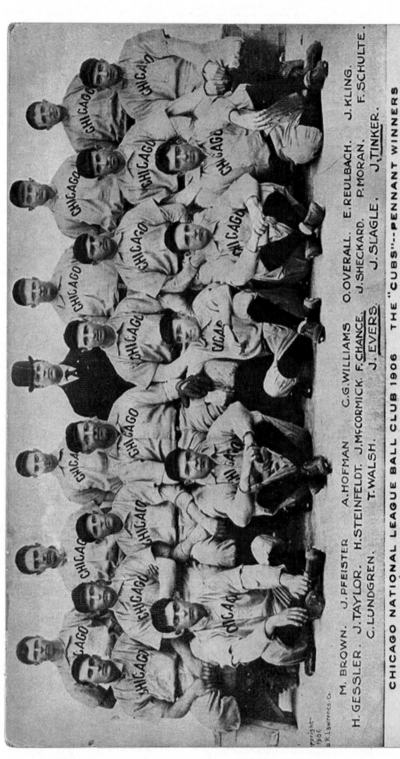

M. BROWN.   J. PFEISTER.   A. HOFMAN   C.G. WILLIAMS   O. OVERALL.   E. REULBACH.   J. KLING.
H. GESSLER.   J. TAYLOR.   H. STEINFELDT.   J. McCORMICK.   F. CHANCE.   J. SHECKARD.   P. MORAN.   F. SCHULTE.
C. LUNDGREN.   T. WALSH.   J. EVERS.   J. SLAGLE.   J. TINKER.

CHICAGO NATIONAL LEAGUE BALL CLUB 1906   THE "CUBS"--PENNANT WINNERS

"Tinker - Evers to Chance,"   1906

V. O. HAMMON PUB. CO., CHICAGO

ning run in the ninth on Harry Steinfeldt's single after the Cubs had blown a 6–0 lead.[23] Chicago followed that win with a remarkable streak of eight more consecutive one-run games, all featuring final scores of either 2–1 or 1–0, and won six of them.

The team was hitting well in 1906, with five men sporting batting averages better than .300—combined with dominant pitching and the spectacular defense of Tinker and Evers, Chicago was threatening to shatter all previous records for winning games. The Cubs were becoming a well-oiled machine, seemingly always positioned in the perfect defensive alignment. In *Touching Second*, Evers revealed the set of signals involved in the placement of the Cubs defense.

Every potential play began with Evers, who considered second base and shortstop as mirror positions—the gateway of the middle of the diamond. After spying Johnny Kling's signal to the pitcher, Evers shifted the outfield to the proper position by the placement of his right hand. Seeing that, Joe Tinker would call out to Harry Steinfeldt and they would shift into final position. Simultaneously, Chance, with his good ear toward second base, listened for a call from Evers that would give him the proper positioning. It was simple yet highly effective, and it relied on Johnny Evers's being able to relay signals in a way that could be rapidly deciphered even as the pitcher was in his wind-up.

That type of precision was the result of constant practice. Evers and Kling drilled for hours on throws; Evers would stand at second base and stick his glove out while Kling would throw until he could hit the glove without Evers's moving a millimeter.[24] Watching them was almost like witnessing military maneuvers.

◐ ◐ ◐

Frank Chance remained concerned about the depth of his pitching staff and decided to trade hard-throwing rookie Fred Beebe to St. Louis for a familiar face, his old roommate Jack Taylor.[25] The veteran pitcher had continued generating controversy following his departure from Chicago; after James Hart had privately accused him of shady play during the Cubs–White Sox series in 1903, Taylor loudly remarked to fans on his return visit to West Side Grounds

Opposite: **No major league team has ever captured more regular season victories than the 1906 Chicago Cubs, who finished eighty games above .500 and won the pennant by twenty games. Top Row: (L to R) Mordecai Brown, Jack Pfiester, Solly Hofman, Charles Williams (team secretary), Orval Overall, Ed Reulbach, Johnny Kling. Middle Row: Doc Gessler, Jack Taylor, Harry Steinfeldt, Jim McCormick (coach), Frank Chance, Jimmy Sheckard, Pat Moran, Frank Schulte. Bottom Row: Carl Lundgren, Tom Walsh, Johnny Evers, Jimmy Slagle, Joe Tinker. (McGreevey Photographs—Boston Public Library.)**

that there was no reason he should have accepted $100 for winning the City series when he would have received $500 for losing it (the series finished in a tie after fourteen games). Hart later publicly accused Taylor of dishonesty when the Browns upset Taylor's Cardinals in the 1904 St. Louis City Series. Taylor was separately accused of betting against his own team in Pittsburgh, and was openly branded a crook by National Commission chairman Garry Herrmann. But the pitcher escaped suspension since charges could not be conclusively proven—he was let off with a warning and a fine.[26]

Chance knew his old roommate would be motivated to avenge what he felt was a wrong done to him by Hart. As an added benefit, acquiring him prevented St. Louis from handing him over to either New York or Pittsburgh. A rotation of Brown, Pfiester, Reulbach, Overall and Taylor could match any in the game.

On August 1 the Cubs led both the Giants and Pirates by five games. Then they went on a tear; between August 6 and September 16, Chicago won an unbelievable thirty-seven of thirty-nine games to blow away the competition. The Cubs eventually won 116 games, establishing a still-standing record for victories in a National League season, while losing only thirty-six times, achieving another record for best one-season winning percentage by a major league team in the modern era. Jack Taylor and Orval Overall justified Chance's faith in them, both recording a 12–3 record for Chicago with earned run averages below two runs per game. Mordecai Brown collected twenty-six wins against only six losses with an incredible 1.04 ERA. Five pitchers boasted earned run averages under 2.00 and the team ERA was 1.76.

The Cubs were the first team in major league history to commit fewer than two hundred errors in a season—including the early days of the National League when teams played fewer than one hundred games. They stole 283 bases. Harry Steinfeldt hit .327, a career high that ranked second in the league behind Honus Wagner. Johnny Kling batted .319—nearly one hundred points higher than a year earlier—and Frank Chance hit .312.

The 1906 Chicago Cubs remain one of the greatest teams in regular season baseball history, and were heavily favored to win the World Series. To accomplish that, they would have to prove they were the best team in Chicago; their opponents would be Charles Comiskey and his White Sox.

Unlike the Cubs, the White Sox had to scratch and claw their way to the American League pennant, riding a nineteen-game winning streak in August to move into contention, and then hanging on by a three-game margin over the New York Yankees. Led by player-manager Fielder Jones, the Sox relied on their pitching—nicknamed "The Hitless Wonders," the team compiled the

Chicago White Sox pitcher Nick Altrock is protected by a cordon of police from a celebrating crowd following his victory in the first game of the 1906 World Series. (McGreevey Photographs—Boston Public Library.)

worst team batting average in the American League at .230, thirty-two points lower than the Cubs.

It was decided that home field would alternate for the first six games of the World Series, with the site of a deciding seventh contest, if necessary, determined by a coin toss. The Series began on October 9 at West Side Grounds; ticket prices ranged from fifty cents in the bleachers to two dollars for reserved box seats.

Frank Chance chose Mordecai Brown to pitch the opener against left-hander Nick Altrock, a breaking-ball specialist who had been the only Sox pitcher to defeat the Cubs in the 1905 Chicago City Series. The American League champs took the field wearing dark blue uniforms on a freezing cold day—many attendees inserted programs into their collars in a futile effort to ward off a howling wind that otherwise whistled unimpeded down their necks. There were even brief snow flurries before and during the game, although not enough to halt play.

The White Sox were somewhat banged up, with star shortstop George Davis relegated to day-to-day status by a bad back, but his substitute, George Rohe, picked up the slack, hitting a triple to lead off the game. After Brown struck out Jiggs Donahue, Patsy Dougherty hit a slow roller in front of the plate. Brown fielded it and tossed to Kling at home plate in time to get Rohe, but the Cubs catcher dropped the ball and Rohe was safe. In the White Sox sixth, Fielder Jones scored on Frank Isbell's single to give the White Sox a 2–0 lead.

The Cubs would only score once, on a wild pitch in the bottom of the sixth. Although a photo of a leaping Johnny Evers snagging a high throw from Kling to tag out Dougherty was published in the *Chicago Tribune*, the game belonged to the White Sox.

When Harry Steinfeldt hit a fly ball with two out in the ninth to Fielder Jones, the Sox manager began jumping up and down and waving his arms in celebration before the ball even got to him. Jones stuck the ball in his back pocket while White Sox fans stormed the field to mob Altrock, who was finally protected by a cordon of police officers.[27]

Game Two pitted Ed Reulbach against Doc White. The Cubs scored three times in the second inning thanks to a wild throw, a squeeze play and an infield hit. Evers and Tinker later worked a neat double steal in the sixth that led to a run, and in the ninth, Evers completed a pretty double play, snatching a hot grounder and tagging out George Rohe running past him before throwing to first.[28] Reulbach was dominant, allowing only one hit, and the Cubs won, 7–1, tying the series at a game apiece. But the victory exacted a price; the Cubs right-hander strained his arm during the game, and the next day he could not lift it.[29]

The third game featured a pitcher's duel between Jack Pfiester and White Sox spitballer Ed Walsh. The contest remained scoreless until the sixth, when third baseman Lee Tannehill, a .183 hitter in the regular season, lined a shot just inside the third base bag for a single. Walsh then drew a walk when Pfiester, who had struck out six in the first four innings, got too careful trying to prevent him from bunting successfully. The next hitter, Ed Hahn, was hit in the face while attempting to sacrifice, the pitch breaking his nose and forcing him from the game. Bill O'Neill took his place on the bases, which were now loaded with no one out.

Pfiester took a deep breath and settled to his task. Fielder Jones brought the crowd to its feet with a line shot down the right field line, but to the relief of Cubs fans it landed just outside the foul line. Jones then hit a pop-up behind home plate that Johnny Kling caught by reaching into the stands. Pfiester followed by striking out Frank Isbell and was suddenly only one out from digging himself out of the hole into which he had dug himself. Up to the plate stepped

George Rohe, hero of the first game. Wanting to get ahead in the count, Pfiester decided to throw a fast ball on the first pitch.

Rohe swung and met the ball squarely, sending it screaming down the third base line over Harry Steinfeldt's head. Jimmy Sheckard tore across to the left field line in an effort to cut it off, but it struck the ground and then bounded high into the crowd for a ground rule triple, scoring three runs. From that point forward it was all about Ed Walsh, who struck out twelve and held the Cubs hitless after the first inning. The White Sox led the series, two games to one.[30]

George Davis returned to the lineup in Game Four, which featured a rematch between Mordecai Brown and Nick Altrock. Evers, who had played sensational defense in the third game, would prove the hero, executing two more sparkling defensive plays; in the fourth inning he cut off what seemed a sure single by Frank Isbell and threw him out, and he saved a run in the fifth, cutting off Patsy Dougherty's bid for a hit while holding the White Sox runner at third.

The Cubs finally broke through in the seventh; Frank Chance singled to right and reached third thanks to a pair of sacrifices, bringing Evers to the plate. Chance impatiently pawed the dirt near third base, all too aware that the Cubs desperately needed his run. Evers swung at the first pitch and laced a shot to left; an exhilarated Chance was nearly across home plate before the ball hit the ground. Cubs fans reacted by waving banners and tossing hats in the air.

Down one run, the Sox had a runner at second with two out in the ninth. Frank Isbell waited out Mordecai Brown and, getting a pitch he liked, smashed a line shot back up the middle. Brown managed to block it with his hands but fell awkwardly. Quickly springing to his feet, he located the ball and threw out Isbell to end the game—a two-hit, 1–0 shutout.[31]

With the World Series knotted at two games apiece, twenty-three thousand people crowded into West Side Grounds for the fifth game, with another six to seven thousand inhabiting rooftops surrounding the stadium. Frank Chance, hoping to end the streak of road teams winning every game thus far, dressed his players in their road grays instead of the home whites. Prior to the start of the game, the Chicago Board of Trade presented Chance with a pair of live bear cubs. Prizefighter Bob Fitzsimmons sent a horseshoe, which the team kept on the bench for good luck.

Luck, however, was not to take up residence with the Cubs. The Sox struck for a run in the top of the first, held only to that thanks to Evers, who fielded a ball hit by Patsy Dougherty deep behind second base and threw him

Frank Chance dives back into first base, avoiding the tag of White Sox first baseman Jiggs Donahue. The 1906 World Series would prove far tougher than the public— or the Cubs—thought it would be. (McGreevey Photographs—Boston Public Library.)

out to end the inning. The Cubs answered with three runs in the bottom of the inning, thanks to two White Sox errors.

But the dead-armed Ed Reulbach could not hold the lead and had to be replaced by Jack Pfiester in the third. The White Sox put the game away with four runs off Pfiester and Orval Overall in the fourth to win 8–6. Frank Isbell smacked four doubles while switch-hitting George Davis hit two-baggers from each side of the plate.[32]

With the Cubs' backs against the wall, Chance asked Mordecai Brown to pitch the sixth game on one day's rest against Doc White. The crowds on the South Side were enthusiastic—at one point they broke down a gate leading to the left field bleachers and one hundred of them poured in before police could stem the tide.

The Cubs scored first, but the White Sox quickly answered in the bottom of the inning, thanks to George Davis's run-scoring double into the crowd—

Frank Schulte protested to no avail that a policeman bumped into him as he attempted to catch the ball. Later in the inning, Jiggs Donahue hit a two-run double and the White Sox led 3–1.

The game, and the Series, was decided in the next round. After Brown retired the first two batters, the White Sox scored four times against the fatigued Cubs ace. As the home fans began to realize their White Sox were going to win the World Series, they began waving banners and blasting tin horns while chanting the score in a manner not dissimilar to a college football crowd. When first baseman Jiggs Donahue fielded Frank Schulte's ground ball and stepped on first base for the final out of the 8–3 victory, the celebration began in earnest. Fans stormed the field, seeking their favorite White Sox player to pat him on the back. Charles Comiskey retreated to his office, where Charles Murphy tracked him down and, shaking his hand, told him, "If I had to lose, there's no one I would rather lose to than you."[33]

The Cubs were in shock. Frank Chance congratulated his opponents, but steadfastly believed the Cubs were the better team and vowed they would repeat as pennant-winners. Johnny Kling and Joe Tinker both admitted the White Sox outplayed the Cubs and deserved to win. Johnny Evers simply muttered, "I can't understand it...."[34]

It was the Cubs that had become "Hitless" without the "Wonder." Jimmy Sheckard was blanked in twenty-one at bats and Joe Tinker went three for eighteen. Johnny Evers had played spectacular defense, handling thirty-two chances without an error. But he too was ineffective at the plate, collecting only three hits in twenty at bats, one of those a double in the ninth inning of the final game. Interestingly, the White Sox won the Series despite committing fifteen errors to only five for the Cubs.

In a lot of ways it had been a successful season for the Cubs—they had been purchased a year earlier by Murphy and his financial backers for $105,000, and had cleared a profit nearly matching the purchase price during the 1906 season. They also had finally gotten past John McGraw and the Giants. But the goal was a World's Championship, nothing less, and fulfilling that objective remained at least a year away.

CHAPTER FIVE

World Champions

The Chicago Cubs may have fallen short of defeating the White Sox, but that did nothing to dampen the pride that the citizens of Troy, New York, had in Johnny Evers. When the impish second baseman returned home on October 18, they treated him as a conquering hero, carrying out elaborate plans that had been in place prior to the World Series. It was claimed that the crush of humanity on hand to greet Evers exceeded the turnout for Charles Evans Hughes, the Republican nominee for governor of the state of New York, who was campaigning in the city at the same time.

When Evers stepped off the train at eight o'clock that evening, he was greeted not only by a throng of admirers, standing on tiptoe and craning their necks for a glimpse of their favorite baseball player, but also by a carriage that was to carry him at the head of a procession through the city's streets to the Rensselaer Hotel, where he would be feted at a banquet held in his honor. Pulling the carriage was his own trotting horse "Cub," named in honor of his baseball team and reflecting his growing interest in the sport of kings. The street lamps of Troy flickered brightly against the moonless autumn night—but no more brightly than the smile on the face of Johnny Evers.

Arriving at the hotel, Evers alighted from his place of honor and was presented a silver loving cup by the St. Joseph's Club. The Elks gave him a diamond ring. Evers offered a few brief remarks during which he congratulated the White Sox, singling out George Davis, a native of nearby Cohoes. He praised Charles Murphy and his teammates, and promised the Cubs would accomplish even more in 1907. Several local luminaries followed Evers to the podium, and afterward the St. Joseph basketball team, which Evers was to coach over the winter, presented him a gold watch.[1]

In addition to coaching the basketball team at his old high school, Evers passed the off-season in his shoe store and promoted the increasingly popular winter sport of indoor baseball.[2] He invited Charles Murphy to Troy for an indoor game he had arranged against a team from New York, starring Philadelphia Athletics outfielder Rube Oldring and captained by Tim Jordan, slugging first baseman of the Brooklyn Superbas. Christy Mathewson's twenty-year-old brother, Henry, pitched for Jordan's team.[3]

Many of Evers's teammates were experiencing eventful winters as well. Johnny Kling became the pool champion of the state of Missouri. Frank Chance tended his orchard in California. Orval Overall played a few games at the end of the marathon Pacific Coast League season for the last-place Fresno Raisin Eaters.[4] Jimmy Slagle operated his feed and grist mill in Worthville, Pennsylvania, while Carl Lundgren ran his dairy farm in Marengo, Illinois. Henry Gessler earned his medical degree over the winter and was now imaginatively nicknamed "Doc." Pat Moran broke his nose playing handball and had to undergo surgery. Reserve catcher Tom Walsh retired at age twenty-one to work for his father on the building of the Panama Canal.[5]

Charles Murphy wanted to sign the core members of the Cubs before spring training, and Evers happily affixed his name to a two-year contract—not that he or any other player of the period had the option of taking their services elsewhere in organized baseball if their team wanted them.[6] Johnny Kling, of course, was a holdout—he always exerted serious effort when it came to avoiding training camp—as was Ed Reulbach, who unsuccessfully applied to the National Commission for free agency because Chicago had not forwarded him a contract over the winter. Charles Murphy pointed out that Reulbach had signed a three-year deal in 1906 and the National Commission sided with the Cubs in the matter, as expected.[7]

Of greater concern was the health of Joe Tinker, who had his appendix removed only days before spring training commenced. It was announced Tinker would be out of action for at least two months—a development that promised to put a definite crimp in the Cubs' plan to repeat as National League champions.

⚾ ⚾ ⚾

Opening Day in Chicago dawned gray and forbidding, as the Cubs prepared to defend their National League title. The wind skidded along the icy surface of Lake Michigan, arriving at West Side Grounds in not-so-gentle puffs, as fans took their seats under a dull sky that threatened rain, or worse. Men ratcheted down hats, folded collars up around their necks and, hands thrust in pockets, prepared to witness the beginning of the 1907 campaign. There were efforts to make the day as festive as possible; in honor of the team's 116-win season, every woman entering the ballpark was given a souvenir stickpin in the shape of a fan, inscribed "Chicago Cubs, World's Record Breakers." Cap Anson was on hand and presented a silk umbrella to each member of the defending National League champions.

After blowing on his hands in a valiant but futile attempt to keep warm, Johnny Evers bunted in his first at bat of the season and appeared to have beaten the throw, but was ruled out. He held his tongue and, other than offering a stern stare, managed not to betray disgust with the call. He later drove in Solly Hofman, who was playing in Joe Tinker's place, with a sacrifice fly—one of four times Hofman scored—as the Cubs won easily behind Orval Overall, 6–1.[8]

The Cubs and Giants sparred for the league lead during the first few weeks and by the time they met for the first time, on the twenty-first of May, it seemed as if neither team ever lost—the Cubs boasted a record of 23–5, one game behind New York at 24–4. The series opener featured the always crowd-pleasing matchup of Mordecai Brown versus Christy Mathewson; McGraw had been saving Mathewson for this game—he'd made only one start in the past thirteen days. Chance had done the same with Brown.

Both teams entered the playing field at the Polo Grounds via the centerfield fence; the unwritten rule had the Giants players walking along the first base side to reach their dugout, while visitors strolled along the opposite fence to access their bench. Evers had a habit of "forgetting" on which side he was supposed to enter, as a result of which he would pass in front of the Giants bench on his way to the visitors' dugout, making sure to utter some remark calculated to get a rise out of John McGraw, who would always fire back.[9]

Brown was a bit ragged at the beginning of the game, allowing a first-inning run, and the Polo Grounds faithful tossed lemons onto the field in an attempt to further rattle the right-hander—the fruit was meant to symbolize that Brown had turned "yellow" in a big game. But the Cubs ace settled down and the contest remained close from beginning to end, featuring a number of controversial calls that afforded both sides the opportunity to howl in protest. Roger Bresnahan had an especially rough day; he committed two errors and was caught on a steal attempt. In the bottom of the ninth, with Chicago leading, 3–2, Bresnahan managed to work Brown for a walk. Dan McGann then smacked a ground ball to Evers for what seemed a certain double play, but Bresnahan avoided being tagged by illegally running out of the base line. Evers successfully completed his throw and both base runners were called out.

Bresnahan rushed toward the umpire on a dead sprint, screaming and holding his hands apart to illustrate by how much Evers's tag had missed him. His argument fell on deaf ears. After Bill Dahlen flied out to end the game, Giants fans swarmed the field and surrounded both umpires; police swooped in to escort them to safety. The crowd was so worked up that at one point a policeman drew his pistol and fired into the air.[10]

The Cubs continued dominating the Giants, and after completing a sweep of New York at West Side Grounds in early June amid rumors that John McGraw was becoming more interested in Wall Street than baseball, Chicago was up by five and a half games. By mid–August their lead had exploded to fourteen. What the Cubs were accomplishing was unprecedented; during an eleven-month period from July 26, 1906, to June 26, 1907, they fashioned a record of 102–20—an .836 winning percentage.

A side effect of their dominance was a lack of attendance—a pennant race devoid of drama, combined with a severe economic recession, conspired to depress the turnstile count at West Side Grounds by one-third. The White Sox, in the midst of a competitive pennant race, would draw eighty thousand more patrons than in 1906, and two hundred thousand more than the Cubs.

The Cubs were involved in another riot in early July, this time in Brooklyn. With two out in the ninth and Chicago leading, 5–0, unruly fans fired pop bottles at Frank Chance, who finally had enough and angrily returned one of the projectiles, accidentally striking a small boy. This enraged the crowd, which threatened to tear down the flimsy wire screen that separated them from the playing field; the fans relented in their desire to attack only after Brooklyn owner Charles Ebbets promised to have Chance arrested. A detective escorted the shaken manager to the clubhouse and advised him to hide out until seven o'clock, at which point an armored vehicle would transport him to the Cubs' hotel. Chance then wisely packed his bags and left town ahead of the rest of the team.[11]

When the Cubs returned to the Polo Grounds in August, Chance received a death threat that included a warning that a bomb would be detonated on the Cubs' train if they defeated the Giants. Chance and his men responded by defeating Christy Mathewson in twelve innings, 3–2.[12]

Despite their lofty position in the National League, Cubs players once again endured what seemed an annual rite of misfortune. Ed Reulbach's wife had a baby girl who died shortly after birth in August.[13] Joe Tinker, having recovered from his appendix operation, injured his knee in an exhibition game at Altoona and missed several games.[14] Chance was forced to sit out for several weeks because of a severe case of the flu. Veteran pitcher Chick Fraser injured his arm, as did Mordecai Brown. Frank Schulte was in and out of the lineup with various ailments. Johnny Kling was sidelined by a hand injury, forcing an already lame Pat Moran back into the lineup.

But nothing was going to stop the Cubs. Their success was rooted in a team approach that sought nothing less than perfection, anchored defensively by Johnny Evers and Joe Tinker. The two men might not have been particularly fond of each other, but that did not impair their performance. In later years Evers would famously say, "Tinker and myself hated each other, but we loved the Cubs. We wouldn't fight for each other, but we'd come close to killing people for our team. That was one of the answers for the Cubs' success."[15]

Evers also felt the team's success was due, in part, *because* he and Tinker did not like each other; he flatly stated that team chemistry was overrated and pointed to his rivalry with Tinker as proof. Evers not only competed with the opposition, he competed with teammates. He wanted to be better than all of them—especially Tinker—and assumed his teammates competed with him as well, although that belief was likely exaggerated by his view of the world more than anything else.

Evers had become an unrelenting competitor—if a teammate made a mistake he was on him in an instant, striking swiftly with a verbal barrage designed to make certain it did not happen again. Not even Frank Chance, whom Evers idolized, was spared by his tongue—opponents were sometimes shocked at the things Evers said to his manager. But Chance understood Evers's behavior was not insubordination; it was the second baseman's way of motivating both himself and the team. Evers's ultimate goal was not individual honors; it was to win. As long as Chance was in charge, the Cubs responded to Evers's prodding, even if they did not always like it—or him.

The Cubs' defense was reliant not only on Johnny Evers's ability to maneuver players into proper position—he was dubbed the first lieutenant of Frank Chance's Board of Strategy—but also on the pitcher's ability to deliver the ball to the plate as expected. The Cubs' defense committed itself on each pitch—moving in tandem almost as if a machine. The players committed as a unit in order to cut off angles, to plug the "gaps." If a pitcher did not put the ball where he was supposed to, he would catch an earful and more from both Evers and Tinker. Their standards were high—perfection the minimum. If a pitcher lacked that kind of reliability, he did not last with the Cubs.

One pitcher who especially groused about being chastised was, not surprisingly, Jack Taylor. After a brilliant half-season for the Cubs in 1906, the grumpy veteran was not pitching as well, and not being used as often, in 1907. Taylor, whose record 187 consecutive complete games streak had ended the previous summer, did not make a start after August 21, a 12–4 loss to New York, and did not pitch at all during the final month of the season.[16]

He was finally released by the Cubs in late September after complaining that the behavior of Evers and Tinker made him want to take the ball and throw it over the fence. "There's no peace of mind in playing for a championship team," he declared. "You've got to go too strong to suit me in order to please everybody concerned. I'd much rather be with a second division aggregation where you don't have a lot of crabs jumping all over you all the time. When I go to work again it will be with some team that hasn't a chance for the pennant. Then I know there will be nothing to worry me, and there'll be some peace and satisfaction to my work."[17] Taylor never pitched again for a contender—in fact, he spent the rest of his career in the minor leagues.

Johnny Evers was struggling at the plate. He had his moments—back-to-back three-hit games against Boston in May, four steals against Brooklyn on June 14, and scoring the winning run while collecting three hits the next day.[18] He had four hits against the Superbas on August 1 and executed a clean steal of home against Cincinnati a month later, jackknifing his body away from home plate toward the pitcher's mound, managing to scrape his toe across the front of the plate to evade the catcher's tag in a daring and spectacular play.[19]

But those satisfying offensive moments were few and far between. Evers had always been a very consistent hitter—never too hot and never too cold; the fact that he was frequently asked to bunt prevented his amassing long hitting streaks during his career. But he had also always avoided long cold spells. This season was different. Between April 22 and May 16, Evers managed only five hits in fifty-eight at bats. He also endured slumps during the summer that reached two for twenty-seven and one for twenty-five.

Defensively he was as brilliant as ever, making only three errors in the Cubs' first twenty-six games for a .980 fielding percentage, and by summer was well on his way to his second five-hundred-assist season. He also reached into his usual bag of tricks—on one occasion in August against Philadelphia, he fooled Phillies base runner Sherwood Magee into thinking a fly ball was a grounder. Evers went through the motions of fielding the ball, even scooping a clod of dirt and tossing it to Tinker. By the time Magee realized what was going on, he was nearly to second base and the Cubs easily doubled him off first.[20]

Evers's batting average sat at .220 on September 8. That day, he was ejected from a game against Pittsburgh and his place was taken by Heine Zimmerman, a talented youngster making his major league debut—Zimmerman had been discovered by Evers while playing in the New York State League.[21] The ejection seemed to wake Evers's bat; he raised his batting average thirty points over the season's final month to a respectable if unspectacular .250— from September 11 to the end of the year, he batted .366.

The Cubs clinched their second straight National League pennant at West Side Grounds against Philadelphia, on a rainy day that twice saw game stoppages. The Cubs turned a triple play and Evers executed a clean steal of home for the second time within a month. Mordecai Brown tried out his sore arm for two innings and, satisfied, retired to the bench in favor of Ed Reulbach. Frank Selee happened to be in town for the Western League's annual meeting and was able to witness his old team clinch its second straight National League title.[22] The Cubs finished the 1907 season with a record of 107–45—nine games below the standard they had set in 1906, but seventeen games better than the second-place Pittsburgh Pirates.

One of their forty-five losses was a forfeit to the Cardinals on the next-to-last day of the season. The Cubs were in St. Louis for a double-header, and in the fourth inning of the first game, Evers attempted to steal third and was called out. No longer adhering to Chance's edict to hold his tongue, Evers argued long and loud enough that Cy Rigler threw him out of the game. In the bottom of the inning, the Cardinals' Shad Barry was called safe on an infield grounder; Chance, Tinker and Steinfeldt instantly surrounded Rigler, and as a result were invited to join Evers on the sidelines. Chance was allowed thirty seconds to make the required substitutions so the game could continue. When he failed to comply, the game was forfeited to St. Louis.[23]

Chance immediately left the ballpark, along with Orval Overall and Jack Pfiester. The three men sprinted across town to scout the recently crowned American League champion Detroit Tigers, who were visiting the St. Louis Browns.[24]

Frank Chance was going to seek every advantage—he was determined not to lose a second straight World Series.

Anything less than winning the World Series would represent failure as far as the Chicago Cubs were concerned. Their opponents, the Detroit Tigers, were led by their twenty-year-old phenomenon, Ty Cobb; the season had begun with most of Cobb's teammates refusing to speak to him and the front office shopping him around to other clubs. But such conflict merely served to fuel the third-year player's competitive streak. The Tigers held off Chicago, Philadelphia and Cleveland to capture their first American League pennant, and Cobb led the league with a .350 batting average; teammate Sam Crawford finished second at .323, and with Cobb constituted a most formidable offensive threat in the middle of the Detroit lineup. The pitching staff was deep, featuring a pair of twenty-five-game winners in Ed Killian and Bill Donovan. Detroit's manager was the ebullient Hughie Jennings, a former star shortstop and teammate of John McGraw with the original Baltimore Orioles.

The Tigers possessed a few faces familiar to Cubs fans—Davy Jones was in left field for Detroit, and Germany Schaefer played the utility role for the

Frank Chance and Detroit Tigers manager Hughie Jennings pose prior to the first game of the 1907 World Series. The Cubs would defeat the Tigers two years in a row in the Fall Classic. (McGreevey Photographs—Boston Public Library.)

Tigers. Forty-one-year-old Bobby Lowe, who after his release to make way for Johnny Evers made good on his promise of a comeback from his knee injury, was closing out his major league career as a bench-warmer for Detroit.

Fans lined up as early as eight o'clock in the morning for the first game, which was scheduled to begin at two-thirty. The Tigers began dribbling into the park around noon. Bill Donovan strolled causally onto the field, a pair of brand-new spikes tucked under his pitching arm. Hughie Jennings took off his cap, rubbed his hands through his bright red hair while glancing around the ballpark, and then posed for photographers. Ty Cobb, with one of his stockings ripped from the heel to halfway up the knee—for him a badge of honor—was accorded a rousing ovation. He responded by removing his cap and bowing to the crowd.

The Cubs' strategy was to run as much as possible against Tigers catchers—they would steal eighteen bases by the time the Series ended, including seven in the first game. Evers made a beautiful play to victimize the Tigers in the top of the fourth. With one out, Sam Crawford on second and Claude Rossman on first, Bill Coughlin hit a high pop fly into short center field.

Crawford thought the ball would fall safely and took off, but Evers made a brilliant running catch and tossed the ball back to Joe Tinker at second to complete an inning-ending double play. A photograph published in the *Chicago Tribune* shows Crawford no more than two strides from home plate when he realizes he is out and the inning is over.

The Cubs took a 1–0 lead in the bottom of the inning, but fell behind in the eighth when the Tigers pushed across three runs against Orval Overall thanks to a couple of singles and a pair of errors—two of five the Cubs would commit that day (including two by Evers), equaling their total for the entire Series against the White Sox the previous October.

But the Cubs knotted the game in the bottom of the ninth to send it into extra innings; the tying run scored when Donovan struck out pinch-hitter Del Howard, only to watch helplessly as the ball skipped past catcher Boss Schmidt, allowing Harry Steinfeldt to score and Johnny Evers to reach third. Evers, who had been watching Donovan closely all day, thought he sensed an opportunity and attempted a clean steal of home on the next pitch, but Donovan delivered the ball to Schmidt in time to tag out Evers and send the game to the tenth inning.

It appeared the Cubs had won the game in the tenth when Jimmy Slagle slid across home plate safely on yet another passed ball, but Harry Steinfeldt was called out for interference on the play and Slagle was sent back to third. Evers made an error on a low throw in the eleventh, but the Cubs held firm. An inning later Frank Chance smashed a line drive that seemed destined to clinch victory, but Germany Schaefer made a leaping grab and completed a spectacular double play. At that point, umpire Hank O'Day deemed it too dark to continue and the game ended as a 3–3 tie.

That would prove the highlight of the World Series for the Detroit Tigers. The Cubs took the second game behind Jack Pfiester, who scattered ten hits in a 3–1 victory. The Tigers replaced Schmidt behind the plate with Fred Payne, but the Cubs stole four bases anyway.

Ed Reulbach started the third game and the Tigers put up little fight, succumbing 5–1. Evers made another throwing error that luckily did no damage, and collected three hits, including two doubles. He also drove in Chicago's first run.[25] At that point he had collected seven hits in eleven at bats in the Series. Ty Cobb had two. The teams moved on to Detroit, with the Cubs up two games to none, plus the tie.

Changing the venue made no difference. Orval Overall started his second game of the Series and easily defeated the Tigers, 6–1. Rain delayed the game at one point with Evers on base and Detroit leading 1–0; once action resumed, Bill Donovan seemed to have lost his touch. Overall hit a line drive to center to score Evers, and momentum belonged to the Cubs after that.

With an opportunity to win his first World Series, Chance asked Mordecai Brown to clinch the championship for the Cubs. Bad weather and bad Tigers play depressed attendance to a little over seven thousand—more people were watching electronic scoreboards back in Chicago than attended the game in Detroit. Chance was unable to play after suffering a broken finger when he was hit by a pitch the previous day, so Del Howard took his place. The Cubs scored single runs in the first and second, with Evers scoring the latter on a ground out after he and Tinker pulled off a double steal. That was all Brown needed—he wasn't perfect, allowing seven hits and four walks, but he kept the base runners scattered and Detroit never crossed the plate.

In the bottom of the ninth, Boss Schmidt popped out to Joe Tinker for the final out and a sea of eight thousand people clogging downtown Dearborn Street in Chicago erupted in celebration, a stark contrast to the silence in Detroit.[26]

The Cubs returned home for a farcical split-squad exhibition game meant as a thank you to 3,500 fans. Frank Chance umpired and Evers manned three different positions during the game, including pitcher.[27] The Cubs were honored at a banquet later that week, with everyone in attendance except veteran pitcher Chick Fraser, whose sister had died suddenly.[28] Three more exhibition games were staged that week against semi-pro teams whose lineups included a scattering of big leaguers, and miscellaneous field events were held before each contest. Evers skipped the final game and headed home.[29]

Johnny Evers returned to Troy and another celebration, this one happier than the one held a year earlier. When Evers's train stopped at Albany, members of the benevolent organization named in honor of his father hopped aboard and accompanied him on the final leg of the journey. He was treated to a band concert at the association's clubhouse and led a procession illuminated by torchlight through the streets of Troy. Bonfires lit almost every street corner as the parade headed for the Windsor Hotel, just a couple of blocks from where Evers had grown up.

The banquet was appropriately festive, with menu cards at each place setting made to look like a collar and shirt and bearing the motto, "All For Troy, And Troy For All."[30] With the mayor's race a mere two weeks away, local politicians were out in force. Johnny Evers was the biggest sports hero the town had ever celebrated, and an inspiration to every kid ever run off Carroll's Hill. Everyone wanted to rub elbows with him, as if his success might in turn rub off on them.

That winter, the National League provided special medallions to each of the Cubs. Evers received his in Troy and hung it in the display window of his shoe store; he joked that it was large enough to be seen for three blocks, making it a great advertisement for his business.

In the *Sporting Life*, W.A. Phelon congratulated the Cubs on their second straight championship and predicted, "The National League race for 1908 will doubtless be much closer and more interesting than was the case for years past. I look for at least three teams to find enough good material to rebuild with and there should be a royal struggle."[31]

Phelon did realize how prescient he was.

CHAPTER SIX

Merkle

The incredible success of the Chicago Cubs was spurring action on the part of their biggest rival. While Pittsburgh largely stood pat for 1908, New York completed an eight-player trade, sending Dan McGann, Bill Dahlen and three others to Boston for Fred Tenney, Tom Needham and Al Bridwell. The Giants also welcomed back outfielder Mike Donlin, who sat out 1907 in order to perform on the vaudeville circuit with his actress wife, Mabel Hite. Boston owner John Dovey attempted to execute another high-profile transaction with Chicago, offering to trade for Johnny Evers with the intention of making him player-manager. But the Cubs refused to consider parting with their twenty-six-year-old second baseman, even as he made noises about sitting out a year after the coming season because of the physical and mental toll the game was exacting from him.[1]

With their roster settled, the Cubs prepared to defend their back-to-back National League championships. Johnny Kling shocked everyone by signing his contract early, as did Mordecai Brown.[2] Joe Tinker, determined to arrive in the best shape of his life, signed a three-year deal, moved to Chicago and bought a cigar shop. Jimmy Slagle and his wife traveled from their remote farm in Jefferson County, Pennsylvania, forced to begin their journey on bobsled in order to rendezvous with a train—an adventure neither had an interest in ever repeating.[3] Solly Hofman threatened to retire to pursue lucrative business ventures, but was taken only half-seriously. Jack Pfiester was late reporting due to the illness of his wife—and a desire for more money.[4]

In March, Chicago baseball fans held their collective breath amid reports that Frank Chance would have to undergo an operation on his foot, but it was decided less drastic measures were called for and the West Side faithful responded with an equally collective sigh of relief. Chance was instead fitted with a special shoe to relieve excruciating pain that had developed between the fourth and fifth toes of his left foot, and he finally began playing toward the end of spring training.[5]

Charles Murphy was determined to claim superiority for his team, not only at West Side Grounds, but on moral grounds as well, and endeavored to demonstrate as such with an announcement that the Cubs would refuse to protest any game, no matter the circumstance.[6] Sportsmanship was Murphy's new watchword. To that end, the Cubs' owner finally fulfilled what most had considered his empty promise to remodel his team's ballpark—including an updating of the visiting clubhouse, long an embarrassment and the target of frequent complaints, especially from Cincinnati president Garry Herrmann. Despite work being halted for a stretch in February due to a freak blizzard that clogged Chicago with a foot of snow, Murphy pressed on. The grandstand was enlarged and additional reserve and box seats were constructed. The remodeled facility was adorned with multiple images of bear cubs, including those of two life-sized bruins cast in cement. The railings in and around the ballpark were supported by posts consisting of baseball bats—more than one thousand of them. There were heroic, inspiring statues of Frank Chance and an anonymous pitcher installed outside the ballpark entrance.

While Murphy was putting the finishing touches on the ballpark, the team traveled to Cincinnati for Opening Day. The Palace of the Fans was festooned with American flags, and more than nineteen thousand people shoehorned their way in—the largest first-day crowd in Cincinnati history to that point. The Cubs broke out new road uniforms—gray with small black stripes. On each player's chest was a brown bear cub standing upright within a capital "C." The warm-up jackets featured a large white bear on each sleeve.

Johnny Evers picked up offensively where he had left off at the end of 1907—collecting three hits in three at bats including a double, while scoring three runs, including the winning tally on Heine Zimmerman's pinch-hit single with two out in the ninth. He handled ten chances in the field without an error as the Cubs rallied from a 5–0 first inning deficit to win, 6–5.[7]

Chicago started out the 1908 season as if determined to make a shambles of the National League race for a third straight year. The Cubs won seven of their first eight games, including a solid 7–3 victory in the home opener on April 22, during which Evers displayed what he proudly labeled his "bulldog tenacity." He made several spectacular plays in the field—handling nine chances flawlessly—while slapping a single, drawing two walks, stealing a base and scoring twice. The *Chicago Tribune* boasted, "The deeds of John Evers on and around second base would increase his shoe sales if the people of Troy could see him in action."[8]

Mordecai Brown did not appear in uniform until May 3; he had been absent from the team to visit his terminally ill mother in Terre Haute. Always in playing shape, Brown tossed a complete-game victory against the Cardinals in his 1908 debut, and Evers continued wielding a hot bat, collecting three hits. But the second baseman committed an embarrassing gaffe, attempting a delayed steal after the third out had already been recorded; when Evers dusted off his pant legs and realized what had happened, he took the ball from St. Louis third baseman Bobby Byrne and used it to whack himself on the head in a public display of self-humiliation.[9]

The Cubs then hit the road, bound for Pittsburgh. Rain had so swollen the Ohio River that floodgates protecting Exposition Park strained in their effort to prevent the ballpark from becoming part of the river itself, succeeding with only a foot, or less, to spare. The Pirates had also acquired a new tarp, custom designed to protect the field against rain—two massive pieces of canvas resting on a truck "wider than a moving van."[10] Pirates manager Fred Clarke had a surprise in store for the Cubs, which they discovered during the game. With two on and no one out in the third inning, Jimmy Slagle sent an innocent little bunt down the baseline. As Slagle stood disgustedly at home plate, watching his effort trickle several inches into foul ground, the ball suddenly took a hard right turn into fair territory. Honus Wagner, playing third base, quickly snatched up the ball and threw out the astonished Slagle.

The Cubs lost the game, 5–2, and afterward, umpire Hank O'Day examined the base path and discovered it absurdly slanted as it meandered toward third—supposedly to allow for better drainage of rainwater from the field of play. He immediately ordered the Pirates to fix it the next day or the Cubs would be awarded the game by forfeit.[11]

Following two days of rainouts, the Cubs exacted revenge thanks to veteran Chick Fraser, Fred Clarke's brother-in-law, who shut out Pittsburgh on two hits under conditions best described as intolerably miserable. Both center and right fields were inundated with water; due to the cresting of the Ohio River at an elevation above that of the playing field, the storm drains had been closed, an action that prevented the evacuation of water already trapped within the park. A bucket brigade was employed before—and during—the game in an effort, largely futile, to prevent the field from being totally swamped. Chance drove in the only run of the game with a double. Evers was later caught attempting to steal home with Fraser at the plate, upending his teammate in the process; of course, Evers protested that the tag had come too late, in the distinctive style for which he was becoming known, but to no avail.[12]

After splitting a double-header the next day, the Cubs moved on to Philadelphia, where Orval Overall tasted defeat for the first time since the previous August—a streak that had stretched to fourteen consecutive victories. Evers collected two more hits and he and Tinker successfully handled eighteen of nineteen chances, but Overall was driven from the mound by the fourth inning.[13]

Because of inclement weather, the Cubs were unable to play again for three days, at which point they returned home to host Brooklyn. Chance had by then decided to shuffle his lineup and move Evers from sixth to lead-off in the batting order. The second baseman responded with a single and also scored a run in his new role, but he also committed a costly error, dropping a pop fly that resulted in two Phillies runs.[14]

After rebounding to win three in a row, including a beautiful one-hitter by Mordecai Brown, the Cubs officially celebrated their 1907 championship by raising a new banner on May 21 at West Side Grounds, prior to a game against Boston. The rest of the day was a disaster. Evers was ejected in the fourth inning; after disagreeing with a called strike, he responded by dusting off the plate to afford the umpire a better view of it. That helpful gesture was not well-received. At the time the Cubs trailed 3–0, and they went on to lose, 11–3.[15]

Despite the loss, the Cubs were showing well in the standings—in first place—although they were not projecting the invincibility that they had in previous years. Chicago was hitting .220 as a team, with only Evers providing much spark with the bat, boasting a fifth-best in the league .299 average. Johnny Kling, at .276, was the only other man above .260. Sensing that the Cubs, while still formidable, were less than what they had been, John McGraw predicted Frank Chance's team would fall short of a third straight championship, insisting that its pitching was not as strong and that Chance's players had never experienced a tight pennant race. McGraw sniffed, "Whether the Cubs are fighters has yet to be proven."[16]

In an effort to spark the team's offense, Chance benched thirty-four-year-old Jimmy Slagle, a six-year regular, and one of the dwindling number of the players dating back to Frank Selee's days. Slagle's replacement in center field was Solly Hofman; with the development of Del Howard and Heine Zimmerman as utility men, Chance felt he could afford to put Hofman in the everyday lineup.

Jimmy Sheckard was the man Frank Chance usually turned to when he needed someone to run the team in his absence. Sheckard also had a tendency to needle teammates, and that tendency nearly resulted in tragedy. On June 2, the Cubs hosted the Pirates and Johnny Evers turned in another stellar performance, hitting a triple and three singles, and falling short of a perfect five-for-five day only because of a close decision at first. But two key players were not in the Chicago lineup—Jimmy Sheckard and Heine Zimmerman—and the Cubs were pounded, 12–6. Mysteriously, neither man boarded the train the next day as the team departed for a road trip. Official word had Sheckard sidelined by an ankle sprain suffered the previous day.[17] When rumors circulated about an eye injury, it was announced that Sheckard was out because an ammonia bottle had exploded in his hands and nearly blinded him. What had actually transpired was finally revealed several weeks later by the *New York Globe.*

According to the newspaper, Zimmerman sat out the June 1 game because of injury—forcing a hobbled Johnny Evers into the lineup. During that contest, Sheckard turned his ankle but remained in the game after being briefly relieved by a courtesy runner. In the clubhouse afterward, Sheckard began needling Zimmerman about being soft and Zimmerman took offense. Before anyone realized what was happening, the two began shouting and punches were thrown. At one point, Sheckard tossed something at Zimmerman, who responded by throwing the nearest item at hand—a bottle of ammonia. Zimmerman's aim was true, the bottle nailing Sheckard in the forehead and splashing ammonia into his eyes. Frank Chance went berserk, attacking Zimmerman, who held his own until Chance shouted for reinforcements.[18]

Chance ordered a team meeting in his hotel room the next day and spent ten minutes chewing out the squad. While those close by heard shouting, what specifically was said proved impossible to ascertain. But the players, obviously chastised, were seen departing the meeting "on tiptoe." Afterward, Chance was said to be red-faced and sweating profusely.[19]

Chance tried trading Zimmerman to the Cardinals for pitcher Arthur "Bugs" Raymond—no bargain in the clubhouse himself—but was unsuccessful. Both Zimmerman and Sheckard, whose eyesight was saved after initial concerns about permanent damage, returned to the lineup a few weeks later.[20]

The fight was indisputable evidence that the Cubs' locker room was divided—hardly a revelation to those aware of the feud between Evers and Tinker. Evers was said to be extremely upset about the treatment of Zimmerman, who he had recommended to the team. Although attempts were made to keep the story quiet, it almost immediately made the rounds in baseball circles. In late June, the Cubs were playing the Giants and Sheckard came to bat. Roger Bresnahan was behind the plate and Sheckard told Bresnahan, "You kick too much." Bresnahan responded, "I guess I don't kick as hard as Zimmerman, do I?"[21]

The Cubs may not have been hitting as well as in recent years, but neither was anyone else as the "deadball" reigned supreme. Chicago's pitchers remained top-notch—especially Mordecai Brown. Between trips home to visit his ailing mother, Brown threw a pair of shutouts, on June 13 against Philadelphia and twelve days later versus Cincinnati. Then he missed another week when his mother died. Upon his return, Brown threw two shutouts against Pittsburgh in three days, stretching his scoreless streak to thirty-seven consecutive innings and his record to eleven wins against only one defeat. The shutout streak finally ended at forty innings on July 10, when the Philadelphia Phillies pushed across a run against him. Shortly after that, Brown received news that his sister had died.[22]

The Cubs could not seem to sustain momentum. Their hitting improved, but then their pitching faltered—Brown losing 11–0 to New York the day after Overall was defeated by Philadelphia, 11–2. Chick Fraser's arm was bothering him and so was Jack Pfiester's. In addition, Solly Hofman dislocated his knee and was out for several weeks—joining Frank Schulte on the sidelines.

In mid–July, the Cubs ceded leadership of the National League to Pittsburgh. The Pirates held onto first place for a little more than a month, at which point the surging New York Giants took over. Throughout the remainder of the season, there would be little daylight between the Cubs, Giants and Pirates. Reveling in his first real pennant race in three years, John McGraw took the opportunity to further needle his Windy City rivals, declaring Larry Doyle to be on the verge of becoming the best second baseman in the National League. "I wouldn't trade Larry even up for Johnny Evers," insisted the Giants' manager.

The Cubs demonstrated they were not quite ready to concede the pennant to McGraw, with Joe Tinker hitting a game-winning inside-the-park home run on July 17 off Christy Mathewson; Tinker was becoming a particular thorn in Mathewson's side. The shortstop's blow coincided with the resurgence of Mordecai Brown, as the Cubs defeated New York, 1–0, behind their three-fingered ace.[23] Tinker delivered yet another game-winning hit the next day to defeat the Giants, 4–3.[24]

By the end of July, the Cubs were leading the National League in batting average, at .254. Johnny Evers was displaying his usual habit of remarkable consistency with the bat, ranking behind only Mike Donlin and Honus Wagner with a .300 mark—one point higher than two and a half months earlier. But Evers, who had been moved to fourth in the batting order by Frank Chance, could not stay out of trouble with umpires. He earned a three-day, four-game suspension thanks to a verbally abusive fusillade hurled at umpire Cy Rigler near the end of a July 27 double-header in Brooklyn. Frustration had boiled over during a day made especially miserable, not only by repeated Cubs base-running blunders, but also because of mosquito swarms so thick that smudge pots were utilized solely to allow the players to sit in the dugout.[25] Following Evers's suspension, Chance offered him a sixty-dollar suit of clothes if he could avoid ejections for the remainder of the season—although Chance quickly added that he did not mean Evers was banned entirely from arguing umpire's calls.[26]

Chance was seeking any edge he could find, without success. The Cubs managed only a mediocre 28–29 record between June 13, when Mordecai Brown threw the first of his four consecutive shutouts, and August 16. At that point, they had fallen six games off the pace. Chicago ended July with five straight wins, including the four games Evers missed due to suspension, but then lost to Boston, 14–0. After defeating Philadelphia on August 3, the Cubs dropped five in a row to the Phillies and Giants, with Evers committing an error to let in the eventual winning run at the Polo Grounds on August 10, a game Orval Overall lost despite allowing only one hit. (Joe Tinker had three by himself as he continued to batter Giants pitching.[27]) In mid–August, Cubs pitchers allowed but six runs total in six games, yet only earned a split of those half-dozen contests. The Cubs needed to make one of their famous runs— but they were running out of time.

When the Chicago Cubs visited Pittsburgh on September 4, Warren Gill was a twenty-nine-year-old rookie first baseman for the Pirates, a week into what would be a one-month-long major league career. The Cubs, playing somewhat better, resided in third place, one-half game behind Pittsburgh and two behind New York. Recently acquired from Grand Rapids of the Central League, Gill was batting fifth on a day that featured a pitcher's duel between future Hall of Fame right-handers Mordecai Brown and Vic Willis.

The game remained scoreless in the bottom of the tenth inning. With two men on and one out, Gill stepped to the plate. Brown promptly plunked him in the ribs, loading the bases. With the game on the line, Brown bore down and struck out Ed Abbaticchio for the second out.

Up stepped another Pirates rookie, Owen "Chief" Wilson, who swung at the first pitch, fisting a soft line drive over Evers's head and into centerfield, bringing Fred Clarke across home plate with the winning run. But Johnny Evers had kept his eye on Warren Gill, who, like some players at that time, had stopped running once he realized his teammate was going to score, ending the game. Rather than jogging all the way to second, Gill turned and ran toward the clubhouse to avoid congratulatory fans. Reasoning that a force play remained in effect, Evers stood near second base and shouted for centerfielder Jimmy Slagle to throw him the ball. Umpire Hank O'Day, after dutifully watching Clarke cross home plate, turned to exit the field. Once Evers received the ball from Slagle, he stomped his foot on the bag and screamed at O'Day that he had recorded a force out. O'Day acted as if he did not hear, so Evers ran over to him. With his jaw twisted one way, his mouth another and his eyes squinting in the late afternoon sun, Evers repeatedly thrust the ball at O'Day while pressing his case that because Gill had not touched second, he had recorded the third out on a force. That meant the inning was over, Pittsburgh's run did not count, and the game remained tied.[28]

Exasperated by Evers's incessant challenges, O'Day snapped, "Cut it out, Johnny, the game is over," and turned on his heels to walk away. Evers shouted after him, "It isn't over until that man touches second base! Why don't you wait until the game is over, you big fathead!"

Evers obsessed over the play, convinced he was right. He chattered about it all night to anyone who would listen before finally cornering Charles Murphy, who proved a receptive audience. The Cubs' owner, who strongly advocated that the National League establish a two-umpire system, saw his opportunity to make a point and—breaking his vow from the beginning of the season not to do so under *any* circumstances—filed an official protest.

National League president Harry Pulliam ultimately denied the appeal because O'Day had not witnessed Gill's failure to touch second base—and not because it was unnecessary for Gill to do so, an important distinction. Murphy, who admitted he had not thought the protest would be upheld, was satisfied he had made his point about the inadequacy of the one-umpire system.

Evers was certain he had made his point as well, and that he had the attention of both O'Day and his teammates. Warren Gill would play only twenty-seven major league games, but his failure to touch second base was about to make him an important footnote to one of the most famous moments in baseball history.

⚾ ⚾ ⚾

A couple of days after the Warren Gill game, the Cubs fashioned a seven-game winning streak, but they could gain no ground on John McGraw's red-hot Giants. On September 18, the Giants swept a double-header from the Pittsburgh Pirates, giving New York eleven straight victories.[29] That same day, the Cubs lost a heartbreaker to Philadelphia and an old nemesis, George McQuillan. The stress was catching up with Evers, who missed the game with a painfully stiff neck that made playing impossible—instead he sat in the stands with Philadelphia Athletics catcher Ossee Schrecongost (the Athletics were well out of contention in the American League and had left most of their veterans home in order to play some youngsters on their last western road trip).

Heine Zimmerman made two errors in Evers's place and miscommunicated with Solly Hofman on a short fly to center that dropped safely for a double. The Cubs, behind Orval Overall, led 1–0 as late as the eighth inning, but

Fred Merkle was a promising teenage prospect in the summer of 1908. He nearly lost a leg to an infection that July but recovered, only to become a victim of a heads-up play by Johnny Evers that forever painted him—fairly or unfairly—as the man who lost a pennant for the New York Giants. (National Baseball Hall of Fame Library—Cooperstown, New York.)

lost to the Phillies thanks to more bad defense in the bottom of the eighth, and a triple and a sacrifice fly in the tenth.[30] The defeat dropped the stumbling Cubs four and a half games out of first with sixteen to play.

The players returned to their hotel after the game in total silence. Moments before reaching their destination, Joe Tinker scooted over next to Frank Chance and gently suggested that the pennant race was likely over for the Cubs and they might as well "break training" and have a few drinks, followed by a good night's sleep. Chance thought for a moment and then replied,

"No. We were good winners last year. Let's ... play the string out. We may win yet."[31]

Fred Merkle was an impressive physical specimen, six-foot-one and nearly two hundred pounds. An outstanding athlete at Toledo High School in Ohio, located in the hometown of Giants star Roger Bresnahan, Merkle made his professional debut as a seventeen-year-old with Tecumseh of the Southern Michigan League. He quickly attracted the attention of major league scouts, and a minor bidding war resulted in his being purchased by the New York Giants in September 1907 for $2,500—a not insignificant sum at the time.[32]

Originally a third baseman, Merkle appeared in fifteen games at the end of the 1907 season for the Giants, showing enough that John McGraw viewed him as the eventual successor to veteran first baseman Fred Tenney. Only nineteen years old in 1908, Merkle nearly saw his career end in midsummer when he developed blood poisoning in his foot. After he was admitted to Good Samaritan Hospital in Cincinnati, Merkle's foot swelled to several times normal size and it was feared amputation would be necessary, possibly up to the knee.[33]

Fortunately, the infection was brought under control. Merkle was released from the hospital in late July and returned to the Giants on August 1. Dodging a bullet, a relieved Fred Merkle had his whole career ahead of him. Little did he know how that career was about to be defined, indelibly, by Johnny Evers.

One of the momentous days in baseball history dawned under cloudy skies. It was a comfortable day for a ball game—about seventy degrees at game time—and there was no indication this day would be different from any other, other than the fact that a game at the Polo Grounds between the Chicago Cubs and New York Giants, especially in September, was always special. It got the adrenaline pumping—which Johnny Evers desperately needed as he woke with his neck again reminding him of its stiffness. It would take time to work out the kinks.

But this day, September 23, 1908, would be different. The Giants had suddenly lost four in a row—including a double-header to the Cubs the day before, moving Chicago into a virtual tie with New York and a game and a half ahead of Pittsburgh.[34] When the players came downstairs from their hotel rooms for breakfast, they ran into a familiar figure, Giants first baseman Fred Tenney, looking positively dapper with his gold-headed cane. Tenney, who lived at the hotel in which the Cubs were staying, politely greeted his rivals and, his back bothering him, walked stiffly to a chair in the lobby to read the newspaper and pass the time before the game.

Once the Cubs arrived at the ballpark, they unloaded their bags and trudged into the clubhouse. After dressing, the players walked across the Polo Grounds outfield, its roped-off area already populated by several automobiles and carriages. They ran the gauntlet of catcalls from the Giants faithful in the reserved seats before taking a few warm-up throws and preparing themselves for yet another crucial game.

It was a large crowd for a Wednesday, although smaller than that of the day before, when Mordecai Brown had once again foiled the Giants by winning the first game in relief and then pitching a complete-game, 3–1 victory in the nightcap. McGraw called on Christy Mathewson, already the winner of thirty-four games, to blunt the Cubs' sudden momentum. Jack Pfiester, whose elbow burned furiously with every pitch because of a damaged tendon, took the mound for Chicago because of his ability to defeat the Giants, earning him the nickname "Jack the Giant Killer." There was one lineup change for New York—Fred Tenney was unable to play because of his back, so Fred Merkle took his place. Since it was an important contest, National League president Harry Pulliam was in attendance, and two umpires, Hank O'Day and Bob Emslie, were assigned to the game.

There was no scoring during the first four innings. Evers made a couple of great plays; in the second with men on first and second he knocked down Al Bridwell's hot smash and recovered to force Fred Merkle, saving a run in the process. That was the same inning in which Pfiester experienced control problems and smacked Harry McCormick in the chest with a pitch, knocking him to the ground. McCormick was revived and remained in the game.

Evers struck again in the Giants' half of the fourth. After Art Devlin smashed a line shot with one out for a single, the next batter hit a line drive destined to fall in right field. Evers made a one-handed leaping catch and doubled Devlin off first to end the inning.

The Cubs struck for the game's first run in the fifth. Joe Tinker hit a low line drive into right center that Mike Donlin thought he might get to. When Donlin realized he would be unable to reach it, he tried using his foot to stop the ball, but it shot past him, skipping under the temporary seats as Tinker steamed around the bases, cap flying from his head and dust trailing in his wake. He was careful to hit the inside of each bag with his foot, allowing him to streak toward the next station without slowing. By the time Donlin retrieved the ball, Tinker was nearly to home plate and the Cubs had a 1–0 lead.

In the bottom of the fifth, Evers made yet another noteworthy defensive play, back-handing another line shot hit by Bridwell, this time behind second base, to rob the Giants' shortstop for a second time.

New York finally tied the score in the sixth. Buck Herzog led off with a sharp grounder that Harry Steinfeldt managed to cut off, but his hurried throw was off the mark and Herzog reached second when the ball eluded Frank Chance. Roger Bresnahan sacrificed Herzog to third, and Herzog then scored on Mike Donlin's clean single to center.

Neither team threatened again until the bottom of the ninth.

There are moments that stick in one's mind. There are also moments that stick in everyone's mind—even when those moments are remembered differently by everyone involved. The ninth inning of this game was one of those moments—a moment that would also define two of the participants for the rest of their lives.

The Giants' half of the ninth inning began innocently enough. Jack Pfiester was gritting his teeth in pain with every pitch, but remained in command. Cy Seymour led off with a grounder to Evers, who threw him out at first. Art Devlin singled, but was subsequently retired on a force play, Evers to Tinker, when Harry McCormick hit a ground ball to second; Devlin slid hard into second base to prevent a double play, and Tinker, covering the bag, took exception. While a cloud of dust hung above their heads, the two traded words but were quickly separated and the game continued.

With two out and McCormick on first, Fred Merkle stepped to the plate. He swung at Pfiester's pitch and felt his bat meet the ball solidly, sending it into the right field gap. McCormick sprinted to third while Merkle, not wanting to take any chance of being thrown out to end the inning, turned cautiously toward second before retreating to the safety of the first-base bag. It was Merkle's first hit of the game and he could not have been more thrilled. The crowd was roaring; the Cubs were on the ropes and he had put them there. It was the biggest moment of his young career.

Al Bridwell, robbed twice earlier in the game by Johnny Evers, was up next for the Giants. Before Pfiester threw his first pitch, Bridwell noticed Merkle was leading too far off first base and backed out of the box. After signaling to the rookie to shorten his lead, Bridwell promptly smacked a solid single into center that Evers could not get to. McCormick crossed the plate with the winning run and Merkle jumped up and down in celebration. The crowd spilled onto the field and Merkle ran for the clubhouse in order to avoid the crush of humanity.

As the *New York Times* put it, "McCormick trots home, the merry villagers flock the field to worship the hollow where Mathewson feet have pressed, and all of a sudden there is doings at second base."[35]

Johnny Evers could not believe his good fortune; once he saw Merkle do exactly as Warren Gill had done nineteen days earlier, with Hank O'Day there to witness it, he felt the Cubs were saved. "I knew I was going to win the

Hank O'Day and Johnny Evers engaged in many battles over the years, but on September 23, 1908, Evers could not have been more pleased to have O'Day as one of the umpires when Fred Merkle failed to touch second. "Here for a change would be an umpire who would be on my side," remembered Evers. (McGreevey Photographs—Boston Public Library.)

argument as soon as I saw Merkle turn into center field," Evers explained. "With any other umpire except O'Day I wouldn't have had a prayer. But I knew from what had happened in Pittsburgh that here, for a change, would be an umpire who would be on my side."[36]

Amid the chaos of celebrating Giants fans, Frank Chance, Joe Tinker and Johnny Evers were all screaming at centerfielder Solly Hofman to get the ball back to the infield. Hofman threw the ball, but it sailed over Evers's head and hit Joe Tinker, who had turned to get Bob Emslie's attention, in the back of the neck.[37]

What happened next has been, and will be, debated forever—everyone was focused on McCormick crossing the plate, not on Merkle running, or not running, to second. Well, almost everyone. What is clear is that Joe McGinnity, coaching third base for the Giants, recognized what was happening and intercepted the ball after it struck Tinker, and before it could reach Evers. He hurled the ball somewhere—some say into the crowd, others say it was retrieved by Cubs pitcher Floyd Kroh after he punched a fan to gain possession of it. In any case, a ball was somehow placed into Evers's hands by either Joe Tinker or Harry Steinfeldt.

On the other side of the diamond, a group of Giants fans celebrated by carrying Buck Herzog off the field, ignorant of the fact that Johnny Evers was standing on second base, raising the ball to the sky as if he were Perseus holding aloft the severed head of Medusa, shrieking to anyone and everyone that he had just recorded the third out to end the inning.

Frank Chance ran over to Hank O'Day, pointed to Evers, and demanded a decision. On-duty police, thinking Chance was about to attack O'Day, swarmed in to protect the umpire. Chance strained against the men in blue, continuing to shout at O'Day while Doc Marshall and Del Howard came to Chance's rescue. O'Day could not hear Chance amid the chaos and was escorted away through the mob by the police. When Chance finally tracked down the umpire, he assured the Cubs manager that Merkle had not touched second and therefore the run did not count. O'Day was declaring the game a tie because it would be too dark to continue once the field was cleared of fans. Harry Pulliam witnessed it all and realized the matter would be coming to him on appeal.[38]

O'Day explained to the press that Merkle had not touched second and had been forced out, meaning the game remained tied, 1–1. Chance said he was glad the Cubs had protested the game in Pittsburgh. Even though he had never expected to see that kind of play repeated, when it was, both the Cubs and O'Day were ready for it.

There were rumors that Pulliam had already declared it a tie game that would have to be replayed, but he denied that. John McGraw argued that it was either a win for the Giants, or a forfeit to the Cubs because the crowd had overrun the field, but it could not be a tie. He added that he was certain the Cubs had no grounds for a protest.

New York newspapers printed standings that reflected a Giants win, while the Chicago press printed standings reflecting a tie. Pittsburgh's newspapers declared the Pirates either a half-game or a full game behind Chicago, depending on the sports editor. The *New York Times* termed the base running mistake, "Censurable stupidity on the part of the player Merkle ... [that] placed the New York team's chances of winning the pennant in jeopardy."[39]

The Cubs argued that under league rules, a double-header would need to be played the next day, but the Giants refused to do so. The Cubs showed up early and then filed another protest, asking that the Giants be forced to forfeit that game. The protest was denied.

Harry Pulliam eventually ruled the Merkle game would be replayed in case the Cubs and Giants ended the season in a tie, accepting O'Day's ruling that Merkle had failed to touch second. O'Day would later try to claim that his decision to call the game a tie was based on McGinnity's interfering with the play—the statement was made at a time when he had become weary of hearing about Evers.

Years later, Al Bridwell was interviewed for the book *The Glory of Their*

Times, and told author Lawrence Ritter that he regretted backing out of the box to get Merkle to shorten his lead. "I often think if I hadn't held Merkle close to first he'd probably have been all the way down to second before the crowd started onto the field." He added, "I wish I'd never gotten that hit that set off the whole Merkle incident. I wish I'd struck out instead. If I'd have done that, I would have spared Fred a lot of unfair humiliation."[40]

It was a game that forever defined the careers of both Fred Merkle and Johnny Evers. Merkle's failure to touch second also wiped out Bridwell's hit, meaning he had been robbed for the third time that game by Evers.

The Cubs continued winning after leaving New York. On September 26, three days after the Merkle game, Ed Reulbach made history by shutting out Brooklyn in both ends of a double-header—to this day the only time that has ever been accomplished in the major leagues.[41]

Chicago then proceeded to take four of five from Cincinnati, giving them a record of 97–55, although the one game the Cubs lost seemed like it might come back to haunt them. On September 30, Jean Dubuc, a twenty-year-old rookie for the Reds, beaned Evers in the first inning, knocking him out cold. After being doused with ice water to snap him back to consciousness, Evers was helped to the bench while Del Howard acted as courtesy runner. Evers returned to the game, but later admitted not remembering much about the contest, which Chicago lost, 6–5, despite a twelve-strikeout performance by Orval Overall, when the Reds rallied to score three times in the ninth.[42]

With that, the Cubs came home to meet the Pittsburgh Pirates for the make-up of an earlier season rainout—the final regular season game for both teams. Chicago had been on the road since September 10, winning eighteen of twenty-two games. The Pirates had won eighteen of twenty-three during the same span, including their last eight in a row. At that point, Pittsburgh was in first, one-half game ahead of the Cubs. The Giants were in third, one and a half games out of first. If the Pirates won, they were National League champions. If the Cubs won, the Pirates were eliminated and Chicago clinched at least a tie. The Giants, who had three games left, would remain alive as long as the Cubs won and they swept their final three games against Boston.

With everything on the line, Fred Clarke chose Vic Willis, who had rested for a week while the Pirates played six games against the last-place Cardinals in a home and away series. Frank Chance went with Mordecai Brown, who had been beaten by Willis in their last confrontation, the Warren Gill contest.

This time, the Pirates were no match for Brown, and Willis was no match for the Cubs. When Chief Wilson hit a ground ball to Tinker in the ninth and Tinker tossed the ball to Evers for a force out to end the game for a

5–2 Cubs win, the Pirates were eliminated, and Cubs fans, thirty thousand strong—the largest crowd to witness a game in Chicago up to that time—poured onto the field. The players sprinted as fast as they could to the protection of their clubhouse.

After the game, an ecstatic Frank Chance shouted, "We simply had to win and we did, that's all there was to it." He praised Mordecai Brown, winner of his twenty-eighth game of the season, and Frank Schulte, who had a pair of key hits. Both Evers and Tinker had great games as well, Tinker collecting two hits and Evers three, along with a pair of sacrifices.

"We will take morning practice each day while awaiting the returns from New York," said Chance. "Whatever the result in New York, we expect to win another pennant and another world's championship."[43]

After dropping a double-header to Cincinnati on September 25, the Giants won ten of thirteen, defeating every pitcher they faced except one—Philadelphia rookie Harry Coveleski, who had appeared in only three games for the Phillies prior to facing the Giants. Despite his inexperience, the twenty-two-year-old defeated the Giants three times in five days—a victory in any of those games would have clinched the pennant for New York. But the Giants still won enough games to end the season in a flat-footed tie with Chicago, meaning the September 23 game would have to be replayed.

The rematch between the Cubs and Giants was scheduled for October 8, featuring the same pitching match-up as before. Jack Pfiester, who had visited famous osteopath Bonesetter Reese to ease the pain in his elbow, would pitch against Christy Mathewson, winner of an incredible thirty-seven games, but nearing four hundred innings pitched for the season. The crowd utilized every tactic imaginable to see the game—one man, a fireman, climbed an elevated railroad pillar and slipped, falling to his death. Another fan, a restaurant owner, was pushed from the top of the bleachers and suffered a broken leg. A gang of small boys broke through a fence and bribed a policeman with quarters in order to sit on the roof of the grandstand.

John McGraw received the biggest ovation from the Polo Grounds faithful and Frank Chance the biggest jeers. There was some gamesmanship—after the Cubs had taken batting practice for only five minutes, Joe McGinnity appeared and began hitting ground balls to Giants infielders, incurring the wrath of Chance, who argued that the Cubs had not been given the opportunity to practice sufficiently. McGraw hoped that Chance would be goaded into a fight and be ejected before the game started—the Giants' manager was not planning on using McGinnity, so if he was chased, it would have no impact on his team. Chance and McGinnity got into each other's faces, but the Cubs

The Giants and Cubs argue after Joe McGinnity interrupts the Cubs' warm-ups prior to the replay of the Merkle game on October 8, 1908. John McGraw hoped McGinnity would goad Frank Chance into a fight that would get him ejected, but Chance proved too smart to fall for the gambit. After some heated remarks and milling about, McGraw made a show of ordering McGinnity to the bench. (Library of Congress—George Grantham Bain Collection.)

manager did not take the bait and McGraw finally made a big production of banishing McGinnity to the bench.

Histrionics out of the way, the game began and the Giants scored first— Pfiester hit Fred Tenney with the first pitch and then walked Buck Herzog after getting ahead of him with two quick strikes. The Cubs then executed a double play, but Mike Donlin followed that with a line shot down the line, scoring Tenney. The Cubs protested that the ball landed foul, to no avail. After Pfiester walked the next batter, Chance pulled him and brought in Mordecai Brown, who struck out Art Devlin to end the inning. The Giants had drawn first blood.

But the Cubs won the game, and the pennant, in the third inning. Joe Tinker tripled to lead off and then scored the tying run on Johnny Kling's single. Mordecai Brown sacrificed Kling to second and Mathewson intentionally walked Evers. Frank Schulte followed with a ground rule double to score Kling, and then Frank Chance singled in Evers and Schulte to give the Cubs a 4–1 lead. Brown shut down the Giants the rest of the way, running into trouble only in the seventh, when the Giants loaded the bases with no one out. Brown buckled down at that point, allowing only one run.

When Al Bridwell grounded out to Joe Tinker, the Cubs bench erupted. Fans mobbed the players, most offering congratulations, although one man landed a punch to the back of Frank Chance's neck before disappearing into the crowd. The *New York World* called Mordecai Brown "The Undertaker," in honor of his burying the pennant hopes of both the Pirates and Giants. The Cubs were going to their third straight World Series.[44]

Frank Chance and his men had finished the season with one of their patented runs—winning forty of their final forty-nine games and twenty-three of their last twenty-seven. It had been one of Johnny Evers's best seasons—he had played great all-around baseball while hitting an even .300 (the same mark he had at the end of July), fifth best in the National League, and by far the highest on the Cubs. He was named to *Baseball Magazine*'s All-National League team.[45] His .402 on-base percentage trailed only Honus Wagner's. He was fourth in the league in runs scored, third in bases on balls, fifth in stolen bases and was the league's second toughest batter to strike out. Plus, he had played a central role that was credited with capturing a third straight pennant for the Chicago Cubs—a moment that had elevated him to stardom.

The 1908 World Series was a rematch with the Detroit Tigers, and it lacked energy in the wake of the heated pennant races staged in both leagues. Ty Cobb had once again battled teammates during the season, first engaging in a public feud with Matty McIntyre, followed by another with fellow star Sam Crawford. In between he engaged in several shouting matches with patrons around the league of such intensity that the Red Sox lobbied to have him barred from playing in Boston for a year. Cobb also won his second straight American League batting title and led the league in hits, doubles and triples.

The first game was played at Bennett Field in Detroit, with Ed Reulbach starting for the Cubs and Ed Killian for the Tigers. It rained heavily during the first six innings, rendering the baselines a muddy mess and footing all over the field uncertain at best. Sawdust had to be spread around the pitcher's mound and home plate prior to the third inning in an effort to soak up the mud.

It was a seesaw contest, with Detroit taking the lead in the bottom of the eighth thanks to Ty Cobb's aggressive base running. With Sam Crawford on third and Cobb at first, Claude Rossman singled to center, scoring Crawford. Cobb, knowing Solly Hofman lacked experience as an outfielder, saw Evers with his back to the infield in the cutoff position. Calculating that everyone would expect him to stop at second and therefore relax, Cobb kept right on going. When Evers heard shouts and turned, he saw Cobb closing in on third base and attempted to put a little extra on his throw, which sailed wide of the mark, skidding past Harry Steinfeldt. Cobb scrambled to his feet and scored to put Detroit ahead, 6–5.[46]

But the Cubs strung together six straight hits in the top of the ninth, including a two-run single by Hofman, to give Chicago a 10–6 lead. The Tigers got a couple of runners on in the bottom of the ninth, but Brown retired Cobb for the last out on a bouncer back to the pitcher's mound.[47] Charles Murphy reacted by saying, "Today's game confirms my opinion that I have the best ball club in the world."

The second game featured a pitcher's duel between Orval Overall and Bill Donovan. Frank Chance ordered the Cubs to take as many of Donovan's pitches as possible, and both teams failed to score for seven innings. Certain Donovan was beginning to tire, in the bottom of the eighth Chance told his batters to start swinging away. Joe Tinker quickly broke open the game with a two-run homer into the bleachers and by the end of the inning the Cubs led, 6–0. Cobb drove in a run in the ninth, but it was far too little and far too late, and the Cubs had a two-game lead in the Series; the Tigers had played seven World Series games and still sought their first win.[48]

In the third game, also in Chicago, the Tigers banished their good luck mascot "Rastus," an African American boy who was forced to sit forlornly in the bleachers rather than on the Detroit bench. Cobb finally played a great World Series game—three singles and a double in five times at bat—and the Tigers, not coincidentally, won. Cobb stole second and third base in the ninth, and then attempted to swipe home on a delayed steal; the Cubs did not fall for it and tagged him out in a rundown.[49]

Game Four in Detroit was all Mordecai Brown. He threw a four-hit shutout and did not walk a batter. The Tigers' only extra-base hit was a double smacked by Sam Crawford in the fourth inning, but he was immediately victimized by a classic Tinker-Evers maneuver. As he took his lead, Evers told Crawford, "You better not wander too far off base or the Jew [Cubs catcher Johnny Kling] will throw down here." As Crawford turned to reply to Evers, Tinker snuck behind him. Kling fired the ball to second, Tinker blocked off the base and Crawford was tagged out. Cobb tried to steal second a moment later, but Claude Rossman struck out to end the inning—Cobb would have been out anyway as Evers made a one-handed catch of Kling's throw and applied a sweeping tag that would have retired him easily.[50]

Chicago clinched the championship the next day before the smallest crowd in World Series history; only a shade more six thousand were at Bennett Field to witness the last World Championship that the Cubs would win for more than a century. Orval Overall allowed only three hits; he struck out four men in the first inning—thanks to a passed ball—a World Series record he still holds all by himself. Overall retired the last twelve batters he faced and was never in serious trouble. Johnny Kling caught Boss Schmidt's foul pop-up for the final out and Cubs fans danced in celebration.[51]

Frank Chance led everyone with a .421 batting average during the Series, while Evers hit .350 and led all players with five runs scored and twenty-one assists. Each Cubs player received $1,400 for winning; team Treasurer Charles Williams was presented an equal share, and trainer Bert Semmens split a full share with pitchers Floyd Kroh and Blaine Durbin, who had not been carried on the active roster for the Series.[52]

Attendance had been so anemic that Charles Murphy allowed the teams to play an exhibition the following Sunday at West Side Grounds so the players could pocket some extra cash. The Tigers won the game, 7–3; in field events held before the contest, Solly Hofman won the baseball throw and Ty Cobb edged Davy Jones in the 100-yard dash. Attendance was 6,664—four hundred more than had witnessed the final World Series game in Detroit.[53]

It was a satisfying end to a satisfying year for Johnny Evers. He had enjoyed his best offensive season in five years, played spectacular defense, and was a World Champion for a second straight season. But the pennant race had taken its toll—he had been hobbled much of the season with a bad neck, a sore leg and a painful stone bruise on his heel, and had missed thirty games due to injury or suspension.

Evers was only twenty-seven years old, but he was mulling over a serious question. Did he really want to come back and play in 1909?

CHAPTER SEVEN

A Sad Lexicon

Tuesday, January 12, 1909, was a joyous day for the Evers clan of Troy, New York—they were welcoming a new addition. At five o'clock in the afternoon, members of two Troy families gathered at St. Joseph's Church for an event that had remained secret to all but closest friends and family—the wedding of Helen Fitzgibbon to Johnny Evers.[1]

The eighteen-year-old Miss Fitzgibbon, like her new husband, was Catholic, Irish, and possessed a fiery personality. The bride walked down the aisle in a taupe wedding suit and a matching "picture" hat—an elaborate bonnet so named for the way the headdress framed the face. Evers's sister Ella served as bridesmaid and his cousin, Edward Wansboro, acted as best man. The ceremony was quiet, simple and dignified. And with that, Johnny Evers, once considered the most confirmed of all Cubs bachelors, had married his very own Helen of Troy.

The ballplayer surprised his new wife with a pair of diamond earrings at their wedding reception, which was held at the family home on Third Street. Following the festivities, he and his bride set off for a three-week honeymoon in Palm Beach, Florida, pausing briefly in Washington, D.C., to visit Evers's uncle, Thomas, and to answer an invitation to call on President Theodore Roosevelt at the White House.[2] During their trip the press hounded Evers about Frank Chance, who was demanding total control of the Cubs both on and off the field as a condition of returning as manager, and Joe Tinker, who was embarking on an eight-week theatrical tour-de-force titled *A Home Run* as rumors swirled, falsely, that he was about to be traded to the Cincinnati Reds.

At the conclusion of the whirlwind trip, Evers and his wife settled into their new home at 133 Second Street in Troy.[3] Set on a street lined with brick

85

buildings, the three-story walk-up was tucked in a neighborhood immediately west of Rensselaer Polytechnic Institute, in the Ida Hill section of town—located only a mile from the house in which Evers had spent his childhood and in the shadow of eighty-acre Prospect Park, with its gorgeous views of downtown Troy and the Hudson River.

Publicly, Evers insisted he was weary from the strain of playing baseball and planned to sit out at least a good portion of the 1909 season.[4] Based on past history, it was notable that neither Frank Chance nor Charles Murphy publicly pressured their second baseman, or branded him a holdout interested only in money. The reason for their restraint was that they understood the real impetus behind Evers's inaction; his mother, who had been distressed by reports of death threats her son had received during the Cubs-Giants playoff the previous October, was terminally ill. In the meantime Evers agreed to coach the baseball team at the Rensselaer Technology Institute, but rejected a five-hundred-dollar-per-week offer from an Albany theater to wax poetic about his baseball career.[5]

While Evers hunkered down in Troy, Frank Chance endured an intense twenty-four-hour negotiation via telegraph before finally abandoning his threat to quit the Cubs. The Peerless Leader agreed to a four-year deal that included his being granted "absolute control" of the team.[6]

Less than a month later, on March 6, Ellen Evers died.[7] The funeral for the mother of Johnny Evers was held at the family home, followed by a mass conducted at St. Joseph's Church. Charles Murphy was in attendance, as was Thomas Evers.[8] Johnny Evers remained noncommittal about his return to the diamond, although he hinted he might come back by mid–June.

Meanwhile, Johnny Kling had opened a beautiful billiard hall in Kansas City, sinking an estimated forty thousand dollars into the venture.[9] He was a no-show at the beginning of spring training, which was not at all unusual, but the Cubs were jolted on March 20 when the catcher wired the team that he was sitting out the 1909 season to take care of his business interests; speculation had it that Kling remained angry at Charles Murphy, who had blocked his attempts to inaugurate a similar establishment in Cincinnati a year earlier.[10] Frank Chance recognized this was not simply a salary gambit; he worried that the veteran catcher would remain in Kansas City for the entire season, forcing the Cubs to face the possibility of a 1909 season without *two* Johnnys—Kling and Evers.

The prospect of losing two stars from the Cubs lineup spurred Chance and Murphy into action. They were soon burning up the telegraph lines between Chicago and Troy, gently prodding Johnny Evers to return.[11] Evers held fast until mid–April, at which point he began gradually yielding to their entreaties. He made sure to delay his departure from Troy an extra day so he could umpire the first game of the Public School Athletic League, where his kid brother Joe was a star. After grabbing several newspapers and a box of cigars, Evers caught the midnight train to Cincinnati, arriving on April 29.[12]

He looked great—tan, healthy and appearing ready for action. But on his first day, he was content to watch Heine Zimmerman single and double in his place as the Cubs defeated the Reds, 5–4. The team then departed for Pittsburgh while Evers returned to Chicago with Charles Murphy to work out the kinks and get settled.[13] Murphy was delighted to have Evers back, and also delighted that the National League, in the wake of the Merkle mess, had adopted a two-man umpire crew for each game.

The Cubs returned home for a double-header on May 2, bringing the Pirates with them. Evers spent the day as first base coach and received a warm welcome from fans thrilled by his return to West Side Grounds. He pleased the crowd by working out on the infield between games, both of which the Cubs lost, dropping them into fifth place with a record of 8–7.[14] Evers made his season debut a day later, pinch-hitting for Chick Fraser in the fifth inning. After drawing a walk, he was eventually stranded at third base and called it a day.[15]

The next afternoon, Chance put Evers in the starting lineup, batting lead-off and playing second base. He had one hit and fielded nine chances without an error, but the Cubs lost to Pittsburgh, 1–0, in eleven innings, dropping below .500 as Babe Adams bested Mordecai Brown.[16]

When Evers arrived at the ballpark on the morning of May 5, he was greeted by a rude surprise. The National Commission was attempting to crack down on holdouts and had declared Evers ineligible due to his failure to report to spring training; he had not bothered applying for reinstatement—a formality the Cubs had thought unnecessary. Evers spent the day in street clothes, sitting in a field box with rabid Cubs fan Kenesaw Mountain Landis.[17] It took a couple of days for the paperwork to be completed, and the payment of a $100 fine, but Evers returned to the lineup against Cincinnati, making a spectacular diving catch of Chick Autrey's line drive to snuff a potential Reds rally.[18] By that time Frank Chance was out of the lineup due to a fracture in his right shoulder, the result of a collision with Pittsburgh's George Gibson; doctors ordered that Chance's shoulder be placed in a cast for several weeks.

Despite these setbacks, the Cubs managed to win ten of eleven games and were solidly in second place behind Pittsburgh by the end of May. Chance worried about the depth of his pitching staff, and Johnny Kling was missed, despite Charles Murphy's continuing praise of Pat Moran. And Johnny Evers was not hitting; following the game against Pittsburgh on May 29, his batting average fell to .151. Still, the Cubs' odds for a fourth straight pennant seemed far from daunting.

On June 30, the Chicago Cubs boasted an excellent 37–22 record, good for second place. Yet they remained a surprising seven and a half games behind Pittsburgh, which had compiled an incredible mark of 44–14. The teams met that day to christen the Pirates' new home stadium, Forbes Field, which would serve Pittsburgh's baseball team for the next sixty-two years.

Baseball had never been more popular and new edifices were all the rage—Philadelphia had one, Charles Comiskey was in the midst of building one on the south side of Chicago, and Brooklyn, Cincinnati, Boston, Detroit and Washington, D.C., were each prepared to follow suit. But Barney Dreyfuss had outdone them all, sinking an estimated two million dollars into his new ballpark, roughly six times what the Athletics had spent constructing Shibe

Barney Dreyfuss spent more than two million dollars on Forbes Field, which opened on June 30, 1909. Johnny Evers collected the first base hit in the new ballpark, which would remain the home of the Pittsburgh Pirates for more than sixty years. (Library of Congress, Prints and Photographs Division.)

Park, and the most spent on any major league facility until Yankee Stadium was built fourteen years later.

More than thirty thousand were on hand, easily the largest crowd in Pittsburgh history to that point, to witness the two best teams in the National League battle in what the *Pittsburgh Press* proudly, and not inaccurately, proclaimed as the "World's Greatest Baseball Park."

Johnny Evers led off the game with a single and later in the inning scored the stadium's first run. Ed Reulbach, whose most recent start had resulted in a one-hitter against Cincinnati, struggled with his control but outdueled Vic Willis to win, 3–2. Despite reaching base three times—on two singles and a hit by pitch—and scoring twice, Evers was nearly the goat of the contest, committing two errors, including a fumble of a grounder in the ninth that allowed the tying run to advance to third with one out. After the game, a Cubs fan leaned over the railing and yelled to Evers, "I'd have murdered you if we'd lost that one!" Evers shouted back, "You wouldn't have had a chance. I would have done the job myself!"[19]

Frank Selee died of tuberculosis at the Elks Home in Denver, Colorado, on July 9, 1909, four years after being forced to relinquish his position as manager of the Chicago Cubs because of poor health.[20] Less than three weeks after Selee's demise, National League president Harry Pulliam sat on a divan in his room at the New York Athletic Club and put a bullet through his head. Pulliam, who had suffered a nervous breakdown at the league meetings in February, had only recently resumed his duties. His last official act was a letter informing teams that the time had expired to have flags flown at half-staff in honor of recently deceased National League owners George Dovey and Israel Durham.[21]

Pulliam had long been afflicted with depression, which had worsened after the Merkle decision and his investigation and subsequent criticism of the Cubs in the wake of a complaint that Charles Murphy had scalped tickets at the World Series. Responses to Pulliam's death covered a wide spectrum. Honus Wagner, a close friend of Pulliam, wept when told the news. John McGraw and the Giants, who never forgave Pulliam for his role in denying them the 1908 pennant, went unrepresented at the funeral.

The Cubs lost both Ed Reulbach and Mordecai Brown for a stretch in mid–July—Brown due to the illness of his wife and Reulbach to ptomaine poisoning. Brown's wife recovered, as did Reulbach, who fashioned a fourteen-game winning streak that lasted until he was defeated by the New York Giants on August 14. The Giants would play a major role in denying the Cubs their fourth straight trip to the World Series, capturing four of the first five games of the series that had ended Reulbach's win streak, and the first three games of a mid–September series.

But when all was said and done, the Pirates were simply too much for the Cubs, and the rest of the league. Pittsburgh won 110 games to Chicago's 104, and Chance's men now knew what also-rans had faced in chasing them in 1906 and 1907. Charles Murphy blamed the lack of a pennant on early pitching woes and Chance's injury. The Cubs manager, while bemoaning the fact he could not set a record of four straight pennants, acknowledged the Pirates as the best team put together besides his pennant-winners. Johnny Evers said, "We lost lots of games on close decisions and we also failed to hit when hits would have copped, but Pittsburgh carried too many guns, that's all."[22]

There was no question that the success of the Chicago Cubs was measured by pennants, not individual accomplishments or near misses. They had fallen short, plain and simple. The pitching remained formidable—a staff earned run average of 1.75—the infield would be back for a fifth straight year, and perhaps they could persuade Johnny Kling to return. The Cubs were not finished yet.

⚾ ⚾ ⚾

Evers had recovered from his slow start, hitting .285 after his low water mark at the end of May to bring his overall average up to a respectable .263. He drew seventy-three walks and struck out only eighteen times, led the team in on-base percentage and was second only to Frank Chance in stolen bases. On the final day of the 1909 season he hit a home run into the right field bleachers at St. Louis in the first game of a double-header, and then sat out the nightcap with the other regulars.[23]

The regular season over, the Cubs challenged the White Sox to a post-season City Series for the first time since 1905—if one does not count the 1906 World Series—and emerged triumphant, winning four of five games. Evers played extremely well, collecting eight hits in seventeen at bats, and then returned to Troy, where he was greeted by family and friends, including his wife and one-day-old son, John Jr.[24]

A month later, the *New York Press* published an article claiming that Evers was quitting baseball in order to devote his energies to his shoe store in Troy. Exasperated by continual predictions of his retirement, Evers fired off a letter denying the story, pointing out he was under contract not only to play the next season, "but a few seasons afterwards."[25]

That December, Evers traveled to New York for the winter meetings and was seen palling around in the lobby of the Waldorf-Astoria with Heine Zimmerman and Jimmy Sheckard—the two apparently having reconciled after their earlier fight—while attending the league confab. During the meeting there were rumors that Sheckard might become Phillies manager and that Zimmerman would go with him in exchange for outfielder Sherwood Magee.[26] Of course, nothing happened; Frank Chance wanted the Cubs to stand pat—after all, hadn't they won 104 games?

The big story involving the Cubs during spring training in 1910 was the status of Johnny Kling and whether or not he would return. Kling whipsawed the press, the Cubs, and the National Commission for weeks, alternating between declaring an imminent return and insisting he wanted to retire in favor of expanding his business empire. He remained in absentia as the season began.

Shortly after Opening Day, Evers and Hugh Fullerton, sportswriter for the *Chicago Examiner*, released a book about the "inside game" of baseball strategy. Titled *Touching Second*, a nod toward the play that had ensured Evers's fame—and Fred Merkle's infamy—the popular work survives as an important primer on baseball as it was played during the "Dead Ball Era."

The book was largely penned by Fullerton while reflecting the views and expertise of Evers, as well as the sportswriter's own observations, and it covered every aspect of the game, including umpiring, managing and building a winning team. It also featured extensive diagrams displaying the range of fielders on certain plays and the timing of various throws and base running attempts. *Touching Second* was extremely popular and increased demand for Evers as a speaker.

On May 2, the Cubs played against the Pirates in Pittsburgh. President William Howard Taft was on hand, entering Forbes Field to the strains of "Hail to the Chief," with "a silk hat brigade" in tow. Fred Clarke, Honus Wagner, Frank Chance and Johnny Evers were accorded the honor of tossing one fresh new baseball apiece to Mr. Taft, who graciously signed each one and tossed them back. The Cubs lost the game, 5–2, dropping them to fourth place a dozen games into the season.[27]

Three days later the Cubs received welcome news when Johnny Kling signed a three-year contract with Chicago; Joe Tinker had finally convinced his friend to apply for reinstatement and return to the fold.[28] Even at age thirty-four, Kling remained in excellent physical condition, and Chance wasted little time returning him to the lineup.

The next day, Chance was incapacitated by another of his searing headaches—an increasingly common occurrence—and asked Johnny Evers to run the club against the Giants. Disobeying doctor's orders to remain in bed,

Chance sat in a box near home plate and watched helplessly as Evers smashed a line shot in practice that accidentally nailed Joe Tinker in the leg, knocking him out of the game that day, and for several more after.

The Cubs played well once the game began. Jack Pfiester lived up to his "Giant Killer" nickname, shutting out New York for a 2–0 win. Evers played impressively, cleanly handling eleven chances and pulling off one of baseball's rarest base running plays by scoring from first base on an infield bunt.

Evers's feat, staged on the eighth anniversary of his first professional game for Troy, began with his leading off the sixth with a walk. Jimmy Sheckard was up next and Evers flashed the bunt signal. Sheckard laid one down perfectly and Evers raced around the bases, never stopping as both first baseman Fred Merkle and pitcher Bugs Raymond pursued and misplayed the grounder, with Raymond finally firing the ball too late as Evers slid across home plate for the first run of the game.

That evening, Evers was asked to speak before the Paulist Athletic Association of Chicago on the subject "How to Become a Baseball Player." As he nervously clutched a cigar in his fingers and glanced at the two hundred teenage athletes present, he apologized for his inexperience in public speaking and allowed his embarrassment about a missing front tooth—a casualty of one of the recent games against the Pirates. He then betrayed that he would not be addressing the advertised topic. "I don't know as there are any set rules to follow," he began, "and if there are I never read them. As a matter of fact, I never read the book of rules of the game. I take the plays as they come up, and my noodle usually tells me the right play to make."

He spoke about the Merkle incident, including the Warren Gill episode that preceded it, and then melodramatically credited three priests with saving his life as he escaped the Polo Grounds following the historic play that changed the course of the 1908 season.[29] In all it was a satisfying day, both for the star second baseman and those gathered to hear him.

Evers had been anxious to get back to Chicago to take delivery of his first automobile, the machine that had become all the rage among ballplayers. Frank Chance purchased his first in the summer of 1908.[30] Christy Mathewson also had one, as did Orval Overall, Jack Pfiester, Honus Wagner, Fred Clarke and Sam Leever. The auto was a symbol of prestige and power, and Johnny Evers found being behind the wheel addicting, as well as a great way to unwind—something he always found difficult.

On May 20, Evers was driving in downtown Chicago with his mechanic, a young African American man who assisted him with driving when he needed help. In the back seat were his best friend, *Chicago Journal* sportswriter George McDonald, and Evers's eighteen-year-old brother Joe, who was living with Johnny in Chicago for the summer.

A melancholy Evers warms up on the infield between innings of a game in 1910—not long after the car accident that claimed the life of his friend, George McDonald. "They didn't blame me for it," said Evers of the accident. "But even so a man can't help blaming himself. I felt a good deal, I imagine, the way a murderer feels ... the shadow of death which was caused by his hand is on him." (Author's collection.)

Evers spied a streetcar stopped on the track to his right and thought nothing of crossing its path, but before he could do so the train began moving—its operator apparently oblivious to Evers's presence. McDonald, sitting in the right rear seat, recognized that a collision was inevitable and attempted to jump from the car, which was knocked onto its side. McDonald was thrown into the right front fender of Evers's automobile, his head wedged so tightly between the wheel and the body of the car that it took three men to free him. No one else was injured in the accident, but McDonald died of a skull fracture and internal injuries without regaining consciousness.[31]

"I had been talking to him but a moment before," recounted a still devastated Evers three years later for a *Baseball Magazine* profile, "...and the next moment he was lying on the ground, fatally injured." He added, "The shock of sudden death was more than I could stand."[32] McDonald's death haunted Evers the rest of his life.

"They didn't blame me for it. It was an accident. But even so a man can't help blaming himself. I felt a good deal, I imagine, the way a murderer feels ... the shadow of death which was caused by his hand is on him."[33] In later years Evers would confide to friends that he could never escape the mental picture of that day: "That man's head was hanging out of my car."[34]

Evers did not drive again for years, often relying on his brother to act as his chauffeur. He explained, "I don't like to ride in an auto ... and I wouldn't be disappointed if I never saw one again."[35]

Following the accident, Evers sat out for ten days as newspapers speculated whether he would ever play again. He remained in the stands with Charles Murphy, attempting in vain to rid himself of the gruesome mental image of his friend and that fateful moment.

While Johnny Evers sat, the Chicago Cubs kept winning—eleven games in a row to be exact—to take over first place. Evers returned to the lineup on June 1 and played well in a 5–1 win over Boston, but the Cubs lost Orval Overall to an arm injury while Frank Chance missed the game because of a broken finger incurred on Memorial Day.[36] At the beginning of the year, Evers had vowed to resist actions that would lead to ejections—but he was a different man than he had been in April. He seemed on edge and more easily agitated than usual.

On June 2, he engaged in several shouting matches with umpire Jim Johnstone.[37] The Cubs then traveled to Philadelphia, hours after Mordecai Brown lost a 1–0, twelve-inning heartbreaker to Boston.[38] Evers was increasingly plagued by insomnia, and traveling more than three hundred miles by train did not help. The Cubs played the Phillies on June 6; Evers failed to survive the second inning, sent packing after screaming at Cy Rigler about his pitch calls on Phillies hitters.[39] The tantrum earned him a three-day suspension.

Three weeks later the Cubs were in Pittsburgh, and Evers jawed with fans throughout the game. When they laughed after an umpire's call went against him, he turned and "made a gesture which is considered the height of insult."

He was threatened with arrest.[40] The Cubs were again in Pittsburgh on July 5, and Pirates first baseman Ham Hyatt accused Evers of attempting to spike him on a hard slide. When the teams changed positions at the end of the inning, Hyatt took up again with Evers, who waved dismissively in Hyatt's direction. Fred Clarke then joined the fray, and soon a dozen players were milling about the infield. Evers waved his hands in Clarke's face while calling him every name he could think of, and perhaps a few he invented on the spot. Clarke began making motions as if to slug Evers when Frank Chance and Jimmy Sheckard yanked their teammate back to the bench.

The next day's game went into extra innings. Chief Wilson led off Pittsburgh's half of the eleventh with a grounder on which shortstop Heine Zimmerman made a great stop, but Wilson was called safe on a close play. A frustrated Evers, who had uncharacteristically struck out twice earlier in the game, snapped at the decision, and Bob Emslie quickly handed Evers his second ejection of the season.[41] Later in the inning, the Pirates had two on and two out; Tommy Leach hit a grounder to Zimmerman who, trying to make sure of his throw, took a little too much time. Emslie ruled the Pirates runner safe at first on a very close play while Wilson scampered across the plate with the winning run.

Frank Chance went ballistic, furiously firing the baseball to the ground, followed quickly by his mitt and finally his chewing gum. But the call was final. Chance, who had tripled twice and scored both Cubs runs, only to see Chicago lose its 2–0 lead and then the game, gathered himself and walked calmly from the field. The Cubs' lead over New York had been shaved by a game, since the Giants had scored five runs in the fourteenth that afternoon to defeat Boston.[42]

In addition to his aggressive and innovative play at second base, there were three events in Johnny Evers's life that made him a star and rendered him worthy in the minds of those later voting him into the Baseball Hall of Fame. One was the Merkle incident, without which the Chicago Cubs would have owned only one World Series championship in the twentieth century rather than two. Another was his captaincy of the 1914 "Miracle Braves."

The third was a poem immortalizing the great Cubs infield. It appeared in the *New York Evening Mail* on July 12, 1910, and was titled "That Double Play Again":

> These are the saddest of possible words:
> "Tinker to Evers to Chance."
> Trio of bear cubs, fleeter than birds,
> Tinker and Evers and Chance.

New York Evening Mail columnist Franklin P. Adams dashed off eight words of verse that began, "These are the saddest of possible words...." Those words helped make Joe Tinker, Johnny Evers and Frank Chance household names and joined them together forever in baseball history. (Harris & Ewing Collection, Library of Congress.)

> Ruthlessly pricking our gonfalon bubble,
> Making a Giant hit into a double—
> Words that are heavy with nothing but trouble:
> "Tinker to Evers to Chance."

The poem, written by popular *Evening Mail* columnist Franklin P. Adams— a Chicago Cubs fan living in New York—became an instant sensation, in much the same way "Casey At The Bat" had after it was performed in New York a couple of decades earlier.[43] Three days later, the *Chicago Tribune* reprinted it under the title "Gotham's Woe," and then answered Adams's poem:

> Ah, no dear friend; these are equally sad:
> "Kling shot the ball down to Evers."
> Throwing to bases is Noisy John's fad.
> "Kling shot the ball down to Evers."
> What though the manager wildly has beckoned?

The chap who on stealing a base has reckoned
Is sure to be caught as he slides to second—
"Kling shot the ball down to Evers."[44]

Soon there were dozens of similar poems flying about the country of different variations, but Adams's piece proved so popular it was reprinted in the *Evening Mail* on July 18 under the title by which it became best known, "Baseball's Sad Lexicon."[45]

The Cubs won eighteen of twenty games between July 14 and August 4, but Johnny Evers continued to unravel emotionally. On July 27 he earned an ejection, and a one-hundred-dollar fine from a fed-up Frank Chance, for arguing with Bill Klem.[46]

Evers's temper only seemed to worsen, even as the Cubs pulled away from the rest of the National League. E.H. Simmons, who covered New York baseball for the *Sporting Life*, praised the machine-like precision of the Cubs middle infield, but chastised Evers for his "ungentlemanly and unsportsmanlike behavior on the ball field." Simmons especially objected to the constant arguing with umpires and the taunting of opponents.[47] Evers did not particularly care, no doubt amused that a writer covering a team managed by John McGraw would comment on such behavior. He was ejected on August 13 in Boston. On August 27 against New York he nearly recorded three outs on a single play, and then was unable to will himself out of bed the next day. He was ejected again against Pittsburgh on September 10.[48] But he was putting together a great September, hitting .469 between the fifth and the twenty-second, while also catching opponents unaware with trapped ball plays and delayed steals. Johnny Evers desperately wanted to get back to the World Series, which it appeared would feature the Cubs versus Connie Mack's Philadelphia Athletics.

Fred Merkle had suffered for two years, hoping for an opportunity to avenge his lapse of 1908, which Johnny Evers had used to his advantage in stealing the pennant from the Giants. John McGraw had never lost faith in Merkle, and by 1910 he was New York's starting first baseman. On September 22, one day shy of the second anniversary of the play that had branded Fred Merkle a "bonehead," the Giants were hosting the Cubs at the Polo Grounds.

Evers drew a lead-off walk in Chicago's half of the fifth inning—his third of the game. Pitcher Louis Drucke made a half-hearted pick-off throw to Merkle, and Evers easily scrambled back. Merkle then made a motion as if to toss the ball back to Drucke, while Evers, grinning at the Giants pitcher as if to say, "Is that the best you've got?" stepped off first base to take his lead.

But Merkle had not thrown the ball to Drucke—he still had it. The first baseman stuck the ball into the ribs of a startled Evers and the umpire called him out. The crowd gave Merkle a standing ovation for catching the great Johnny Evers with one of the oldest tricks in the book. It did not make up for 1908, not by a long shot. But it was still satisfying for Fred Merkle to victimize Evers on a "bonehead play" of his own.[49]

On October 1, 1910, the Cubs were visiting Cincinnati, counting down the days before they could claim their fourth National League pennant in five years. With the Cubs ahead, 3–1, Evers singled to lead off the fifth and was sacrificed to second. The next batter, Solly Hofman, lined a pitch to center; Evers was off at the crack of the bat with only one thing in mind—to score.

As he rounded third, Evers focused his attention on Reds catcher Tommy Clarke. Not wanting to take a chance that Clarke might bluff him into thinking there would be no throw, Evers decided to slide. But a momentary uncertainty led him to do so a fraction late and he felt his right cleat awkwardly catch the plate, forcing his leg one way and his foot the other. There was an audible crack as fans behind home plate recoiled from what they saw. Evers screamed out in pain, having broken his right fibula just above the ankle, a particularly nasty fracture that left the bone protruding through the skin.

The first person to check on Evers was Hank O'Day, who took one look at Evers's leg and frantically waved for the Cubs bench. O'Day was so disturbed by the sight of the injury that he could not eat that night. Evers was carried from the field on a stretcher, and a doctor summoned from the stands instructed that he be taken to the hospital immediately. Despite intense pain, Evers wired his wife that he expected to play the next day—a missive no doubt meant to ease any anxiety she might have experienced on hearing about the injury.[50] Ironically, there had been no throw to the plate; Evers's season ended during a play on which he could have scored standing up.

Evers, who said he had been nagged all season by a feeling something would prevent him from playing in the World Series, was transported to Chicago and admitted to West Side Hospital. It was determined he had also suffered extensive ligament damage and that the leg could not be re-set until the swelling subsided. So Evers sat in the hospital with his wife acting as nurse-maid, his leg wrapped in blankets and ice packs while his teammates officially clinched the 1910 National League pennant with an 8–4 win over Cincinnati.[51] Frank Chance told the team that they could drink whatever they wanted to that evening—Charles Murphy would pick up the tab. Chance also arranged to have two bottles of wine delivered to Evers in the hospital so he could feel a part of the celebration, a gesture Evers never forgot.[52]

Evers's leg was finally repaired four days after the injury, with doctors re-breaking it in order to properly set it before casting. Charles Murphy, Harry Steinfeldt and Heine Zimmerman visited Evers and were allowed to witness the procedure. Knowing of Evers's notorious sweet tooth, Zimmerman handed him a five-pound box of candy—one of two that had been awarded Zimmerman for hitting a pair of home runs in a recent game. Evers was told to expect a hospital stay of ten days, followed by at least six weeks on crutches.[53] Of course, doctors could not keep him down that long. Three days later, Charles Murphy packed Evers into his car and drove him to a game between the White Sox and Tigers.[54] The next day, Evers sat in an automobile in centerfield watching his teammates defeat the St. Louis Cardinals.[55]

Evers had another reason for getting out and about as quickly as possible—he was scheduled to open his new shoe store in Chicago in less than a week, in partnership with team secretary Charles Williams. The men had signed a twelve-year lease at seven thousand dollars a year for a Monroe Street storefront. Plans were made for Evers to be propped up in a chair by the store window for the grand opening.[56] He was allowed to go home. Publicly, doctors proclaimed optimism about his full recovery. Privately, there were concerns.

⚾ ⚾ ⚾

The opening of Johnny Evers's shoe store on the eve of the World Series was a true event. Frank Chance, Heine Zimmerman, Frank Schulte and several other Cubs joined Evers in the store window, causing a crush of fans on the sidewalk that spilled into the street, bringing traffic to a complete halt. "If we keep up this clip, I won't have time to play ball anymore," a beaming Evers exclaimed. "Our opening has been a bigger success than I looked for."

Charles Williams was unable to attend, busy making final travel arrangements for the Cubs, who were leaving for Philadelphia that night. Evers accompanied his teammates to the train station, a forlorn figure on his crutches, to bid goodbye and good luck. He explained that physically he could have traveled, but mentally, it was another story.

He admitted to Ring Lardner, "I'd go crazy if I had to sit up in the stand and watch those games. I suffered enough looking at those St. Louis affairs out on the west side. If I went to Philadelphia I'd be trying to tip Chance to some things, and I probably would go wild in the effort or get put out of the place for yelling too loud."[57]

Evers anxiously gathered with Cubs fans around the ticker at Al Tearney's restaurant for the games in Philadelphia. He did attend the contests in Chicago and was accorded a rousing cheer by Cubs fans. But Chicago lost the 1910

World Series in five games, many of them lopsided victories for the Athletics, as it appeared age had finally caught up with one of the greatest teams of all time. Orval Overall was talking retirement, Frank Chance was playing less and less, Mordecai Brown was thirty-three years old, as was Harry Steinfeldt, and Johnny Kling was about to turn thirty-five.

As for Evers, he began working to rehabilitate his leg. He remained in Chicago with his brother Joe over the winter, in order to keep an eye on his shoe store. It was there that he received a telegram in December that brought bad news.

Despite his public optimism about the shoe store in Chicago, Evers had been forced to accept less than advantageous terms on his stock, which was then delayed in transit, costing him much of the lucrative fall business. The partner/manager of the Troy store was unhappy with Evers's decision to open the outlet in Chicago, but Evers paid no mind until a telegram arrived on December 16. It was from the partner in Troy and read, "If you want your store open next Monday you can open it yourself."

Still on crutches, Evers caught the next available train home, only to discover the store locked. He acquired the key from one of the boys who worked there and, upon examining the books, discovered them in such disarray he had to call in an expert to decipher what had happened.

The upshot was that his partner had mismanaged the business and fled. Johnny Evers was financially wiped out. Once creditors discovered the problems in Troy, they feared the ballplayer was going to declare bankruptcy, and they put additional pressure on the Chicago store. Evers approached friends for assistance in keeping creditors at bay and his Chicago outlet open for a while, but ultimately it too went under, along with twenty-five thousand dollars Evers had sunk into the business.[58]

Evers had originally been promised his release when his two-year contract was up after the 1910 season, but he needed to stay close to Chicago and said he would sign for another year, determined to overcome his leg injury.[59] In the meantime he remained busy, bouncing between his stores in Troy and Chicago, trying in vain to keep both, or at least one, open. He was offered coaching positions by Yale University and the Naval Academy, as it was thought he would likely miss spring training anyway in order to allow his leg to heal.[60] He made a December appearance at the College Theater in Chicago, insisting during a monologue that the Cubs would return in 1911 largely intact and ready for another run at a championship.[61]

It was during the winter that American League umpire Billy Evans wrote an article about Evers, insisting that he and other umpires thought him a wonderful player and a warm and generous person—off the diamond—but "an awful crab" on it. During his playing career, Evers was more often referred to as "The Trojan" or "Jawn," the latter a reference to his prodigious chin; today he is most often remembered the way Evans portrayed him, as "The Crab."[62]

During the same winter, Evers was profiled in the magazine section of the *New York Herald* and, after praising his wife, uttered his famous line, "My favorite umpire is a dead one," closely followed by the remark, "And I think Chicago has the prettiest girls in the world."[63] It is safe to say that these were not the wisest remarks Johnny Evers had ever made.

Evers was back in the lineup on Opening Day in 1911, but the Cubs were beginning to look different. Harry Steinfeldt held out and was sold to St. Paul of the American Association—Heine Zimmerman took his place. Orval Overall retired to pursue gold mining interests in California. Johnny Kling lost his starting job to Jimmy Archer. This was a team that had averaged an incredible 106 wins per season between 1906 and 1910—the equivalent of 112 per year in a 162-game schedule—yet were without a win four games into the 1911 season.

They then seemed to catch their old spark, winning eight of nine to move into second place, one game behind Philadelphia, before losing Frank Chance at the end of that streak when he sprained his ankle in Cincinnati on a play nearly identical to the one that resulted in Evers's gruesome injury. As he attempted to score from second, Chance's foot caught in the dirt and twisted near home plate. It was feared that he too had broken his leg. Thankfully, X-rays revealed only a severe sprain, but it was enough to keep him out of the lineup for a while.[64]

Evers was asked to run the team in Chance's absence, but by the fourth inning of his second game in charge got kicked out of yet another game in Pittsburgh.[65] Less than a week later, it happened again, against Cincinnati.[66] It was clear there was something wrong. Evers's batting average was hovering at the .200 mark. He was not sleeping, appeared constantly nervous, and lacked an appetite. The day after his ejection against the Reds, he refused to get out of bed; worried friends, thinking back to Harry Pulliam two years earlier, described Evers as having suffered a nervous breakdown.[67] The pressures of winning, his attempts to keep his business afloat, to rehabilitate his leg, to handle his guilt about the accident that claimed his friend's life, and his own driven personality had conspired to bring him down.

Evers was granted permission to go home to Troy and rest for a few days.[68] When the Cubs visited New York in mid–May, Evers's brother Tom stopped by to inform Chance that the second baseman was spending his days in bed, nerves shot and face swollen.[69] There was public speculation that his physical problems were tied to his habit of eating up to a pound of fudge each day and smoking a dozen cigars.[70] Heine Zimmerman was shifted to Evers's position, and twenty-nine-year-old rookie Jimmy Doyle took over at third.

A week later, Evers suddenly appeared at Comiskey Park in a White Sox uniform, cavorting around second base. He claimed to feel better and insisted he was prepared to rejoin the Cubs when they returned from their road trip for a series against the Giants beginning June 2. But he did not play against the Giants.

Sportswriter F.C. Lane saw Evers about this time, knowing of his trials, and was shocked by the player's haggard appearance and trembling hands. Evers confided to Lane, "I don't feel very well. I can't seem to sleep. I didn't close my eyes at all last night. The doctor says I have nervous prostration. I have had touches of the same disease before, but never like this."[71]

He attempted to play again, on June 11 against Boston, entering the game in the eighth inning with the Cubs leading in a 20–2 rout. He was accorded a standing ovation when he took his position, and another when he came to bat in the bottom of the inning and struck out against rookie Bill McTigue.[72] After that appearance, he sat day after day on the bench, in uniform, rumors swirling that his return was imminent. But it was abundantly clear to those close to Evers that was not the case.

Chance and Murphy sat down with Evers and ordered him to take a sabbatical in the Adirondacks. Murphy offered him use of his car and a driver, and arranged for him to stay at a resort. There, he lived out in the open air, went to bed each night at eight o'clock, and cut back to one cigar each day. In early August he wrote a friend that he was feeling much better and expected to play in the World Series—taking for granted his team would make it.[73]

Meanwhile, the Cubs were playing Brooklyn on August 5, and Joe Tinker made a couple of poor plays that in the eyes of Frank Chance resulted from a lack of effort. When Chance called him on it, Tinker barked back, and Chance, not one to put up with insubordination, fined Tinker $150 on the spot and suspended him for the remainder of the season.[74] Chance immediately wired Evers that Tinker was out and he needed him back. Thinking Tinker had been injured, Evers hurried to Chicago. While he was en route, cooler heads prevailed and Chance lifted Tinker's suspension, and even rescinded the fine.[75] It was likely not coincidental that the day following his "suspension," Tinker faced his favorite pitcher, Christy Mathewson; he belted two singles, a double and a triple, and also stole home.[76]

Evers rejoined the Cubs on August 7 and seemed to have regained his old spark. With the Tinker emergency resolved, he could take his time working into shape, so his first public appearance in uniform came on the coaching lines, on August 21. As predicted by Sam Weller a day earlier in the *Chicago Tribune*, Evers returned but did not last long, ejected by Bill Klem after three innings.[77] Evers was back in the lineup as a player on September 2 against Cincinnati at third base, as Chance wanted to ease him back into the lineup. He made an impressive return, smashing a single and a triple and scoring two of Chicago's three runs as the Cubs defeated Cincinnati, 3–1. He then surprised Chance by asking if he could continue playing third, as he was enjoying it. Chance did so, leaving Heine Zimmerman at second.[78]

The Cubs continued to play well, as did Evers. He had two hits the next day against St. Louis, and four more against the Cardinals on September 6 during a 9–0 rout that moved the Cubs to within two and a half games of the first-place Giants. A day later, Chicago swept Cincinnati for its eighth win in the ten games since Evers's return, and was only one game behind.

But Evers began to unravel again. He was ejected on September 8 for arguing with Hank O'Day that a Reds base runner had used his arm to deliberately knock a ball away in order to score. When O'Day refused to listen to the argument, Evers stood on tiptoe and yelled into his ear.[79] The Cubs lost five of seven to drop five games off the pace, and a week later Evers was ejected again, this time in Pittsburgh by Bill Klem.[80] That episode earned him a suspension, and Evers did not play again—save for two pinch-hitting appearances—until October 3.

The 1911 season had been a lost one for Evers—he ultimately appeared in only forty-six games. It had been a lost season for the Cubs as well, the team winning only ninety-two games and finishing seven and a half games behind the New York Giants, who subsequently lost the World Series to the Philadelphia Athletics.

There were those who wondered whether Evers, despite a respectable September, had anything left as he readied to begin his eleventh major league season. He was about to surprise everyone, maybe even himself.

CHAPTER EIGHT

Comeback

It is often difficult to predict what will motivate a professional athlete; Johnny Evers found his motivation to play an eleventh year for the Chicago Cubs in the wake of his darkest season. Playing in September had re-energized him, creating certainty in his mind that he could come back. Maybe, he thought, he could even control his temper. Evers was also a father for the second time; Helen gave birth to a girl they named after her. Evers wrote Charlie Williams in January from Troy that he was "going to come back with a whole head and with both hands and feet to play second base ... without a skip."[1]

After reading the letter Williams mused, "I think Johnny Evers ... was the quietest fellow I ever saw the first season he came to Chicago. He seldom opened his mouth. Now you couldn't keep it closed with a club."[2] Not even Evers's closest friends could imagine him holding his tongue for an entire season.

Meanwhile, the Cubs were a team in transition. Frank Chance was hesitant about continuing as a player—he had appeared in even fewer games than Evers in 1911 due to searing headaches that limited sleep to no more than two hours each night. After collapsing prior to a game against Cincinnati, he was warned by doctors that one more blow to the head could kill him.[3] Not long after that, a somber Chance confided to Hugh Fullerton that he could not see the ball anymore and thought it might be time to quit.[4]

Chance was forced to further consider his own mortality when, on the first of February, third baseman Jimmy Doyle died following an operation for appendicitis.[5] There were other changes afoot for the Cubs. Johnny Kling had departed for Boston to become player-manager of the Braves. Mordecai Brown, coming off his sixth straight twenty-win season, was threatening to retire. Ed Reulbach had surrendered a run more per game over the past two seasons than he had in his first four. And, of course, Evers had suffered a nervous breakdown and a broken leg. The National League was no longer intimidated by the Cubs—Hank O'Day, the umpire recently named manager of the Cincinnati Reds, insisted that the only quality pitcher the Cubs had was Mordecai Brown. He quickly added that should the veteran follow through on his threat to retire, the Cubs were finished.

But the Cubs' cupboard was not completely bare. Although a hothead who threatened to sit out unless he received a salary increase, Heine Zimmerman was a talented player. Jimmy Archer was developing into an excellent catcher. Frank Schulte had slugged twenty-one home runs in 1911, capturing the National League's Most Valuable Player Award. Jimmy Sheckard remained a solid outfielder. And the team still boasted a middle infield of Joe Tinker and Johnny Evers, if the latter could make a comeback.

Mordecai Brown changed his mind about quitting, signing a three-year contract and joining the team at training camp in New Orleans. With Brown, Reulbach and Leonard "King" Cole—winner of thirty-eight games versus only eleven losses over the past two years—it seemed, at least on paper, that the Cubs would contend once again.

Ignoring repeated warnings, Frank Chance attempted to continue playing—his stated goal was to appear in at least half of the Cubs' games in 1912. He lasted only two before the headaches returned.

"I owe Chicago a great deal," declared the Peerless Leader, "but I don't owe baseball or the great Chicago public my life. They tell me that another blow on the head or another collapse like last year's [in Cincinnati] would finish me. I wanted to stick in the game until after the [home opener] in Chicago, but after my experience in yesterday's game I felt that I was liable to give in any minute."[6] Chance became a bench manager only; he would never again play for the Cubs.

Chicago opened its 1912 season as if in a trance, losing the first three games of the season and, after winning the fourth, suffering a ghastly 20–5 defeat at the hands of the St. Louis Cardinals. In that contest, Evers committed an incredible five errors as whispers intensified that the second baseman had, in the parlance of the time, "gone back."

Following a stern lecture from Chance, the Cubs boarded a train that evening in a heavy downpour, bound for a make-up game in Cincinnati. As the players discussed the latest news about the recent *Titanic* disaster and prepared to retire for the evening, they were abruptly jolted off their feet, belongings sent hurtling in every direction. This was accompanied by the shrieking of metal grinding against metal and the groaning sound resulting from the unnatural twisting of rigid railroad cars. All plunged into darkness as motion ceased and the grating sounds were replaced by the weary hiss of an exhausted steam engine and the rapping of steadily pounding rain on the outside of the sleeper car. The train had derailed, with all but one its twelve cars leaving the track. After several shouts of, "Is everybody all right?" the shaken players stumbled from the wreckage, not yet comprehending their great fortune in escaping serious injury—the accident occurred on level grade, so the cars remained largely upright. The passengers were instructed to remain on board until six o'clock the next morning, when a crew would repair the track and reset the train onto the rails.[7]

One could not help but wonder whether the wreck would prove a metaphor for the Cubs season—it certainly seemed apt to that point.

Bitter rivals Johnny Evers (right) and John McGraw share a quiet moment before a game during Evers's amazing comeback season in 1912. Evers would have by far his best offensive season that year, even as he confessed to friends that he never felt quite the same after his nervous breakdown. (George Grantham Bain Collection, Library of Congress.)

On May 6, Johnny Kling returned to West Side Grounds with the Boston Braves. Cubs fans were pleased to see him, but his ex-teammates showed no mercy, scoring three runs in the first inning on their way to a 5–3 win.[8] Chicago winning streaks, however, appeared only intermittently. Chance shook up his lineup, moving sore-kneed Solly Hofman from centerfield to first, Heine Zimmerman—who was leading the National League in hitting—from first to third, and Ed Lennox, replacement for the late Jimmy Doyle, from third to the bench.[9] When that failed to improve the team's fortunes, Chance traded Hofman and Leonard Cole to Pittsburgh for veteran outfielder Tommy Leach and twenty-eight-year-old pitcher Albert "Lefty" Leifield, and moved Vic Saier to first base.[10] A month later, the New York Giants' record stood at 50–11 while the Cubs sat in third place, fifteen and a half games behind.

Chance did discover a pair of useful pitchers in June—right-hander Larry Cheney, a twenty-six-year-old out of Kansas, and spitballer Jimmy Lavender, a twenty-eight-year-old rookie from Georgia—and the team began stringing together some victories. In early July, Lavender threw three consecutive shut-outs and then defeated New York's Rube Marquard, 7–2, ending the Giant left-hander's nineteen-game winning streak.[11] That win marked the seventh in eight games for the Cubs, and after Mordecai Brown lost to Christy Mathewson, Chicago won seven more in a row. Brown, who prior to the loss to Mathewson had thrown shutouts in consecutive starts, pitched a heroic game on July 15, relieving Jim Moroney in the first inning and tossing nine and one-third innings of relief to gut out an 8–7 victory. But Brown's third win of the season was a costly one; he twisted his knee so badly while stealing a base in the tenth inning that he had to be helped from the field. Joe Tinker then drove in the run that won the game.[12] A day later, the Cubs had sliced New York's lead to nine games. But the advance stalled, even as Chicago continued winning.

Joe Tinker and Johnny Evers were playing as well as ever; Evers was surprising everyone with his play. After his five-error game, he committed only two over his next twenty-two games. As July gave way to August, he had not missed a single game and was ejected only once, after becoming angry at Cy Rigler about a walk issued to Fred Merkle, and then exploding when Rigler called a strike on him later that inning.[13]

There were frequent comments about Evers's defensive resurgence, and he was hitting the ball as never before. He and Vic Saier smacked back-to-back home runs against Philadelphia. He went five for six plus two walks in a double-header against Brooklyn on July 21, and three for three the next day, including a double, a triple and yet another walk; Evers reached base eleven times in three games.[14]

On August 3, again against Brooklyn, Evers stole home cleanly in the ninth inning to key a four-run, game-winning rally for the Cubs. At that point his batting average was at .307, one point behind Honus Wagner (Heine Zimmerman led the league at .399), and it would only increase as the season wore on. From July 1 to the end of the year, Evers would hit .388; between July 18 and September 27—a span of two hundred at bats—he hit an incredible .430.

⚾ ⚾ ⚾

The Cubs had won twenty-seven of thirty-five, but on the morning of August 4 still trailed the Giants by ten games. Then the Giants stumbled a bit at home against Pittsburgh and St. Louis, allowing Chicago to close the gap.

Following a sloppy win on August 10 against Boston, Evers engaged in a post-game argument with umpire Bill Finneran. The incident received little notice at the time, but two days later, as the Cubs prepared to leave their hotel to take on the Braves, a telegram arrived from league president Thomas Lynch announcing that Evers had earned five days' suspension for the altercation with Finneran. Frank Chance was livid, as was Evers, whose enforced absence would carry through the first two games of a key three-game series at home against the Giants. Lynch claimed the suspension was because Evers had "passed his hand in front of Finneran's face after the game in question." Evers retorted that Finneran had pushed him in the face first and wondered why he was not being suspended as well. Chance fired off a telegram to Lynch, accusing him of hurting the Cubs to help the Giants. "There is no doubt in my mind," insisted Chance, "what the New York club runs the league."[15]

The Cubs won three of the next four anyway, and Evers returned on August 17 for the final game of the Giants series, smacking a pair of doubles and contributing to the scoring of three runs as Chicago defeated Christy Mathewson, 6–5, in a hard-fought eleven-inning game. Lew Richie, who had defeated New York in the series opener, pitched a complete game on one day's rest; in the clubhouse afterward, Chance awarded the pitcher a one-hundred-dollar bonus.[16] The Cubs were only five games back.

Johnny Evers was playing as if he were a man possessed; in the fifteen games following his suspension he batted an even .500. Not only that, after winning a fifth game in a row on August 22, the Cubs were within four games of the lead. But Ed Reulbach injured his side against Philadelphia and was unable to make another start for two weeks. The Cubs dropped three in a row. After a four-game winning streak, they lost seven of nine. It would have made a great story had the Cubs rallied from so far behind to overtake the Giants, but fighting uphill all season had taken its toll; with less than a month remaining, they had dropped to nine and a half games off the pace. There would be no miracle comeback for the Cubs in 1912.

⚾ ⚾ ⚾

Once Chicago fell out of contention, Johnny Evers reverted to his previous bad behavior. On September 3 in Pittsburgh, he turned to question a strike called by Bill Brennan. While he argued, the Pirates pitcher tried to quick pitch him. Evers was hit by the next delivery and accused the Pirates of doing so intentionally, resulting in the exchanging of harsh words with Honus Wagner.[17]

On September 8, he was ejected in Cincinnati after being tagged out at home plate while attempting to escape a rundown. During the ensuing row, he was accused of putting sand down Bill Brennan's back.[18] Another telegram from President Lynch awaited the Cubs in Boston, informing them that Evers was suspended for another five days and fined fifty dollars.[19]

Frank Chance had little patience left. He was not feeling well; the headaches—which had never completely subsided—returned with a vengeance. The Cubs were out of the running, so Chance consulted a specialist in New York and put Joe Tinker in charge. On September 17 the Cubs manager underwent successful surgery to remove a blood clot on his brain.[20]

That same day, Johnny Evers was ejected once more, in only his second game back following his second suspension. He had attempted to stretch a single into a double and, realizing the play would be close, executed a hook slide that he felt got him in safely. Umpire Brick Owens ruled otherwise, and when Evers refused to surrender the field, the infielder was directed to the showers.

Two days later, between games of a double-header against Brooklyn, Joe Tinker accused Evers of loafing on a force out. They exchanged words and Tinker took a swing at Evers. Suddenly the men were wrestling while teammates attempted to pry them apart. A plainclothes policeman was finally able to separate them, and they managed to play the second game without incident.[21]

The season ended with a whimper—the Cubs lost two of three to Cincinnati and were swept by Pittsburgh, dropping them to third place. They won the final two games of the season against St. Louis to finish with a record of 91–59. While still a very good baseball team, the Cubs had most definitely slipped a notch.

Meanwhile, had there been a Comeback Player of the Year Award, Johnny Evers most definitely would have won it. He batted .341, fourth best in the National League, with a career-high thirty-five extra-base hits, including eleven triples. His on-base percentage of .431 was second-best in the league, and he continued to be almost impossible to strike out. He established a career high for turning double plays, and at age thirty-one, had not missed a single game due to injury.

Big changes were coming to the Cubs—third place was not where Charles Murphy wanted his team to finish, and he felt it was time for a shake-up. The first thing he wanted to do was change managers; within days of Chance's surgery, Murphy announced that the team would have a new leader in 1913.[22] Word first leaked that Chance had resigned but he disputed that, contending, "I have not resigned; I never will resign, and what's more, I'm ready to sign a contract and manage the Cubs next year."[23]

Wanting to force Murphy's hand and become a free agent, Chance declared he was willing to take any contract Murphy offered, regardless of the amount, and return as a utility infielder if that was what the Cubs owner desired.[24] No one believed that would happen, as stubborn as Murphy might be. There were rumors Chance was headed to Cincinnati, Brooklyn or the New York Yankees—or that he might even stay home and tend his orange grove.

Chance managed the Cubs during the City Series against the White Sox in mid–October, and Murphy used the occasion to further shake up the team, releasing Mordecai Brown, who had won only five games because of his knee injury. Brown cleared waivers and was transferred to the Cubs' American Association farm team in Louisville.[25] In nine seasons Brown had won 186 games for Chicago while losing only 83 with an earned run average below 1.80.

Rumors swirled in October, with Joe Tinker and Johnny Evers being the most prominent names mentioned as Chance's successor. Tinker was emphatic that he did not want the job—claiming that he had turned down an offer earlier in the year from Murphy because he felt the pressure to win immediately would be too great. On October 22, Tinker was granted permission to pursue the possibility of becoming manager of the Cincinnati Reds, provided he could work out a player exchange acceptable to the Cubs. The announcement immediately fueled speculation that Evers would be named Chicago's new manager.[26]

The next day, Evers returned from a meeting at Charles Murphy's home and confirmed that he had agreed to succeed Frank Chance. Addressing the issue of Joe Tinker, Evers said, "I don't want to deprive Joe of a chance to manage a club if he can get the job, but there is no shortstop in the league today I want as much as Tinker."[27] Evers was formally introduced in his new role on October 24, signing a five-year contract, one year longer than Chance's last deal.[28]

Two days later, Frank Chance boarded a train with his wife, bound for his ranch in California. After issuing a statement of thanks and a farewell to the baseball fans of Chicago, he waved goodbye to Mordecai Brown and his wife, who came to the station to see him off.[29] Johnny Evers remained in Chicago for a week for some dental work and then set off for Troy, where yet another banquet was to be held in his honor. Before departing Chicago, Evers reiterated that he would not trade Tinker unless the deal made sense for the Cubs. While admitting that he and Tinker did not always get along, Evers maintained that they had always played well together and could continue to do so.[30] Tinker was equally adamant that he would not weaken the Cincinnati Reds to take the job there, and added that remaining with the Cubs was not an option.[31] "I can't play the same kind of baseball under Evers that I did for Chance," he insisted.[32] It was obvious neither of them would play for the other.

Frank Chance's future was resolved when Murphy finally allowed the Cincinnati Reds to claim him on waivers.[33] The Reds in turn dealt Chance to the New York Yankees to fill their manager position, leaving open the same slot for Joe Tinker in Cincinnati, pending a deal acceptable to Chicago.

Evers returned in mid–November for a banquet at the Hotel Sherman to celebrate his selection as manager. The fete started a good hour and a half late so Evers could dutifully autograph program after program before taking his seat of honor. Hank O'Day, recently hired by Charles Murphy as an advisor to the Cubs, began the official proceedings by ordering Johnny "out of the game" just to make him feel at home. Evers toasted Frank Chance and said that his goal was to put together a team that would prove a worthy successor to those led by the Peerless Leader.[34]

Three weeks later Joe Tinker was finally traded to Cincinnati, officially becoming player-manager of the Reds.[35] That sent everyone scrambling for a National League schedule to determine when the Cubs and Reds would first meet in 1913.

CHAPTER NINE

Managing the Cubs with Neither a Tinker Nor a Chance

It was unquestionably a season of adjustment for Cubs fans—the triumvirate of Tinker, Evers and Chance, after a decade together, was no more. It had always been suspected that absent Chance, Tinker and Evers could not coexist—the Peerless Leader had been, for lack of a better analogy, the father figure in the relationship. Tinker and Evers had pushed back at times, but without question they respected him. With Chance on hand, Tinker and Evers functioned like a machine, despite their personal differences. Without Chance, the two were having fistfights in the dugout.

Charles Murphy had settled on Evers, allowing the more likeable Tinker to go. Evers still revered Chance, and was especially hurt whenever he felt his old boss favored Tinker—however slight that favoritism might have seemed to outsiders. He also disputed Tinker's contention that he had been disloyal to Chance and had failed to say goodbye to his former manager before his departing for California.[1]

In the off-season, Johnny Kling had his billiard hall, Joe Tinker chased the footlights, and Frank Chance tended his orange groves. But Johnny Evers was all about baseball, all the time, and he was invariably sensitive to criticism when it came to anything about the game that was his life.

Evers had defied the odds in 1912, overcoming injuries as well as financial, emotional and physical obstacles to play some of his best baseball at a demanding position past his thirty-first birthday. Now he faced his greatest challenge, managing a team many perceived as being on the downside while at the same time following in the footsteps of a legend. It had to seem strange to Evers, realizing he would be unable to look in either direction on the diamond and see Tinker or Chance.

Evers nevertheless looked forward to the challenge and planned to manage as he played—unconventionally with fire and attitude. The team was his. "All I ask is a fair chance, one good opportunity to show what I can do," he told the *Chicago Tribune*. "I think I can hold down this job. I expect to make mistakes; every manager makes them. I expect to be criticized; every manager is. But I am going on about my business, doing the best I can, and I want the fans to withhold judgment for a while. Don't count me out before I enter the ring."[2]

Evers wanted his team to be based on speed, smarts and aggressiveness. The Cubs acquired five players from the Reds for Joe Tinker, including outfielder Mike Mitchell and infielder Art Phelan. Shortstop Al Bridwell was purchased from the Braves; the former Giants star, who had smacked the game-winning single that wasn't because Fred Merkle failed to touch second in 1908, was available after an injury-plagued season.[3]

The Cubs added catcher Roger Bresnahan in early January, yet another former Giants star victimized by Johnny Evers in 1908. Bresnahan had been released as player-manager of the St. Louis Cardinals; Chicago outbid Cincinnati and Pittsburgh to land him. Evers insisted that in Bresnahan and Jimmy Archer, the Cubs possessed the two best catchers in the game.

Charles Murphy was so enthused that he had the lives of Evers, Bresnahan and Archer insured for fifty thousand dollars each. He exclaimed, "I do not think I could replace either of these three players for $50,000. I decided to insure their lives ... for my own protection."[4]

Evers announced that the Cubs would depart for spring training in Tampa, Florida, on February 15.[5] Before leaving Chicago for a quick trip home prior to training camp, he asked Murphy to construct a pit of sand in Tampa so he could instruct Vic Saier and some of the other young players in the finer techniques of sliding.[6] Evers's enthusiasm aside, experts were not particularly impressed with the Cubs roster, pointing out that their pitching was suspect; conventional wisdom had the team finishing in the bottom half of the league for the first time in a decade. It was widely predicted that of the two Frank Chance understudies, Joe Tinker was more likely to bring his team home in the first division. For his part, Chance advanced the opinion that Tinker would do a good job in Cincinnati, but that Murphy had likely brought in Roger Bresnahan as insurance should Evers prove unsuccessful—a statement that aggravated Evers to no small degree.

Pitching was indeed a concern—so much so that when Orval Overall began making noises out in California about a comeback thanks to a new spitball, Hank O'Day was dispatched to see if the veteran was indeed in shape and, if so, to convince him to return to Chicago. (Published reports quoted Overall as saying he did not want to play for Murphy and would only stage a comeback with Tinker in Cincinnati.)

Tinker caused a flap when he visited Kansas City in February and met with Cubs holdout Larry Cheney, who had won a league-leading twenty-six games as a rookie. Tinker called on Cheney after Murphy reportedly had granted the pitcher permission to make his own deal—if he could find someone to pay him what he was asking. Evers nonetheless viewed Tinker's actions as tampering and labeled them as such.[7]

The ho-hum of a humdrum spring training was broken the moment the Cubs returned to Chicago—a fight broke out before the train even came to a complete stop. As the Cubs pulled into Polk Street Station, Evers rose from his seat and ordered trainer Doc Semmens to coordinate the unloading of the players' luggage. Semmens refused and Evers responded with an insult "which means a fight anywhere off the diamond." Semmens answered with a left cross to Evers's jaw, knocking the manager back into his seat. Evers then repeated the insult as others stepped in to prevent an escalation of hostilities. Semmens resigned on the spot and was immediately hired by Joe Tinker as trainer for Cincinnati.[8] The Semmens episode provided fodder for those inclined to doubt Evers's ability to rein in his infamous temper.

It was absolutely frigid on Opening Day in Chicago, perhaps appropriately so on a day that marked the first time in nearly eight years that the Cubs would be led by someone other than Frank Chance. Not only was there no Chance—there was no Brown, no Tinker and no Kling. In addition, Jimmy Sheckard sat on the opposition bench, having been sold to the St. Louis Cardinals a few days earlier after losing his centerfield job to Otis Clymer. Yet another link to the great Cubs teams of 1906–1910 was gone.[9] The day's festivities were highlighted by the presentation of a 180-piece sterling silver set encased in a mahogany chest, given to Evers during a ceremony emceed by Mayor Carter Harrison, Jr., whose father had held the same office when Cap Anson was a young first baseman for what were then called the Chicago Colts.

Both Al Bridwell and Roger Bresnahan were in the lineup, with Jimmy Archer subbing at first base in place of Vic Saier, who was recovering from a sprained ankle suffered while sliding in the final exhibition game. Jimmy Lavender started for Chicago, but the Cardinals jumped on him for two runs in the first, and he left after six innings, trailing 4–2. Evers slapped a pair of singles, was safe on an error and drew a walk, but made a crucial third out on a foolish attempt to stretch one of his singles into a double—Jimmy Archer would have scored easily on the play had Evers stopped at first base. Mike Mitchell was later caught at home plate on a double steal, costing the Cubs yet another tally. Evers never surrendered, using three pitchers including Larry

Cheney in the ninth, to no avail, as the Cubs dropped their opener, 5–3.[10] It was not the debut Evers wanted, but it was out of the way.

The Cubs did play better after Opening Day. They took two of three from the Pirates and two of three at the outset of their first road trip, in St. Louis.

The first game of the Cardinals' series featured a beautiful game pitched by Larry Cheney; going into the ninth inning he had allowed only a scratch infield single. Evers hit a two-run inside-the-park home run and made a great play on a bounder up the middle, leaping behind second base to spear the ball with his bare hand and throwing the ball in the same motion to retire the batter. The Cubs won, 7–1.[11]

After St. Louis it was on to Cincinnati to face Joe Tinker and his Reds— Frank Chance's words about the presence of Bresnahan representing a supposed lack of faith on Charles Murphy's part still ringing in Johnny Evers's ears.

Twenty thousand were on hand at year-old Redland Field to see the first-ever battle between the former teammates. The ballpark itself was an absolute mess thanks to floods that had swept the region earlier that month— mud had so caked the field that the grass died and the teams were playing on an all-dirt surface that would not be re-sodded until the Reds went on the road. The floods had also wreaked havoc with the railroad schedule; the Cubs arrived in Cincinnati only a couple of hours before game time, sans bats. After a quick trip to the local sporting goods shop, they arrived at the ballpark.

Both managers used their best pitchers, Larry Cheney for Chicago and Rube Benton for the Reds, with the Cubs winning, 3–2, thanks to a pair of runs in the eighth inning. Joe Tinker played a spectacular defensive game for Cincinnati, while Evers pulled himself from the lineup in the fourth inning in favor of Art Phelan so he could employ another right-hand hitter against the left-handed Benton. The loss dropped Cincinnati into sole possession of last place.[12]

The second game of the series was an eleven-inning slugfest finally captured by Chicago when Evers brought in Larry Cheney to pitch with two on and no one out in the eleventh inning. Cheney retired Joe Tinker for the final out; after working the count to three and two, the Reds manager flied out to end the game.[13]

The next day the teams used thirty players—with Evers making a triple lineup switch in the seventh inning—as the Cubs came from behind again. At one point, Evers sent Ward Miller to bat for Lefty Leifield and Tinker coun-

tered with pitcher Gene Packard. Evers reacted to Tinker's maneuver by recalling Miller and sending Tommy Leach to the plate. While this strategy is routine
now, it was almost unheard-of at the time—the two men definitely wanted to
get the best of each other.[14]

In the series finale, Evers got greedy and called on Larry Cheney for the
fourth game in a row, but his ace could not hold a three-run lead after relieving
Jimmy Lavender in the eighth inning, and the game ended in a tie.[15] The Cubs
left Cincinnati in a virtual deadlock for first, while the Reds dropped to 1–7
and a share of last place.

After Chicago captured three of four from the Pirates, Tinker and Evers
met again, this time at West Side Grounds. The Cubs had misplaced their bats
on the way to Cincinnati; this time it was the Reds whose equipment disappeared—their uniforms failed to arrive when Doc Semmens forgot to check
the team baggage—an incident that no doubt amused Evers. Joe Tinker contacted Charles Comiskey and arranged to borrow some White Sox uniforms
for the day.[16]

The Reds dropped the first two games of the series—stretching their
winless streak against Evers and the Cubs to six—before finally winning thanks
to Mordecai Brown, who had been acquired in January after the Cubs had
shipped him to Louisville.

Starting pitcher Chief Johnson had been rolling along for Cincinnati,
taking an 8–3 lead into the ninth, but then the Cubs scored a run and loaded
the bases with one out. Desperate not to lose another game to Chicago, Tinker
called on Brown to make his season debut. It was the type of dramatic appearance reminiscent of the pitcher's glory days on that very diamond; Cubs fans
had been rooting wildly when their team began to rally—but they seemed to
switch allegiances once they saw their former hero trudge across the grass and
ascend the mound.

Old Mordecai stared in at Al Bridwell and threw one of his trademark
sidearm curveballs for a strike. He then threw another, which Bridwell took
for strike two. Brown wasted a fastball outside before throwing another curve,
which Bridwell bounced to the first baseman, who threw home for a force out.
Brown then retired Jimmy Archer on a pop fly to end the game amid a robust
round of applause.[17]

Another mainstay of the Cubs' championship years made his season debut
in the final game of the series—Orval Overall had finally been persuaded by
Hank O'Day to play for the Cubs instead of the Reds and began his comeback
attempt against Cincinnati. Despite rainy weather, a large crowd was on hand
to see Overall, who was definitely rusty but held his own, carrying a 4–4 tie
to the eighth inning before the Reds broke open the game.[18]

Despite winning two of their last three, as the Reds departed Chicago it was the Cubs sitting in first place and the Reds that were in last. Critics were beginning to wonder whether they had underestimated Johnny Evers.

May 10, 1913, was Johnny Evers Day at the Polo Grounds; a contingent from Troy, some six hundred strong, poured into the ballpark to honor their hero. The Cubs had stumbled a bit, losing five of six to fall to third place, but Evers remained confident and upbeat. The delegation from his hometown entered via the center field gate, marching across the wide expanse of grass to home plate, where Troy's mayor greeted them. Both Evers and John McGraw received loving cups, and every player on both teams was presented a box of brand-new collars, direct from the Collar City. Charles Murphy gave Evers a gold-handled cane and umbrella, making sure everyone realized it had cost three hundred fifty dollars. Evers delighted his fans by smashing the game-winning hit, an eighth-inning double.[19]

On his "day," Evers had been warned by Bill Klem to stop holding his nose in response to calls he did not like. Two days later he repeated the gesture, earning an instant ejection from umpire Al Orth. Of course, Evers made no effort to depart quickly—he took his time walking the length of the bench, dispensing advice and instructions. A couple of innings later, Klem spotted Evers sitting by the outfield fence and halted the game until he removed himself.[20] That stunt earned him another suspension from league president Lynch in the midst of a big series, this time for three games.[21]

But Evers had surprised many baseball "experts." His team was in the first division while Frank Chance and Joe Tinker's languished at the bottom of their leagues. But, as Evers's critics had asked, could the Cubs' fiery second baseman continue to control his own temper, or would that temper prove his undoing?

Evers was having a difficult time with Heine Zimmerman. Coming off an incredible 1912 season that had unquestionably gone to his head, Zimmerman seemed to be getting into trouble every other day. He was ejected on June 13 against Brooklyn, broke Dodgers catcher Tex Erwin's arm the next day while attempting to steal home, and then closed out the Dodgers series with another ejection, this time for arguing a tag play at home plate.[22] Two days later Bill Klem thumbed Zimmerman again, apparently for comments made about a call Roger Bresnahan had disputed.[23] It was Zimmerman's fifth ejection of the season.

The next day an anonymous letter arrived at the offices of the *Chicago Tribune*. Enclosed was a one-hundred-dollar gold note, cut in half.

Heine Zimmerman was never easy to handle, but during the summer of 1913 he was more out of control than usual, until an anonymous fan challenged him to avoid being ejected for two weeks. If successful, he would earn a $100 reward. (George Grantham Bain Collection, Library of Congress.)

With it was a letter that began, "I'm Irish and haven't much use for the Dutch. But there is one Dutchman I think a whole lot of and his name is Heine Zimmerman."

The letter instructed that one-half of the note be given to Zimmerman with the proviso that if he could avoid ejection from a ball game for two weeks, he would receive the other half. It was signed "A SPLIT CENTURY."[24]

Bill Klem summoned Zimmerman to home plate prior to the beginning of the game on June 19 and handed the Cubs third baseman an envelope. Indeed, it contained one-half of a $100 gold note. Zimmerman, who had suspected the story to be a gag, greedily stuffed the note into his back pocket. He was not ejected that day. After the game, he crowed, "That $100 is as good as mine already, for I'm through fussing with umpires. Two weeks is easy. I won't get thrown out of a game all year."[25]

The next day Zimmerman was sent to the bench—not by an umpire, but by Johnny Evers. In the third inning, the Cardinals had a runner on third and two out. The batter hit a smash to Zimmerman at third, who started to throw home instead of to first base. Roger Bresnahan, catching for the Cubs, screamed at Zimmerman to throw to first, which he did. In the dugout, Bresnahan and Zimmerman got into it, and when Evers told Zimmerman to pipe down because he had nearly committed a bonehead play, he cursed Evers. When Evers dared him to repeat the epithet, he did. Evers fined him one hundred dollars, at which point Zimmerman said it a third time. He was immediately banished to the clubhouse and the fine was increased to two hundred dollars.

Zimmerman was in a somber mood after the game, worried he had lost his chance at the one-hundred-dollar bill. When assured it only applied if he was ejected by an umpire, he appeared visibly relieved. Zimmerman apologized to Evers the next day and all was forgiven; the fine was rescinded.[26]

Zimmerman behaved after that, continually aware of the hundred-dollar bill in his back pocket. The Cubs visited Cincinnati in late June and Joe Tinker asked to see the bill. Thinking it a joke, Tinker tore the half bill in half again. A horrified Zimmerman snatched back the pieces and stuffed them into his pocket.

Zimmerman nearly lost his temper on the final day, on a close play at the plate, screaming "No!" when the ruling went against him. But he held himself in check, walking away as the crowd watched breathlessly, knowing the reward was on the line.[27]

The next day, July 3, umpire Bill Brennan summoned Zimmerman to home plate and handed him an envelope. Inside was the other half of the gold note. He examined it, kissed it, and handed it to Johnny Evers, who looked it over and pronounced it genuine. Hoping to discover the identity of his bene-factor, Zimmerman examined the folded sheet of paper that had enclosed the bill, but found it blank. After the game, Zimmerman asked reporters to relay the message that he had learned his lesson and wanted to thank the fan who had sent him the currency.[28]

The identity of the anonymous benefactor was never revealed, but one cannot help but wonder whether the "Irishman" of the original letter was none other than Evers himself.

The Cincinnati Reds visited Chicago over the Fourth of July holiday, but the intensity of the rivalry between Joe Tinker and Johnny Evers had cooled. Tinker's wife had fallen seriously ill during the summer, and the Reds manager was further shaken when trainer Doc Semmens died of heat stroke the day after leaving the hospital following an operation for appendicitis.[29]

The Reds were struggling, but Evers came to Tinker's defense. "Joe has made good," said Evers. "He has done all with that club that a human being could do. There is nobody who could have done any better. He has had to begin from the beginning and make the club over, and I know something of the task that is."[30]

Evers and Tinker huddled later that week and discussed the possibility of rounding up their old teammates for an exhibition game to benefit the widow of Jimmy Doyle.[31] Those witnessing the conversation came away feeling that the two seemed closer than they had been in years.

Johnny Evers had gotten Heine Zimmerman under control, but there was another player he could not seem to keep in check, and that player was Johnny Evers.

On July 6, Evers earned his team a forfeit loss. Chicago was hosting St. Louis in a double-header; after the Cubs won the first game, 6–0, it was agreed that the nightcap would end by five o'clock so the Cardinals could catch their train to Boston. The second game did not begin until fifteen minutes to four, and Evers began stalling after St. Louis scored three times in the first, hoping there would not be enough time to play the four and a half innings required for the game to count. When he ignored repeated warnings, the umpires announced the game forfeited to the Cardinals. Evers responded by grabbing umpire Mal Eason by the shoulders and screaming in his face, but at that point the home crowd turned against Evers and began jeering.[32]

He was ejected on July 11 for arguing a close play at second base.[33] Three weeks later he was tossed again in a game against Boston, but still managed to order double lineup switches from the door of the clubhouse.[34] He earned three more ejections in August, including one that swept up Heine Zimmerman.[35] That's not to imply Evers lacked productive moments—on August 21 he had three hits against Christy Mathewson, including a home run into the right field bleachers. Unfortunately for Evers, Mathewson won the game, 8–2.[36]

At mid-season, Charles Murphy began jettisoning the team's older, high-salaried players. On August 6, Ed Reulbach was traded to Brooklyn and Mike Mitchell was sold to the Pirates. Reulbach had been unhappy for some time, declaring that he could not be successful pitching for a team that had lost confidence in him.[37] Orval Overall showed flashes of his old self, including a shutout of Boston, but by early August had won only four games and was sold to San Francisco of the Pacific Coast League. Lefty Leifield followed him there in short order.

There were rumors that Evers and Bresnahan were not speaking, and that Evers and Tommy Leach had been at odds.[38] Mike Mitchell, after joining the Pirates, said, "It is impossible for anyone to get along with Evers. I never had a word with any other manager I ever worked for, but I couldn't please Johnny."

Johnny Evers in July 1913. The strain of managing is clearly taking its toll. He would be ejected from five games in less than two months and players traded away that summer began taking potshots at him. (George Grantham Bain Collection, Library of Congress.)

He added, "Nearly every other player feels the same way as I do about him ... the feeling that pervades the team is one of resignation, all the boys just simply waiting for the season to be over, with the hope they will be traded elsewhere."

An obviously pained Evers replied, "Many times I have been fired out of games when I should not have been punished. Then again I have done things that should have caused me to be put out of baseball. After I have got back to the hotel and cooled down I have been ashamed of myself, and if the umpire had come around I would have apologized. There is one thing, though, that I don't like. This is the talk that I am always giving my men call-downs on the field. It has got so that every time I speak to one of my players I am accused of crabbing at him. This is not so. Before I was manager of the Cubs I got after other players and they got after me. Why, I even fought with Chance when I thought he was in the wrong. I'm out there on the field working for the best interests of my club."[39]

Despite the controversy, the Cubs played much better than expected in 1913. Although they were never a threat to win the pennant, they finished with a more than respectable record of 88–65, thirteen and a half games behind the New York Giants, winners of their third straight National League title. They were only one game behind the second-place Phillies. Joe Tinker and his Reds finished a distant seventh.

Evers also had a solid season as a player, hitting .285 and striking out only fourteen times in 446 at bats. He had kept the team in the first division all year—extending his own record of never finishing lower than third place in any full major league season he had played. With more pitching, it was felt the Cubs could contend again; indeed, Evers thought he had discovered another good young pitcher to pair with twenty-one-game winner Larry Cheney in James "Hippo" Vaughn, a failure during previous trials with New York and Washington. Vaughn won five of six starts with a 1.45 earned run average for Chicago after being acquired from Kansas City for Lew Richie.[40]

Evers was looking forward to his second year as manager and declared that his goal was nothing less than a pennant: "We will start right at the opening of the season and have them all on the defensive before the next season is a month old."[41]

Meanwhile, the Reds fired Joe Tinker. An excited Evers immediately wired Charles Murphy, who was traveling in Europe, about the possibility of bringing the shortstop back to the Cubs. Tinker was said to be equally excited about the opportunity.[42] Cubs fans were ecstatic at the suggestion of such a reunion.

But when Opening Day arrived in 1914, one of the men would be in Chicago, the other in Boston, and neither of them would be with the Cubs.

CHAPTER TEN

The Miracle Braves

Two days after Christmas 1913, Charles Murphy called Johnny Evers into his office. A week earlier the Brooklyn Dodgers had agreed to acquire Joe Tinker from Cincinnati, but the transaction remained on hold because of Tinker's demand for a ten-thousand-dollar bonus; Evers hoped Murphy would tell him that the shortstop was back on the market.[1]

Instead, Murphy asked Evers whether he "would be willing to play under an older man." Evers, who knew that Murphy and Hank O'Day had been conferring quite frequently, told the Cubs owner he would have to think about it.[2]

Although irritated by Murphy's question, Evers heard nothing further over the next several weeks and went about his duties, signing players and preparing for his second spring training as manager. He had not been entirely surprised by Murphy's inquiry, confiding to friends that he had not felt secure in his job; Murphy was angered by the Cubs' loss to the White Sox in the City Series in October, complaining that the defeat had cost him $50,000. Evers told friends, "I replied by asking him how much he thought I made for him in 1908 when Merkle forgot to touch second. When he said, 'Probably $200,000,' I said, 'Well, that's more than even up.'"

But in early February, Murphy began publicly criticizing Evers for the City Series loss, terming him "too impulsive to be a manager and a player at the same time."

Four days later, via a typed press release, Murphy announced he was relieving Evers of his duties as manager and replacing him with Hank O'Day. Evers was in New York, where the National League was holding its meeting to set the schedule for the 1914 season, and he was furious when he heard the news.

"I will never play for Murphy again under any conditions," he declared, adding that he had been approached by the Federals but would rather sign with Frank Chance in New York.[3] Out in Los Angeles, Chance was informed of Evers's dismissal and exclaimed, "Well hell, is that so?" Chance then called Murphy "a menace to baseball" and added he would love to land Evers. "I don't care what the Federal League offers. I will pay more. Evers is a great ballplayer."[4]

An outlaw league moving from independent status to direct competition with the National and American leagues in 1914, the Federal League had money to spend and was targeting established players possessing name recognition—Mordecai Brown was named player-manager for St. Louis, and Joe Tinker agreed to serve in the same role for the new Chicago franchise, owned by restaurateur Charles Weeghman. Weeghman also hired Evers's close friend Charlie Williams as team secretary and announced he would construct a new ballpark at Sheffield and Clark on the north side of the city.[5] Johnny Evers was another of the league's intended targets.

An alarmed cadre of National League owners summoned Evers to a secret midnight conference, where he presented both of his five-year contracts—one for his services as a player and the other as manager. Evers claimed the agreements were interlocking and that his dismissal as manager severed his player contract, making him a free agent.

Hank O'Day attempted in vain to meet with Evers and convince him to stay with the Cubs as a player. Boston Braves owner James Gaffney, eager to transform his team into a contender, offered $25,000 to secure Evers.[6] New Brooklyn manager Wilbert Robinson, John McGraw's former right-hand man, was equally eager to secure Evers for his infield, offering to move second baseman George Cutshaw to shortstop to make room for him. Dodgers owner Charles Ebbets announced he would outbid the Braves.[7]

Evers was finally convinced to go to Boston. Charles Murphy preferred an exchange of players rather than cash, so Gaffney agreed to swap infielder Bill Sweeney and pitcher Hub Perdue for Evers, who once again balked—not because he did not want to join the Braves, but because he did not want Murphy to profit from trading his services.[8]

Worried that Evers would jump to the Federal League, the National Commission declared the second baseman a free agent, and league presidents Ban Johnson and John Tener began discussing how to resolve the situation and at the same time rid baseball of Charles Murphy—who had long been at odds with other owners.[9] Following several days of intense negotiations, Evers reached agreement with James Gaffney on a deal that included a $25,000 signing bonus and assumption of the remainder of his five-year playing contract. With that, Johnny Evers was the highest paid player in baseball.

"I am going to begin all over as a player," Evers proclaimed. "I will take my orders from [Braves manager George] Stallings just as though I was never a manager. It's up to Stallings as to what position I shall play, but, no matter where I am placed, I will give the best efforts that are in me and will do everything I can to assist the success of the Boston club."[10] When asked about the possibility of being named team captain, Evers insisted there had been no agreement about that, but admitted he would likely accept if it was offered.

A few days later Charles Murphy was forced to sell the Cubs to Charles Taft, bringing an abrupt end to Murphy's tenure at the helm of the franchise.[11] With Murphy out of the way, the Braves complied with a league request to send Sweeney to Chicago in order to make the Cubs whole.[12] For his part, Evers rarely ever mentioned Charles Murphy again.

The Boston Braves were beginning their forty-fourth season in 1914, and their few remaining fans could be forgiven for not remembering that the team had once been the game's dominant franchise, capturing four consecutive National Association championships under baseball pioneer Harry Wright, and eight more in the National League before 1900, many of those under Johnny Evers's first major league manager, Frank Selee. Since then, the team had finished in the first division only once.

The ball club played at South End Grounds, which dated to the National Association days. The facility had been upgraded in 1888, the remodel featuring a fanciful double-decker castle-like motif for its entrance and grandstands.[13] After burning down in 1894, the ballpark was hurriedly replaced on the same site using the same theme, but on a smaller scale.[14]

The Braves floundered after the turn of the century, and in the aftermath of a 1912 season that resulted in the Braves' fourth consecutive last-place finish, Gaffney fired Johnny Kling and hired George Stallings, a successful minor league manager and a veteran of less successful stints with the Philadelphia Phillies, Detroit Tigers and New York Yankees.

Born in Augusta, Georgia, the forty-six-year-old Stallings was a stereotypical Southern gentleman away from the baseball diamond, holding court at the plantation his family had owned for generations, "The Meadows," located just outside Macon, Georgia.

Unlike most managers, Stallings sat on the bench in street clothes, always impeccably dressed in an expensive coat, a butterfly bow tie and—depending on the time of year—a flat-topped straw skimmer or a fedora. To characterize Stallings as intense was an incredible understatement; to him, winning was heaven, losing was hell, and there was nothing in between—he was Johnny Evers in a bow tie. Despite his debonair appearance, which by all accounts reflected his off-field demeanor and ability to charm women, Stallings was incessantly profane around his players and they wisely kept their distance when the score was against them.

More than anything else, Stallings prized players who could think on their feet and detested losing as much as he did. He held regular "skull sessions" to review opposition weaknesses at a time when that was very uncommon. To aid these strategy discussions, Stallings consulted a diary he faithfully maintained with notes on nearly every player in baseball—including how to best unnerve each one. Stallings's objective was to apply pressure to the opposition and never relent.

Stallings was also famously superstitious—perhaps the most superstitious man in a notoriously superstitious profession. He carried a rabbit's foot that he had rubbed bald, never took a two-dollar bill if he could help it, and avoided any numbers that could be combined to add up to thirteen. When his team was winning, he would go out of his way to do things exactly the same way every day. He would even freeze in position if a rally started, and not move until the side was retired.[15]

George Stallings recognized that acquiring Evers was nothing short of a bold stroke that provided him the equivalent of having a second manager on the field—exactly the prescription for a young team. The Braves had improved under Stallings in 1913, finishing a respectable fifth. He hoped the addition of Johnny Evers would result in a first-division finish.

Evers arrived for spring training in Macon on March 4 to don a Boston uniform for the first time. Disembarking at the train station shortly after noon with his wife and two young children in tow, Evers was on the diamond less than two hours later, working out his timing with diminutive twenty-two-year-old shortstop Walter "Rabbit" Maranville, who was amazingly four inches shorter and a good fifteen pounds lighter than his new double-play partner.

Evers steeled his emotions as he squinted into the warm Georgia sun, the crow's feet growing deeper under and around his eyes. Thoughts briefly drifted back to his old team, but just as quickly his attention shifted to his new one. Evers was immediately impressed with his new teammate's athleticism and baseball acumen; a year earlier he had passed on an opportunity to acquire the young shortstop for Chicago because he saw nothing special in him.[16]

Rabbit Maranville and Johnny Evers could not have been more different. Evers was abrasive, confrontational, and a man who, despite being a proven star, constantly challenged himself—and everyone else. Relentlessly. Mercilessly. Evers was an unquestioned general on the field—a ruthless competitor always on the attack, both literally and figuratively. On the other hand, Rabbit Maranville was gregarious, always ready and willing to party, and never seemed under pressure at all; he was not about to miss out on what life, and fame, had to offer.

Johnny Evers, shortly after arriving for his first spring training with the Boston Braves in Macon, Georgia, poses with his son, John Jr., who is wearing a replica Cubs uniform. (Reproduced from the original held by the Department of Special Collections of the Hesburgh Libraries of the University of Notre Dame.)

Maranville *was* like Evers in one way—he was an unorthodox athlete, whose play was based on feel. He utilized a distinctive technique for catching pop flies, always making a basket catch with his hands held at his belt buckle, no matter the situation. Stallings was aghast when he first saw his young short-stop's unique style and ordered him to change it. After dropping several pop flies, Maranville begged to resume his preferred method; Stallings waved him off and told him to go ahead. The Braves' manager had not been sold on Maranville—only after his nephew, Art Bues, contracted strep throat before the start of the 1913 season did Stallings give the youngster a chance.

Evers and Maranville became roommates in the spring of 1914 and despite their different personalities, they developed into an outstanding middle infield combination; Evers sensed Maranville was a talent he could meld with as he had with Joe Tinker.

Maranville was no less impressed with his new mentor. "Evers and I worked at second and short like a charm," Maranville related in his autobiography, *Run Rabbit Run.* "It was just Death Valley, whoever hit a ball down our way. Evers with his brains taught me more baseball than I ever dreamed about. He was psychic. He could sense where a player was going to hit if the pitcher threw the ball where he was supposed to."[17]

At the end of the first day's workout, Stallings invited Evers, Maranville and James Gaffney to "The Meadows" for a special evening of entertainment and relaxation, including barbequed pig and a tour of his plantation.[18] Evers was feeling rejuvenated, ready to take the anger he felt toward Charles Murphy out on the rest of the National League. A new chapter that would cement Johnny Evers as one of the great winners of his era was about to begin—he and the Braves were the perfect match at the perfect time, although it would not seem so during the season's early stages. By the end of spring training Evers was named team captain, an announcement that surprised no one.[19]

The Boston Braves opened the 1914 season at Ebbets Field against the Brooklyn Dodgers. Since the team was starting on the road where George Stallings could not control conditions, the ever-superstitious manager outfitted his team in special caps bearing swastika symbols for good luck.[20] But the Braves played uninspired baseball and lost, 8–2.[21] After winning the second game of the season, Boston dropped its next two, plus an exhibition against the International League Baltimore Orioles in which a teenaged Babe Ruth pitched three innings.[22]

The Braves managed to win their home opener, 9–1, but then dropped twelve of their next thirteen games and suffered a string of injuries, including to the thirty-two-year-old Evers, who was hobbling around on a banged-up knee that had bothered him the year before—even as he forced himself not to limp at the ballpark in order to disguise the fact he was in great pain.

By May 21, when the Braves reached Chicago for the much-anticipated return of Johnny Evers to Chicago, the Braves' record was an abysmal 4–18.[23] Evers was accorded a spirited standing ovation by Chicago fans after leading off his "day" by drawing a base on balls. Rabbit Maranville followed with a triple to score Evers standing up, and then crossed the plate himself moments later on an error. Evers added a sacrifice fly in the fourth to complete the scoring for Boston's 3–1 victory. The crowd could not get enough of their former hero—Evers was given another standing ovation following a routine single in the seventh inning.[24] The Braves won again the next day thanks to a surprise shutout from sore-armed veteran left-hander Otto Hess, marking the first time Boston had won consecutive games. Evers and Maranville combined for thirteen assists and four putouts without an error, and Maranville made a spectacular, over-the-shoulder diving catch while sprinting into the outfield with his back to the plate. Hess allowed only four hits, all singles, and did not walk a batter.[25] A couple of wins had sparked hope—had the Braves turned the corner? In short, the answer was no.

The Braves split a Memorial Day double-header in Philadelphia before moving on to Brooklyn, where they dropped four of five games to end their road trip with a record of 11–26. The upcoming month-long home stand was a sorely needed return to Boston; Maranville was suffering from a sprained wrist and tonsillitis. Evers and young third baseman Charlie Deal were hobbled.

Coach Fred Mitchell had been tutoring Hank Gowdy, who was in the process of converting from first base to catcher. One of the obstacles was Gowdy's reputation for laziness—at one point he complained that Stallings was playing him too much. Evers fixed him with a withering stare, and in a voice tinged with disdain reminded the young player, "I play every day, don't I? And Maranville and Schmidt, and the rest of us, except the pitchers. Why shouldn't you work every day?" A chastised Gowdy ceased complaining and donned the mask every time he was told.[26]

Evers also took Rabbit Maranville to task. In a game against Cincinnati, Evers fielded a double-play grounder and tossed the ball to Maranville, who was covering second. But when the Reds' base runner came in with a hard slide, Maranville threw around him and was late delivering the throw to first, allowing a run to score.

"My delay in trying to throw around [the runner] let out a blast of curses [from Evers] I have never heard since," remembered Maranville. "I said to Evers after the ballyhoo, 'What should I have done?' I told him I didn't want to hurt [the runner].

"He said, '...the next time anyone comes down at you to stop a double play, you hit him right between the eyes.'"[27]

The Braves finally began improving, manufacturing a five-game winning streak in early June. Evers played an outstanding game against the Pirates on June 12, handling twelve chances without an error, including one particularly beautiful play in which he ranged far to his left onto the right field grass to throw out Pittsburgh's Mike Mowrey to end the game.[28]

A week later, Bill James pitched the Braves to their ninth win in eleven games, a three-hit, 3–2 victory over the St. Louis Cardinals. Otto Hess played first base in place of Butch Schmidt, who had injured himself sliding the previous day, and hit a home run.[29] Boston's record was 22–30; it was the closest the Braves had been to the break-even mark since May 9.

But they dropped the series finale to St. Louis. A bad throw from back-up catcher Bert Whaling, who was attempting to complete a double play with the bases loaded, allowed a run to score in the eighth inning of a close game, and the other Cardinals runners moved up to second and third. With the score tied, 2–2, the infield moved in and the next batter hit a line shot through the space in which Evers would normally have been positioned, giving St. Louis a lead they never relinquished.[30] A furious Evers blamed Bill James for pitching to the wrong spot. James was equally angry, convinced that Evers had made a mistake and refused to own up to it. After exchanging heated words in the dugout, the two did not speak again that season.

With his team still in the basement, George Stallings took stock; he had been debating whether to revamp his roster for two months. James had been a surprise, making up for the loss of Jack Quinn to the Federal League to give Boston a strong third starting pitcher along with Dick Rudolph and Lefty Tyler. But the outfield remained a great concern. Stallings was in the habit of keeping a journal at his bedside to jot down thoughts that came to him. One night in late June, he was drifting off to sleep when an idea suddenly snapped him to consciousness. He managed to write it down, so as not to forget it. The concept involved expanding on the practice of utilizing pinch-hitters by playing to their strengths against particular pitchers, especially righties against lefties and vice-versa. Stallings thought, "Why not do it for an entire game?" It was the birth of the modern platoon system.

"I would shift my whole outfield," he said, "according to whether a right-hander or left-hander was working against us."[31] To accomplish this, Stallings would have to shuffle his roster. He sold thirty-six-year-old Jim Murray to St. Paul. He shipped Hub Perdue to the St. Louis Cardinals in exchange for out-fielder Ted Cather and utility man Possum Whitted, who could play both third base and the outfield.[32] He then purchased the Phillies' left-handed-hitting outfielder Josh Devore, a veteran of multiple pennant chases thanks to his years with the New York Giants.[33] Combining the new faces with Larry Gilbert, Les Mann and Joe Connolly, George Stallings had his platoon out-field.

Despite the new system, the Braves dropped their July 4 double-header against Brooklyn and sat in last place with a record of 26–40. That day, all of Boston celebrated Independence Day, with the city serving six hundred gallons of ice cream and more than fifteen thousand popcorn balls to the children of Beantown. Police officer Frank Rooney put on a pair of exhibitions in which he boxed a kangaroo. Open air band concerts were staged and the bell chimes of the Mission Church played patriotic music during the day. Amateur track and field events were staged on The Common, with thousands in attendance. But the fireworks celebration that unfolded that evening proved far less explosive than George Stallings after his team embarrassed itself in an exhibition game in Buffalo three days later. It was an episode that many—in hindsight—felt had marked the turning point of the season.

The Braves arrived in Buffalo on July 7 for a game against the International League Bisons, which had been struggling to compete for attendance with the Federal League team also representing the city. George Stallings had been a popular and successful manager there, and it was thought he would bring out the fans—which he did.

But Stallings's return was not a happy one. The Braves were listless and sloppy, committing four errors and losing to the minor leaguers, 10–2.[34]

That night Stallings lit into his players, challenging their manhood and questioning their status as major leaguers. Years later, in what was undoubtedly a highly sanitized version of the diatribe, Rabbit Maranville remembered Stallings, oblivious to the presence of onlookers, shouting at the players as they silently boarded the train. "Big league players, you call yourselves, eh!" screamed Stallings. "You're not even Grade 'A' sandlotters. I'm ashamed of you all!"[35]

The day after their post–exhibition game tongue-lashing from George Stallings, the Braves knocked off the Cubs in a hard-fought eleven-inning contest. Evers was particularly feisty, his nose bloodied in a collision on the base paths with Larry Cheney, and later earning an ejection after arguing too stridently that Rabbit Maranville had beaten a throw to second base.

The Braves added four more wins in a row; the team was indeed hitting its stride—Maranville was providing heroics every day and Evers was maneuvering the infield like an Army general, forcing hitters to bat into the teeth of the Braves defense. Boston may have been ten-and-a-half games out of first place, but Stallings was far from giving up on the season.

On July 19, the Braves defeated Cincinnati to move out of last place for good. Attendance was beginning to improve to the point that the team was turning away fans at South End Grounds. At the end of the month, the Braves were suddenly sitting in fourth place, having won fifteen of twenty games since Buffalo, and the baseball world was beginning to take notice. William Weart, Philadelphia correspondent for *The Sporting News*, noted, "Three weeks ago the Braves' chances looked to be about one in a thousand. Now the Stallings outfit has gotten dangerously close to the leaders. If Stallings' men keep up the pace for the next ten days that they have set for the past four weeks, the map of the National League is likely to undergo quite a change."[36]

Grantland Rice chimed in: "In an ordinary season the possibility of the

Johnny Evers sits in the dugout next to George Stallings—two of baseball's most
intense personalities. Together, Evers and Stallings drove the Boston Braves to one
of the greatest upsets in baseball history. (George Grantham Bain Collection,
Library of Congress.)

Boston Braves winning a pennant would never be considered. But 1914 is no
ordinary season."[37]

The Boston Braves were suddenly the hottest ticket in a rabid sports
town, and were finding it increasingly difficult to accommodate their fans at
the cramped and outdated South End Grounds. A few home games had been
scheduled the year before at the larger and more modern Fenway Park, but
the rent charged by the Red Sox had proven too expensive for the Braves to
book the venue more than a handful of times. Lacking alternatives and concerned about the ramifications of continually turning away large crowds, James
Gaffney approached new Red Sox owner Joseph Lannin about reducing the
rent at the new ballpark. Lannin, owner of a small stake in the Braves before
purchasing the Red Sox in December 1913, did even better than that, providing
Gaffney use of Fenway Park for the remainder of the season at no cost.

The Braves continued winning. On August 4, Dick Rudolph threw his
second two-hit shutout in five days, defeating Pittsburgh, 1–0.[38] Evers made
a sparkling defensive play to save the day, a leaping stab five feet behind the
second base bag, followed by a throw to first in the same motion while remain-

ing airborne.[39] Evers's revival as a player since his nervous breakdown three years earlier was remarkable; he was fielding better than ever, hitting .295, and showing no signs of slowing down.

But Johnny Evers was about to receive terrible news that threatened to derail his season.

On August 7, Evers received a telegram informing him that his two-year-old daughter, Helen, was seriously ill with scarlet fever she had contracted a week earlier.[40] His son had caught the disease first, so his daughter was sent to stay with relatives. However, the attending physician insisted on having Helen return so she could be exposed to the disease and develop immunity. Despite her trepidation, Evers's wife followed the doctor's instructions with disastrous results. A worried Evers played that afternoon before leaving for Troy, and by the time he arrived at the train station his daughter had already died—in fact, she had succumbed shortly after the telegram arrived.[41] The funeral was held on Saturday, August 8.[42]

After saying he was sure the distraught Evers would recognize his responsibility to his teammates and return as soon as possible, Stallings turned from business to personal feelings about his team captain, remarking, "He knows how we sympathize with him without our telling him. The death of his little girl is a hard blow, but Johnny Evers will bear up under it as he has under all his other trials, you can be sure of that." As Stallings predicted, the day after the funeral Evers wired the Braves to let them know he was returning immediately. Before he left Troy, his entire wardrobe and baggage were fumigated to ensure that the disease would not be spread to others.[43] His grieving wife and son would shortly join him in Boston.

During Evers's absence, Stallings acquired third baseman James Carlisle "Red" Smith from Brooklyn.[44] Smith's first game with the Braves was on August 10; batting sixth in the order against Cincinnati, he drove in Boston's first run with a single to score Rabbit Maranville. Bill James pitched a complete game and the Braves won, 3–1, to capture their twenty-fifth win in thirty-one games.[45] In a span of only twenty-three days, the Braves had moved from last place to second. The team completed its home stand against Cincinnati with a thirteen-inning, scoreless pitcher's duel between Red Ames and Lefty Tyler; it would be the final game the Braves ever played at South End Grounds—the remainder of their home contests in 1914 would be staged at Fenway Park.[46] The team continued on to New York, where Johnny Evers was there to meet them.

The confident New York Giants, led by their iconic and cocky manager, awaited the Braves; few gave any thought to the notion that the league-leading, three-time defending National League champions would fail to put the upstarts in their place. John McGraw had been growing testy—he had been ejected three times in a recent series against Cincinnati, during which the Giants dropped four of five at the Polo Grounds. The third time, McGraw was threatened with forfeit if he didn't leave the playing field. When umpire William "Lord" Byron reached for his watch to issue McGraw a time limit, the Giants manager tried to snatch the timepiece and was summarily dismissed.[47]

McGraw's mood did not improve after the Braves swept the Giants, with Lefty Tyler closing out the series by defeating Christy Mathewson, 2–0, in ten innings. Boston was only three and a half games out of the lead.[48]

George Stallings gathered his players after the final game and told them that the Giants "were done." He explained that New York could be overtaken and challenged them to do it. He warned them not to become overconfident and not to get down if they went through a streak where the breaks went against them.[49]

The Giants were scheduled to embark on a three-week road trip that would conclude with three games in Boston, a series that now seemed key to the entire season. Maranville had wowed the New York press with his defense, Red Smith had boosted the offense, Johnny Evers was back, George Stallings seemed to be inside the heads of his opponents, and the pitching had been spectacular—Bill James had not lost since July 4. Since June 1, the Giants had played break-even baseball over a seventy-four game stretch, while the Braves had won forty-nine of seventy-three.

The Braves visited Chicago on August 26, playing on the diamond where Evers had spent a dozen years of his life. During the game, Evers and Heine Zimmerman engaged in a fistfight after Zimmerman swung his arm in an attempt to knock the ball loose on a play at second base, igniting a brawl that emptied the benches. Stallings worried that suspensions of his best players might be forthcoming, but league president John Tener did not want to disrupt the pennant race and instead doled out fines to the participants.[50]

Maintaining momentum was important to Stallings—over the preceding forty-seven days, the Braves had rocketed from last place to sole possession of first. Since dropping the Fourth of July double-header, Boston had won thirty-eight of forty-nine games, capturing the attention of the sports world with an unprecedented leapfrogging to the top of the standings. Incredibly, the Braves would play even better over the final forty-one games of the season.

On the eve of the big rematch between the Braves and Giants, John McGraw was interviewed about the upcoming battle and the manager allowed his admiration for George Stallings. Then, when asked about Johnny Evers, he said, "You only find a man of his natural ability and brains once in about ten years." McGraw added that while he felt Stallings a genius on the bench, he feared Evers because he was the spirit of the team on the field.[51]

Evers was facing yet another key series against the Giants—a rivalry that had defined his career. His stomach was giving him fits again—it always did in times of stress. The come-from-behind nature of this pennant race, the end of his career with the Cubs, the death of his daughter, and now the nerve-wracking pair of series against the Giants—they were all taking their toll. In addition, when the series began, Evers was forced to deny a patently false story quoting him as saying that the Braves were not championship caliber and had no real chance of overcoming the Giants.[52]

Thirty-five thousand were on hand for the morning game at Fenway Park, with several thousand more left on the outside after tickets stopped being sold. It was one of the largest crowds ever to witness a baseball game up to that time.

The Braves found themselves trailing Christy Mathewson, 4–3, in the ninth inning when Evers filled the role of hero with a two-run, walk-off line shot that bounced into the crowd. Evers ran for his life to the clubhouse— after touching first base, of course—while fans celebrated by rushing onto the field and into the Braves dugout.

Even though the Giants routed Boston in the nightcap, the Braves had proved they could stand toe to toe with the defending champions.[53] Boston took the rubber match the next day behind Bill James; Evers smacked three hits and executed a sensational defensive play, snagging a tough pop fly and then whirling quickly to catch the Giants runner off first. Boston had an edge on New York it would not surrender.[54]

Everything was going right for the Braves; in the nightcap of a double-header against Philadelphia, Stallings started a young pitcher out of Harvard named George Davis. He threw a no-hitter.[55] Davis's start was a godsend to George Stallings, who had used Davis in order to give an extra day's rest to his three best starting pitchers.

September 16 was Johnny Evers Day at Fenway Park, and rarely had such an honor been more deserved. Before the game he was presented a silver tea service as twelve thousand fans showed their appreciation for the man they called "The Trojan."

Unfortunately, as if to punctuate how tough a year it had been for Evers personally, he received word that his home had been ransacked from top to bottom by burglars, who stole the nearly identical silver service he had received from the Chicago Cubs a year earlier; since Evers's wife and son John Jr. had left Troy shortly after his daughter's funeral, the house had sat vacant for several weeks.[56]

A large contingent of National Guard was in the stands, as was the Ninth Regiment Band, which struck up "When Johnny Comes Marching Home" after Evers scored what proved to be the winning run. The 6–3 victory helped the Braves maintain what had expanded to a three-and-a-half game lead over New York.[57] John McGraw pinned his hopes on a five-game series between the teams the last week of September.

But the unstoppable Braves would end the pennant race before then. On September 24 the team was feted at a dinner hosted by the Filene Men's Club. George Stallings addressed the more than one thousand in attendance, crediting the fighting spirit of the team for its success. Evers appeared next at the rostrum and praised Stallings, comparing him favorably to Frank Chance, who had recently resigned as manager of the New York Yankees.[58]

As Boston's lead continued to widen, making the Giants' elimination all but inevitable, John McGraw saluted the Braves as a team that would contend for years to come: "In two years [George Stallings] has turned one of the worst collection of ballplayers I ever laid eyes on—and I have seen some pretty bad ones—into a championship contender." He also praised Evers as being like a manager on the field—not only positioning the infielders based on pitchers and hitters, but the outfielders as well.[59]

The Braves officially clinched the pennant on September 29, with Evers scoring the run that made them National League champions in a game against, most appropriately, the Chicago Cubs—it was the first time since 1900 that a team other than the Giants, Pirates or Cubs had won the National League pennant.[60] The jubilant players boarded a train bound for New York, with James Gaffney tagging along so he could meet with the National Commission, which was making final arrangements for the upcoming World Series between the Braves and the Philadelphia Athletics. Upon arriving in New York, Stallings, already anticipating questions from reporters about his team's being an underdog to the Athletics, pointed out that the Braves had won sixty-one of their last seventy-seven games. He then proclaimed, "Anyone who thinks the Athletics are not going to have a fight on their hands is laboring under a misapprehension."[61]

For his part, Evers continued to fight all the way through the final day of the regular season. Not one to let what he considered an injustice pass without comment—even with the pennant long since clinched—in the penultimate game of the season Evers argued that he had tagged out a runner attempting to steal. When the umpire disagreed, Evers tossed his glove straight up into the air in a show of disgust. Somehow, he lasted another inning. But, after continuing to bark at the umpire, he earned his ninth ejection of the season. Before leaving, Evers hit his first home run of the year, a blast far over the head of the centerfielder.[62] Stallings, who had lectured Evers about his repeated ejections, let this one slide, recognizing that the blow-up was Evers's way of gearing up for the upcoming battle against Philadelphia.

The Braves suffered a major blow in the same game when Red Smith slid awkwardly into second base and caught his spikes, causing him to dislocate his ankle and fracture both his tibia and fibula.[63] The injury and its timing were reminiscent of that suffered by Evers prior to the 1910 World Series.

George Stallings remained upbeat: "I am extremely sorry that such an unfortunate incident should deprive us of Smith's services at such a critical stage," he said. "But we are singularly fortunate in having a reliable substitute in [Charlie] Deal for third base." He added, "We are well prepared.... I am glad to be in a position to say there is not a place on the team into which we could not put a substitute at a moment's notice."[64]

Evers seconded Stallings, declaring, "Don't think for a moment that the loss of Smith will weaken our infield. No one knows better than I what Deal is made of and, take it from me, barring his lesser batting power, Charlie will fill Red's place to the entire satisfaction of everyone interested in the welfare and success of our team." But it was abundantly clear the Braves were going to miss Smith, both for his bat and his aggressiveness.

On the regular season's final day, Johnny Evers was named the National League's Most Valuable Player, earning a brand-new Chalmers automobile that went with the designation in a close vote that saw him edge Rabbit Maranville for the honor.[65] Even though he still was not driving, Evers was especially proud of the award. But his attention soon shifted to the Athletics and the war he planned to wage against them.

⚾ ⚾ ⚾

The heavily favored Athletics arrived at Shibe Park, focused on winning their fourth World Series of the decade; Evers had missed the first of those because of a broken leg, and he was determined to avenge the loss the Cubs had suffered in his absence. Few gave the Braves much of a chance—even Frank Chance said he did not see any way Boston could win the Series, remarks that only served to fuel Johnny Evers's competitive fire.[66] Connie Mack chose Chief Bender, winner of six World Series games in his career, to start the first game, while George Stallings countered with twenty-seven-game winner Dick Rudolph, appearing in his first World Series.

A controversy erupted when Stallings asked Connie Mack for permission to work out his team at Shibe Park the afternoon before the first game. Mack reportedly said no, insisting he wanted the afternoon but would allow Stallings the morning. That did not suit Stallings, who wanted the Braves to practice in the same conditions, including the position of the sun, they would experience at game time. Stallings went to great lengths to voice his displeasure with what he deemed poor sportsmanship on Mack's part; many suggested the episode was a ruse to distract the Athletics and fire up the Braves.[67]

If it was, it worked. Stallings's men were certainly not lacking in confidence; Hugh Fullerton was covering the event and spent several hours with the team the day before the start of the Series. He reported that, to a man, the Braves were confident they would win.[68]

Stallings ate breakfast with his players in the hotel lobby at nine o'clock on the morning of the first game before reporting to the Baker Bowl, where the team would practice prior to heading to the Athletics home park. Well aware that he had already mined what he could out of the incident, Stallings waved off further questions regarding the practice controversy with Connie Mack: "I said all there was to say yesterday," he insisted to a reporter seeking more grist for his publication. But Stallings was not hesitant to talk about his team's chances. "I will tell you now," he exclaimed, "that these Athletics are going to get the biggest surprise of their life this afternoon."[69]

⚾ ⚾ ⚾

Shibe Park was sold out for the first two games of the series. A capacity crowd of 20,562 arrived, ready to cheer on the Athletics in unseasonably hot weather, and thousands more perched on rooftops across the street in seats sold to them by enterprising building owners for up to a dollar a spot. Many of those were Boston rooters, who had arrived in town only to find there were no tickets available.[70] Thousands more Braves fans remained in Boston, gathering around manually operated scoreboards displaying the action relayed via Western Union. Countless others called the *Boston Globe*, taking advantage of the newspaper's telephone service that provided updates on the half-inning.

During warm-ups, New York sportswriter Bill Hanna approached Evers, who was apparently still angry about Mack's supposed practice snub and the opinion of "experts" that he did not measure up to Philadelphia's great second baseman, Eddie Collins. Evers, who had just posed for a photo with Collins, pointedly told Hanna, "We are going to beat them and we are going to give them the worst showing any club ever got in a World's Series.... We are going to win because we are a better ball club and because we have more fight in us than they have."[71] As the Athletics took the field, Stallings walked up and down the bench firing up his team before finally pointing to Athletics starter Chief Bender and yelling, "Get in there and beat that big Indian!"[72]

The Most Valuable Players of their respective leagues, Johnny Evers (right) and Philadelphia Athletics rival second baseman Eddie Collins shake hands before Game One of the 1914 World Series. Evers had already declared, "We are going to beat [the Athletics] and we are going to give them the worst showing any club ever got in a World's Series." (Cleveland Public Library Digital Gallery.)

Bender completed his warm-ups, and umpire Bill Dinneen—a hero for the Boston Red Sox in the very first World Series eleven years earlier—gave the order for the teams to play ball.[73] Stallings was already pacing the dugout, anxious to decipher the Athletics' signals. He also instructed his players to completely ignore their opponents—if confronted with a "hello" or an extended hand, they were to completely ignore it. But that order did not carry over to behavior on the bench. There, the Braves kept up a steady stream of invectives aimed at their opponents—especially Bender, Eddie Collins and Wally Schang—constantly hurling insults calculated to get under their skin.

Bender was not sharp in the second inning and the Braves reached him for two runs on a walk, a Hank Gowdy double and a Maranville single. The Athletics responded with a run in the bottom of the inning; Evers cut off a second tally by making a great stop on a grounder and alertly firing the ball to the plate to cut down Amos Strunk trying to score.

Before the World Series, George Stallings quizzed Christy Mathewson, who offered that at this stage in his career, Bender was likely to start off batters with curves and change-ups, and then rely on his fastball late in the count. Hank Gowdy followed that advice, working the count full in the fifth inning before slamming a fastball over the head of the centerfielder, coasting into third with a lead-off triple. Maranville then slapped a single over first base into right field, scoring Gowdy.[74] Boston maintained a 3–1 lead going into the sixth.

Philadelphia's Jack Barry opened that inning with a spectacular defensive play; Herb Moran lifted a short fly ball behind third base and Barry took off like a rocket. Just as he crossed the left field line into foul territory, the Athletics shortstop stuck out his bare hand and caught the ball. It was one of the most incredible defensive plays ever witnessed in the World Series; even Boston's official rooting section, the famous Royal Rooters, had to cheer. But the Braves would use the rest of the inning to break the game wide open.

Evers singled sharply through the box before Bender could even react to the ball. The veteran right-hander then walked Joe Connolly. With two on and one out, Possum Whitted drove in Evers and Connolly with a triple. Whitted then scored on Schmidt's single past Barry. Boston added another run later in the game on a double steal.

Once the final out was recorded, the Royal Rooters vaulted onto the field and marched around the stadium singing "Tessie." Boston mayor John "Honey" Fitzgerald led the procession, joined by his daughter Rose and her husband, Joseph Kennedy. After completing their parade about the grounds, the Rooters hopped onto buses while James Gaffney and George Stallings waited in their automobiles to lead a celebratory procession back to the hotel.[75] As the group neared its destination, Johnny Evers, Hank Gowdy and Rabbit Maranville roared up in an automobile and insisted on joining the assembly.

A subdued Connie Mack said that Bender had not seemed himself and allowed that the team had not hit well against Rudolph. But he added that the Athletics were not discouraged. When asked whether the team would hit better against the other Boston pitchers, Mack replied, "I should hate to think that we won't."[76]

It was extremely hot and muggy the next day, so much so that three fans collapsed during the game. Connie Mack chose his other great veteran, Eddie Plank, to start Game Two while Stallings countered with Bill James, winner of twenty-six games, including nineteen of his last twenty.[77] Standing room in the bleachers was at a premium an hour before the two o'clock start, and it seemed as if everyone carried a camera to record the historic moments about to unfold. Near the Boston dugout, a band supporting the Athletics began to play ragtime. When the musicians switched to a tango, Josh Devore emerged from the dugout and began an impromptu dance—the Braves were definitely not feeling pressure.

The game was a tight one, scoreless into the ninth inning, when the Braves finally pushed across a run thanks to a fly ball hit by Charlie Deal that Amos Strunk lost in the sun. Deal coasted into second with a double, but was nearly picked off by catcher Wally Schang when he subsequently wandered too far from the bag. Instead of running straight at Deal to force him to commit to one direction or the other, Schang threw behind him. Seeing this, Deal broke for third and reached easily.[78]

Les Mann then hit a soft liner in the direction of Eddie Collins, who made a leap for it. Collins felt the ball hit his glove, but when he came down his mitt was empty. The ball bounded on into centerfield as Deal trotted home with the first run of the game.

Adrenaline up, Bill James threatened to squander his slim advantage when he walked Jack Barry to lead off the bottom of the ninth. Wally Schang then attempted a sacrifice bunt, but fouled it off. Standing out at second base, Johnny Evers was shocked—where was the killer instinct in the champions? He thought to himself that the Athletics knew they were defeated, trying for one run rather than a big inning—after all, Schang had been the only man who had hit James hard all day. James struck him out.

With a runner on first and one out, Evers called time. Eddie Murphy was the next batter and, knowing Murphy habitually hit the ball up the middle, Evers instructed Maranville to play next to the second base bag, and told Charlie Deal to shift toward shortstop. On the next pitch, Murphy did exactly what Evers said he would do, slapping a ball up the center of the diamond that deflected slightly off James's leg. Maranville grabbed the ball, stepped on second as the runner slammed into him, and fired to first to complete a beautiful double play to end the game—a play he was in position to make because Evers had placed him there.

"They all cheered for Rabbit," Maranville recalled during a 1948 interview, "but it was Evers' generalship that won the game. If he hadn't called time, the Athletics could have won."[79]

The Royal Rooters celebrated the victory by hoisting a sign four feet tall and ten feet wide they had smuggled in and placed face-down atop the Boston dugout. It proclaimed the Rooters' loyalty to the Braves and they marched it across the diamond toward the Athletics bench. Representing Boston's previous baseball conquests—plus another they anticipated—the sign read: Baltimore, 1897; Pittsburgh, 1903; New York, 1904; New York, 1912; and Philadelphia

1914.[80] While the Rooters marched, a joyous mob grabbed a protesting Johnny Evers and carried him on their shoulders.

A capacity crowd of 35,520 filed into Fenway Park for the third game of the World Series. Prior to the teams' taking the field, Evers was presented his Chalmers automobile as the National League's Most Valuable Player and he proudly paraded the car around the stadium with most of his teammates riding along at one point or another—it was the only time he would ever drive it.

The game itself was a pitcher's duel between Philadelphia's Joe Bush and Boston's Lefty Tyler that entered the tenth inning tied at 2–2; at that point the Athletics appeared to take command. With runners on first and second, Evers made a great stop of a grounder, saving a run by keeping the ball on the infield and retiring the batter, whose out advanced the Athletics runners. Eddie Collins was walked to load the bases and the Braves crowd grew nervous as one of the game's great clutch hitters, Frank "Home Run" Baker, walked to the plate.

Tyler could not fool Baker, who smashed a line shot that Evers was unable to gather cleanly and had to play off his chest. The lead run scored, and Evers, upset at himself for failing to make the play, proceeded to retrieve the ball mechanically, forgetting the other base runners. Eddie Murphy was on third and realized Evers was not paying any attention to him. Murphy slowly inched down the baseline and when Evers still failed to look in his direction, he sprinted home to score a second run without even drawing a throw, giving Philadelphia a 4–2 lead. At the end of the inning, a dejected Evers trudged to the bench after having made what he freely admitted was a "bonehead" play— distraught that he had fallen asleep at such a key moment.[81]

But, as seemed the case so often in his career, Evers would gain a reprieve. Hank Gowdy opened the bottom of the tenth with a home run into the centerfield bleachers. After pinch-hitter Josh Devore struck out, Herb Moran walked, bringing Evers to the plate. Joe Bush fed Evers two fastballs for strikes and then tried a curve on the next pitch, but Eddie Collins missed Schang's sign. Evers promptly singled through the spot in the infield where Collins should have been, moving Moran over to third. Joe Connolly then hit a fly ball deep enough to score Moran and the game was again tied, 4–4.

Bill James took the mound in the eleventh and retired the Athletics easily, allowing only a walk to Schang. Bush likewise had no trouble with the Braves in the bottom of the inning as darkness became a concern. The umpires conferred and decided that one more inning could be played.

After Philadelphia failed to score in the top of the twelfth, the red-hot Hank Gowdy took his big black bat and brought the crowd to its feet with another ground-rule double into the bleachers to lead off the bottom of the inning. When Gowdy reached second base, an incredulous Jack Barry walked over and asked, "Say, for the love of Mike, what *can't* you hit?"[82] Les Mann came in to run for Gowdy and the next batter was walked intentionally to set up a force play. Herb Moran then bunted, and as Bush fielded the ball, he recognized he had a chance to get Mann at third. But he also recognized Mann was the fastest player on either team and rushed his throw, which sailed wide of Baker and up the left field line. Mann scored the winning run and the Braves had a stranglehold on the World Series.

That night, Boston's traveling secretary encountered Stallings and told him he was making arrangements for the Braves' return to Philadelphia should they lose the next day. Stallings ordered him, "Cancel it. Cancel it right away. It is bad luck and I don't want any reservations on that train, even if we have to go over there on day coaches, or Mr. Gaffney has to hire a special. I haven't even packed a bag and I don't intend to, either, because I won't need it."[83]

The Athletics were staying in the same Boston hotel in which Johnny Evers and his family were residing. Precocious five-year-old Johnny Jr. was becoming something of a hotel pet. After the third game of the Series, Eddie Collins's wife ran into Johnny Jr. in the hallway and said, "I bet you don't know who won the ballgame." The youngster replied, "Sure I do. My father!"[84]

Game Four had the feel of the anticlimactic and the inevitable; the only question was whether the Athletics would become the first team ever swept in the World Series. The teams entered the bottom of the fifth tied at 1–1; with two out, Dick Rudolph singled and then went to third on a double to left.

Connie Mack then chose to pitch to Evers rather than loading the bases for Les Mann. The Braves captain worked Bob Shawkey to a full count, and when the Athletics pitcher delivered a fastball down the middle, Evers pounced on it, dropping a single into center field to score both Rudolph and Moran, giving the Braves a 3–1 lead. The Athletics were beaten.

A confident Rudolph easily retired Eddie Collins, Home Run Baker and Stuffy McInnis in the ninth; the final out of the series was McInnis's grounder to Charlie Deal, who threw to Butch Schmidt at first. Fans stormed the field as Schmidt's teammates rushed over and attempted good-naturedly to get him to relinquish the ball—a trophy that always went to the man recording the last out. Schmidt smiled and refused.[85]

Connie Mack praised the Braves, admitting his team was outplayed from the start, and expressed hope that his players would learn from their defeat. But he did betray bitterness: "I am sorry I cannot congratulate George

Stallings. He has too much of the Jack Johnson style.... Johnny Evers and the other Boston players beat us on the field, and they cannot get too much credit, but when I think of Stallings' attempt to have me put before the world as lacking in sportsmanship, I feel that it would be lowering myself if I showed any other attitude than that of contempt for a man bringing such methods into baseball."[86]

Stallings branded Mack the poorest of poor sports and crowed, "I did not think we would win in four straight games, but I never had the least doubt that we would beat the Athletics."[87]

The upstart Boston Braves, without any big names other than Johnny Evers, had not only defeated the mighty Athletics with their celebrated $100,000 infield and future Hall of Fame pitchers, they had done so exactly as Evers had said they would, giving them "the worst showing any club got in a World Series."[88] The dynasty of the Philadelphia Athletics was at an end. Mack would lose many of his best players over the winter, and the team would spend the next eight seasons in last place.

Meanwhile, Johnny Evers was again atop the baseball world. Without him, the Cubs had finished a distant fourth in 1914 while the Braves were champions. He had hit .438 in his fourth World Series—second to Hank Gowdy's incredible .545 average for the four games. He had delivered the Series-winning hit, and in the last fourteen World Series games in which he had played, he'd only lost one. Johnny Evers was as popular as he had been after the Merkle play, and it seemed as if the world was his.

CHAPTER ELEVEN

Too Much Electricity

Johnny Evers returned to Troy on October 19, 1914, for the grandest welcome-home celebration he had ever experienced. Provided a personal escort from the train station in Albany to Monument Square, he was stunned by the outpouring of affection from five thousand well-wishers, assembled for a parade that included ten bands and several drum corps. Marchers wore large buttons "the size of tea saucers" adorned with Evers's face. The proud athlete joined the mayor at the head of the parade route before taking his place on a reviewing stand at City Hall.[1] A special gold baseball bat and the uniform he wore during the World Series were on display in the window of the C.E. Wilson store, where his brother Thomas was in charge of the shoe department.[2] The city itself seemed to glow during the procession, as crackling bonfires on every street corner released embers that danced skyward into the night, and red light torches cheerfully illuminated the streets.

A banquet was held afterward at the Armory, with more than five hundred people in attendance including George Stallings, Joseph Lannin, John McGraw, James Gaffney, Hugh Fullerton and Rabbit Maranville. Stallings and Gaffney each raised a glass to Evers, proclaiming Chicago's loss as Boston's gain. The irrepressible Maranville then clambered onto the seat of his chair— souvenir Indian headdress precariously perched atop his scalp—and heaped credit on Evers for making him a better player.

Evers replied, "If I am a great ballplayer, as you so kindly refer to me, it is because of the 'Rabbit' here. When I found Maranville working alongside of me I found that if I wanted to keep up with him I had to let myself out a bit. I consider him the greatest ballplayer in the world. To know him is to love him, and if you could know him as I do, you would love him too."[3]

But gratifying as this homecoming was, it became difficult to overlook that when it came to Johnny Evers, bad times always seemed to hitch a ride along with the good ones. That was the case in 1902, when Evers's father died a week before he was sold to the Chicago Cubs. It had happened in 1908 and 1909, when he became a star and married, only to have his mother fall seriously ill and pass away the next spring. In 1910, the year the Cubs clinched an unprecedented fourth National League pennant in five years, Evers was involved in an accident that claimed the life of his close friend. Then he broke his leg and missed the World Series, and shortly thereafter lost everything he owned when his business went under. And again, during perhaps his biggest triumph, the "Miracle Braves," Evers lost his daughter and his home was ransacked by thieves.

In addition, his marriage was under severe strain; he and Helen were spending more time apart each year. He sat out a road trip when his father was near death in 1902, and skipped the beginning of the 1909 season due the poor health of his mother. But when his daughter died he was home barely long enough to attend the funeral, let alone grieve, before departing once more.

The morning after Evers's celebratory return to Troy, his mother-in-law died after a long illness at age forty-nine.[4] Twenty-four hours later Evers was in Springfield, Massachusetts, attending a banquet honoring Rabbit Maranville and Les Mann.[5] Evers had built a new house in Troy for his wife and son, thanks to the small fortune he earned in 1914—roughly $45,000 when his World Series share was added—but it would not be a home filled with singing and laughter.

After the World Series, sportswriter Charles Stack traveled to Troy to meet Evers and his brother Joe for a *Baseball Magazine* profile. Evers still refused to drive—he confessed to not even wanting to ride in an automobile. Joe acted as chauffeur for Johnny, who constantly shouted out warnings regarding obstacles or speed—the younger brother always remaining patient with his famous sibling. "You know he met with an accident in an automobile and has never liked them since," said Joe Evers—never mentioning he was in the same accident. "But I don't mind it. I know he is nervous and doesn't mean all he says."

Stack met Evers's wife and son at their new two-story home, and was then whisked away for a tour of Troy, during which Evers pointed out the hilltops and vacant lots where he had learned the game—and had been chased off for trespassing more than once by police. Everyone waved and shouted "Johnny!" as they passed, and Evers seemed to take pleasure in being Troy's most visible celebrity.

There was a stop at the cemetery, where Evers's daughter was buried. The

Joe Evers served as friend, protector, chauffeur and later business partner for his brother. He also had a baseball career of his own, lasting more than a decade and including one game in the major leagues, as a pinch-runner for the New York Giants in a game against the Philadelphia Phillies on April 24, 1913. (George Grantham Bain Collection, Library of Congress.)

base of the marble monument marking the family plot was already in place as Evers noted that he too would be buried there one day. Stack's piece, "A Day With John Evers," depicted a pleasant, even gracious man, an image seemingly at odds with the profane, win-at-all-costs athlete everyone thought they knew.[6]

That is not to say Johnny Evers was in any way less competitive than his public persona. Christy Mathewson claimed that Evers was so high-strung he could not wear watches—according to the Giants star, Evers's nervous energy generated a mysterious electrical charge that prevented his timepieces from operating properly. He simply had too much electricity.[7] Evers's intense make-up left him prone to episodes of restlessness, anxiety and persistent insomnia that had resulted in his nervous breakdown in 1911. Friends recognized those same signs during the winter of 1914–15 and worried for him.

In December 1914, while attending the league meetings, Evers collapsed and was confined to the Hotel Somerset in New York for two weeks with a severe case of pneumonia—considered so serious that Helen was called down from Troy to be at his side. Doctors released Evers two days before Christmas to spend what had to have been an especially melancholy holiday at home— the first for the couple since the deaths of their daughter and Helen's mother.[8]

After Christmas, Evers returned to Camp Totem—where he had recovered from his nervous breakdown three years earlier. Taking up residence near the aptly named Lake Burden, Evers hiked and let the stubble grow on his face while "the mercury played tag with the bottom of the thermometer." Evers told a correspondent from the *Syracuse Post-Standard*, "I feel stronger than I have ever felt." He also vowed that 1915 would be his best season yet.[9] Before reporting to spring training, Evers stopped at Pinehurst Country Club in North Carolina to play some golf, a sport that was becoming all the rage among the baseball set.

Unlike the previous year, the Boston Braves entered the 1915 season as one of the favorites to win the National League pennant.[10] They had lost Charlie Deal and Les Mann to the Federal League, but had acquired a true star from the Philadelphia Phillies, fiery Sherwood Magee.[11] The thirty-year-old outfielder had spent eleven years with Philadelphia, winning the National League batting title in 1910, and leading the league in hits and doubles while batting .314 in 1914. A potent bat the Braves had been lacking, Magee was a smart player, physically gifted and, like Johnny Evers, quick to let his opinion be known, especially to umpires.

Evers was experiencing a productive spring training, apparently fully recovered from his illness and manning the keystone sack like a youngster. His weight was up and he seemed in better shape than he had been in years. The Braves also looked better than ever. Unfortunately, Magee broke his collarbone while chasing a fly ball almost immediately upon hitting the practice field with the Braves, an injury that sapped his power during the season.[12] Magee originally thought it to be a strained shoulder and attempted to play through it; he was in the lineup on Opening Day.

So was Evers, who started off as if he was serious about the 1915 season being his best. He had two hits off Grover Cleveland Alexander and stole a pair of bases in a 3–0 loss.

The Braves hosted Brooklyn for the season's third game and finally landed in the win column, although the victory cost them Johnny Evers. With Boston leading in the eighth inning, 2–1, Evers forced Herb Moran on an attempted sacrifice. Joe Connolly then hit a bouncer up the middle that Dodgers short-stop Ollie O'Mara knocked down but couldn't handle cleanly. Still hoping to complete a double play, O'Mara rushed his throw, striking Evers as he slid into second. Bracing for impact, Evers slid awkwardly, his heel catching the bag.[13] He had to be helped off the field with what was initially diagnosed as a sprain; a week later Evers remained confined to bed and doctors confirmed that the ankle was broken. Evers laughingly denied rumors that the injury was career-ending, but it was more serious than the Braves let on—more than two months would pass before Evers could play again.[14] There was little he could do but wait.

Evers returned to Boston in early June, hobbling about on a cane. During his absence, James Gaffney had overseen construction of a new ballpark in the Allston neighborhood; designed with a record seating capacity of forty-five thousand, it was scheduled to open in mid–August. A proud Gaffney recognized that his fiery second baseman was a major reason the project had come to fruition—the Braves needed him back in order to fill those seats.

On June 27, an off-day in the middle of a series against the New York Giants, the Braves visited Troy for an exhibition game against Evers's old minor league team, which the second baseman and two friends had agreed to purchase out of civic duty when it ran into financial difficulty.[15] The game drew a large, enthusiastic crowd to Center Island Grounds and Evers took advantage of the opportunity to test his ankle. He batted lead-off and played the entire game, reaching base twice—on a single and a walk—and scoring a run. Although the Braves lost to the locals, Evers was encouraged.[16]

At the time, Boston sat in fifth place, two games below the break-even mark, as the league's smaller twenty-one-man roster limit, adopted prior to the season, interfered somewhat with George Stallings's outfield platoon system. In addition, Bill James had been sidelined much of the year with a sore arm, and Evers had been out of the lineup for two months. But John McGraw still feared the Braves, especially with Evers. "Stallings is a great manager," lectured McGraw, "but Johnny is a pepper shaker. He makes men play ball whether they want to or not while he's alongside them."[17]

Evers knew he was not at one hundred percent—his ankle was extremely sore after the Troy exhibition—but he wanted to get into at least one game of the back-to-back double-headers against the Giants. Nothing defined Evers more than his battles with John McGraw and the New York Giants. He was determined to play, and Johnny Evers on one leg was more valuable in the lineup than most of his teammates on two.

Unable to play the first day, he coached the baselines and engaged in a profanity-laced exchange with New York fans who booed Red Smith after an aggressive slide.[18] Evers finally played in the nightcap of the second double-header on June 29. The Braves had lost the first contest, their third in a row to the Giants, and between games George Stallings read the riot act to his men. Evers immediately put a charge into the team by leading off the game with a double, although he tweaked his ankle sliding into second base and limped through the rest of the day. He made a great defensive play in the sixth when Chief Meyers attempted to stretch a single into a double. Larry Gilbert's throw from the outfield was low and off the bag, but Evers handled it and used a swipe tag to retire Meyers, even as he was sent spinning by the force of Meyers's slide.

Evers then won the game in the seventh inning with a two-run homer into the right field grandstand. The Giants' home crowd was so impressed with Evers's performance, he was obliged to leave the dugout twice to doff his cap.[19]

But Boston continued to struggle, forced to play eight double-headers between June 28 and July 13 with a thin pitching staff and Evers unable to play two games in one day. The Braves fell to last place—exactly where they had been a year earlier. Frustrated by his inability to contribute as he wanted, Evers reached the boiling point. During a loss to St. Louis, a close play at the plate went against the Braves and Evers shouted, "They're trying to get the crowds out. They've ordered a close race. Leave them alone, boys, they're only following instructions."

Evers's remarks were interpreted by some as an accusation that the National League race was fixed. League president John Tener summoned Evers to his office, demanding an explanation. The contrite ballplayer explained that he sometimes said things in the heat of battle that he did not mean—and admittedly should not say—but assured the league president that he did not feel the race was fixed. Tener gave Evers a pass.[20]

With the Braves floundering, Evers felt he had no choice but to ignore the pain in his ankle and hold down second base as long as he could. On July 16, he played fifteen innings and collected three hits as the Braves defeated Pittsburgh thanks to eight innings of superb relief pitching by Tom Hughes. Evers gritted his teeth, set his jaw, and played both games of a double-header against Cincinnati the next day and stroked a key single in the nightcap. The team responded to Evers's presence, winning fifteen of sixteen games to rocket from last place to third by the end of July—reminiscent of the team's rise during the "Miracle" season.

But Evers's increasingly volatile nature kept poking to the surface. On July 22, he took exception to Ernest Quigley's called strike. After drawing a walk on the next pitch, a still-furious Evers flung his bat toward the dugout, then reached down and grabbed a handful of dirt and threw it into the air. Some of the dirt accidentally landed in Quigley's face—not that Evers felt particularly guilty about it—and within moments the two stood nose to nose. Suddenly, Quigley landed a left hook to Evers's chin. Roger Bresnahan, catching for the Cubs, yanked Evers away to prevent him from charging Quigley. Braves fans were so angry that the umpire was forced to withdraw after the game under police escort. John Tener again investigated, fined both men one hundred dollars and ordered them to shake hands.[21]

On July 27 the Braves were in Brooklyn, where Evers had engaged in a long-running feud with a group of fans dubbed "The Eight Little Managers," who always sat behind the visitors' bench and mercilessly rode the opposition. Evers singled to drive in the first run of the game, but later made an error that led to a three-run inning for the Dodgers. The "Managers" began singing over and over, "Johnny lost the ga-ame. Johnny lost the ga-ame." Soon the rest of the crowd joined in. When Evers came to bat in the ninth, he began shouting at Brooklyn pitcher Phil Douglas, warning him that he had better duck unless he wanted his arm torn off. Evers subsequently smashed his fourth hit of the game, and upon reaching first base turned to make faces at the crowd as a pinch-runner was dispatched to take his place. Joe Connolly then singled and Sherwood Magee doubled, and the Braves won, 4–3. Evers had won the game, lost it, and then won it again; mocking the singing fans, the *Brooklyn Eagle* headline blared, "Johnny Evers Shows the Fans How Not to Lose a Ga-ame."[22]

A week later, Evers was tossed in Pittsburgh. Instead of departing immediately for the clubhouse, he sauntered toward a drinking fountain near the Pirates' bench. When he lingered a little too long for the liking of Pirates manager Fred Clarke, Evers playfully flicked water in Clarke's face and the two began throwing punches. Evers was suspended—not for the fight with Clarke, but for what he said to umpire Bob Emslie that precipitated his ejection.[23]

A frustrated Evers threatened to retire from the game immediately. "I am tired of being made the butt of a lot of unwarranted criticism," he complained. "I'm not a rowdy, and have never done a thing to bring discredit upon baseball. These attacks upon my character have hurt." James Gaffney defended his star second baseman, and after retreating to Troy for a couple of days, Evers calmed down and returned to the Braves.[24]

The Boston Braves opened their new stadium on August 18—more than forty-six thousand were on hand for James Gaffney's triumph. The lush infield grass of South End Grounds was transferred over. The clubhouses were placed under the grandstand, eliminating the need for players to run the gauntlet of fans after games. The facility housed team offices and held more than forty thousand comfortably; a spur from the public transit system enabled large crowds to easily enter and exit. The playing surface was spacious, 375 feet down the foul lines, 520 feet to right-center and 440 feet to the centerfield scoreboard—decidedly pitcher-friendly, it was designed for inside-the-park home runs, which Gaffney considered the most exciting play in baseball. There was no advertising on the walls, which were painted green to provide a better background for hitters.[25]

Inspired by their new surroundings, the Braves went on another tear, this time behind their pitching staff, which threw seven shutouts during the first home stand in their new park, including three in a row against Cincinnati. At the end of August, Boston was in third place, only three and a half games behind first-place Philadelphia.

But Evers's temper got the best of him once again; he engaged in a prolonged harangue of William "Lord" Byron and was sent to the showers. As he walked to the clubhouse, he held his nose the entire way. That earned him a five-game suspension at a key point in the pennant race.[26]

The enforced sabbaticals did not hinder Evers's performance, although his bad ankle prevented him from collecting extra-base hits—he would end up with only six in 278 at bats. He was hitting around .280 while playing every day—when not under suspension—and continued to play stellar defense on his one good leg. At West Side Grounds in Chicago on September 13, Evers made one of his greatest plays; Chicago's Bob Fisher hit a looper into center that seemed destined for a two-out, two-run single. Braves centerfielder Pete Compton made a mad dash but was going to come up short. Evers had broken with the pitch and managed to spear the ball one-handed while running at "breakneck speed," somehow avoiding a collision with Compton. Because of his momentum and bad ankle, Evers made a wide arc after making the catch, continuing to run at full speed while holding up the ball as if a trophy for all to see. James Crusinberry wrote in the *Chicago Tribune* that it appeared as if Evers "wanted to throw his cap in the air and give three cheers." He settled for tipping his cap to the cheering crowd.[27]

But Evers, who typically finished his seasons on a high note, seemed to run out of gas in mid–September—as evidenced by an uncharacteristic twenty-nine at bat hitless streak between September 19 and September 30. Boston continued playing well, winning eleven of fifteen down the stretch, including four in a row against New York (putting the Giants into last place, where they finished), but could not mount a sustained push to vault them past the Phillies. There were many who believed that had Evers not been injured the Braves would have won their second straight pennant, and there was something to be said for that point of view. With Evers making a heroic effort to play on one leg, Boston's record was 51–28 when he was in the lineup. Without him, the Braves were only 32–41.

For the second straight year there would be a Philadelphia-Boston World Series, only this time it was the Phillies versus the Red Sox rather than the Athletics against the Braves. James Gaffney returned the favor of the previous year and allowed the Red Sox to use Braves Field, with its larger capacity, for the Series, which the Red Sox won in five games to keep the World Championship in Boston.

Johnny Evers confided to close friends that he had never felt quite the same after his breakdown in 1911. He always felt nervous and on edge, and rarely slept. He sold his hometown baseball franchise, and there were rumors he was planning to retire to assume the position of head baseball coach at Yale. There were also rumors he might manage Cincinnati, or even in the Federal League.

There were changes coming to the baseball world—especially after the war with the Federal League was settled. The Cubs had merged with their Federal counterparts, the Whales, with Federal League owner Charles Weeghman taking over the amalgamation. As a result, Joe Tinker and Mordecai Brown were returning to the Cubs and the team was getting a new home, Weeghman Park; today it is known as Wrigley Field and remains headquarters of the franchise a century later. Joe Tinker was named manager and Weeghman procured a new live bear cub as mascot.[28]

The Boston Braves had new ownership as well. James Gaffney stunned the baseball community by selling to a group headed by Boston banker Arthur Wise and Harvard football coach Percy Haughton, who pledged to strive for nothing less than another National League pennant. Haughton also announced that George Stallings would be granted total control of the team and a brand-new five-year contract.[29]

Before selling the Braves, Gaffney had publicly vowed to change the team's rowdy image. Haughton said he agreed with Gaffney about the need to turn around the Braves' reputation. Upon hearing that, Evers declared with a straight face, "I heartily endorse clean baseball. There has been entirely too much wrangling on the ball field to please the fans, and I say the umpire should chase all the players who always try to make a show on the ball field."[30]

Indeed, the team behaved much better as the 1916 season got underway. Evers remained positively serene during arguments, keeping himself far removed from the fray. He seemed relaxed and was ejected only once during the first three months of the season, and even in that instance managed to hold his temper.[31] Evers successfully ran the team for a few days in early June, when George Stallings left town to attend the funeral of close friend Bud

Sharpe. But while Evers and the Braves were behaving themselves, they remained stuck in the middle of the pack.

That all changed on July 5, when Evers was ejected by Lord Byron over called balls and strikes. After spewing a few choice words within earshot of John Tener, and pointedly referring to criticism of players supposedly made by the league president's wife, he was suspended indefinitely.[32] Tener admitted he was at a loss about Evers. "I don't know what I can do with him," he complained. "I don't think he is civilized."[33]

Three weeks later Evers had a run-in with Mal Eason after a called third strike. When Cubs third baseman Rollie Zeider piped in, demanding that Eason eject Evers, Evers strode toward Zeider, bat in hand, and began measuring Zeider's nose with it. Being sensitive to the size of his olfactory organ, Zeider retaliated by stomping on Evers's toes. Evers then cracked Zeider on the knee with his bat. The Three Stooges–like fiasco concluded with punches flying as players and umpires separated the combatants; perhaps owing to the entertainment value, neither man was suspended.[34]

Soon after that, George Stallings earned a three-day suspension and a stern lecture from Percy Haughton due to a post-game run-in with Cy Rigler.[35] Haughton was unhappy, but critics noted the Braves had climbed into second place since regaining their "fighting spirit." On August 3, that fighting spirit turned inward when Evers and Red Smith engaged in fisticuffs.

The flash point was reached after Smith was called for interfering with a base runner. He was immediately chewed out by Evers, whose bad throw in the first game of the double-header had led to a Braves loss. When Smith attempted to explain what had happened, Evers accused him of making excuses for "dirty play." With Stallings absent due to his suspension, there was no one to defuse the situation, and it only escalated.

Evers was banished to the clubhouse by the umpire, but he and Smith resumed fighting in the dressing room after the game. Evers was later seen leaving the ballpark, tears streaming down his face as he declared his teammates were against him. Stallings asked Evers to meet with him that evening, but he failed to show. Evers finally calmed down and settled his differences with Smith through a handshake the next afternoon.[36]

But Evers had been injured in the fight with Smith and began suffering severe pain shooting down his left arm to his fingertips, leaving him unable to sleep for three straight nights.[37] After resting at home for a few days, Evers returned, and on August 23 earned an indefinite suspension for what he claimed was a misunderstanding while coaching third base.[38] He went home again. Finally, on September 4, George Stallings announced Evers was out for the rest of the season with a sore shoulder—he'd received word from Helen Evers that the family doctor insisted it was useless for her husband to play again that season; he had managed to appear in only seventy-one games and batted a career-low .216.[39]

Boston actually played well in Evers's absence. The day Stallings received Helen's call, the Braves moved into a tie for first place, having won fifty-five while losing twenty-eight since the first of June—after they resumed battling with umpires. But they fell short of the pennant in 1916, coming in third with a record of 89–63, finishing one position ahead of the New York Giants, who somehow only placed fourth despite amassing winning streaks of seventeen and twenty-six games.

The Braves would begin the 1917 season facing more questions than answers, with number one being whether Johnny Evers could pull himself together again at age thirty-five. Or was he becoming like his watches, which according to Christy Mathewson, could only keep time for so long before going haywire?

During the winter, Evers offered Grantland Rice his philosophy about hard times: "Too many people are inclined to fall off in their work ... when the breaks come from the wrong direction. This is, of course, the time to try and hustle all the harder. When the break is coming your way there isn't the same need to keep on your toes. But when they are coming from the wrong direction, the only help then is to meet the occasion with all you have."[40]

Evers wanted to give it all he had, and going into his sixteenth season he remained a hot commodity. He attended the World Series between Brooklyn and the Boston Red Sox amid rumors that he would return to the Cubs as manager, replacing the recently dismissed Joe Tinker. Evers did nothing to discourage such talk, claiming that negotiations were underway to secure his unconditional release from Boston.[41] There were also rumors about James Gaffney's attempting to purchase the Pittsburgh Pirates and, if successful, naming Evers manager.[42] The Yankees tried acquiring him but abandoned the effort when it became clear he would never pass waivers. George Stallings claimed to have no interest in parting with his star: "Evers will be in fine shape the coming season and will play great ball for us."[43]

When training camp rolled around, Evers arrived in good spirits and declared he wanted to play until he had logged at least twenty big league seasons.[44] He cut back on the more than one dozen cigars he smoked each day. His wife and son arrived a few days later, accompanied by Rabbit Maranville.[45] Vowing to control his temper, he took to yelling at himself during games, rather than at teammates, opponents or umpires, so as to better focus his energy on his own efforts and keep himself out of trouble.[46]

Then, during an exhibition game at Dothan, Georgia, against the New

Johnny Evers (left) with Phillies manager Pat Moran. In July 1917, Evers was released to the Phillies, who hoped his fire and winning attitude would propel Philadelphia to a second pennant in three years. They would finish in second place. (Photograph courtesy of Robert Warrington.)

York Yankees, Evers's left shoulder popped out of socket during an at bat—the same shoulder that had caused him to miss the last two months of the 1916 season. This latest setback cost him twenty-seven of the team's first thirty-eight games, at which point he was hitting an anemic .176. While sitting on the bench he ran the team for a few days when George Stallings left the team to get married.[47]

It was clear that Evers was not the same ballplayer—time and injuries had taken their toll. Stallings turned to former Federal Leaguer Johnny Rawlings while at the same time insisting he was holding Evers in reserve for warmer weather. Evers did play more in June and had his moments, including back-to-back two-hit games against Pittsburgh and Chicago, and three hits in the nightcap of a double-header against New York.

But Evers also recognized the truth—he was slowing down. "I hit an infield grounder ... against the Giants and I felt like I had a base hit," Evers recalled in a 1943 interview. "But I was thrown out by a step. I'd beaten out hundreds like it in my day. The very next time I came to bat the same thing happened. And when it happened a third time I knew the truth ... the years were marching faster than I was marching. It's that last step that makes the difference. You may fool some of the people after that, but you don't fool yourself. For when your legs go, it's a sure pop that you've got to follow."[48]

Johnny Rawlings soon returned to second base and Evers returned to the bench. As it had for Bobby Lowe fourteen years earlier, Evers's time had come. Rawlings was simply the better ballplayer.

During the second week of July, Stallings approached Evers and told him the Philadelphia Phillies were interested in acquiring him. Evers said he would have to think about it. The next day he agreed to meet with Phillies manager Pat Moran, an ex-teammate who had taken the Phillies to the World Series in 1915. Three weeks earlier, the Phillies had been playing tag with the New York Giants for first place in the National League. Now they were a half-dozen games off the pace, and Moran hoped that even with Evers sporting a sub-.200 batting average, employing John McGraw's longtime nemesis would spark his team's chances—or least give McGraw something to think about.[49]

Evers was honest with Moran, explaining that he had a bad left (non-throwing) arm, but thought he could still play semi-regularly. The second-place Phillies agreed to assume Evers's $10,000 salary; his signing was front-page news in Philadelphia.[50] He also addressed the criticism his original Braves contract had received in light of his sub-par performances the past couple of years.

"I suppose Boston owners think I have been getting a good thing off them.... It is true that I had a good contract with Boston. But it is also true that they wanted me at that price, or they wouldn't have paid me."[51]

Evers made his Phillies debut against Cincinnati on July 16, playing second base and hitting in the lead-off spot. He initially played as if a little rusty, collecting only six hits in his first forty-three at bats for Philadelphia—plunging his overall batting average to .169. He earned his first ejection with the Phillies in a game against Chicago on August 20; his replacement, Bert Niehoff, went on a hitting streak, putting Evers on the bench for two weeks.[52] But Evers received another chance and finished strong, batting .292 over the final four weeks of the season, raising his overall average forty-five points to .214. He went five for twelve in a four-game series against the Cubs; collected three hits, including a home run, against the Cardinals; and went four for nine in a double-header against the Giants on October 2. As had been his habit throughout his career, Evers ended the season playing his best baseball. But Philadelphia could not close the gap and the Giants won the National League pennant by ten games; in the past fourteen seasons, either McGraw or Evers had captured the pennant eleven times. In addition, one or the other had finished second nine times during that period.

Evers did maintain an amazing streak when the Phillies finished second— in his fifteen full major league seasons, he had never finished lower than third place.

The question was whether he would have an opportunity to extend that streak.

Chapter Twelve

When Johnny Comes Marching Home

It is incredibly difficult for a professional athlete to know when to quit. Johnny Evers was no different—there were days when he played as well as ever. He did not *feel* different. He knew he still had greatness *in* him. But he was not *great* anymore.

The Philadelphia Phillies had decided not to bring Evers back for 1918, even with the war in Europe sapping major league rosters of talent as players enlisted or were drafted into service for their country. Always jealously guarding his independence, Evers made sure to paint the situation as one of his own choosing, declaring that the end of his five-year contract made him a free agent.[1] He did have offers—the St. Louis Cardinals were strongly interested, as were the Boston Red Sox, although the latter was pursuing him only as a coach.

After Boston opened the door slightly to the possibility of his playing, Evers chose the Red Sox despite their offer being $1,000 less than that of St. Louis, because they were only a year removed from back-to-back World Series championships and afforded him the opportunity to return to the scene of one of his greatest triumphs.[2] He would serve as right-hand man to new manager Ed Barrow, who was hired after incumbent Red Sox player-manager Jack Barry joined the Naval Reserve. In addition, Evers was to coach the bases full-time and play second base—in an emergency.[3]

But the scent of freshly cut grass is powerfully seductive in the spring—especially to an old ballplayer—and within a week of his signing, Evers was talking much more about playing than coaching. He requested permission to arrive with pitchers and catchers in the first wave of personnel reporting for spring training and caught a train at Albany, along with Barrow, Red Sox owner

Harry Frazee and pitcher Dick McCabe.[4] The always gregarious Babe Ruth was there to greet them, the twenty-three-year-old having already boarded in Boston with several teammates.[5] The party arrived at Hot Springs, Arkansas, on March 11 to work out the kinks in weather eighty degrees warmer than they had left behind in New England.

Evers was happy to be with the Red Sox—a strong contender with a young and talented pitching staff. The team's five best pitchers, Carl Mays, Sad Sam Jones, Dutch Leonard, Bullet Joe Bush and Ruth—already a star of the first order both for his stellar pitching and freakish ability as a hitter—were each between twenty-three and twenty-six years old. They would win more than eight hundred major league games between them, despite the fact that Ruth pitched full-time only three years. Evers also recognized that he was receiving the opportunity to extend his career because of unusual circumstances; during an exhibition game in late March, he good-naturedly shouted to Brooklyn pitcher Jack Coombs, "You know where we would be only for this war!" Coombs nodded and replied, "I get you, Johnny."[6]

Evers roomed with Ruth—and it's almost too obvious to point out the dichotomy the two men represented as baseball's past and its future. Two years later, Evers would declare Ruth "the most wonderful hitter in the history of the national pastime," but in April 1918 he seemed to him an aberration, albeit an extremely talented one. Evers was focused on his own future, not Ruth's, and from the start of training camp acted as if he were a colt that had been penned up all winter. He fielded everything, hit aggressively, and warmed to his task of "bringing pepper" to the Red Sox, chattering incessantly while executing his trademark one-handed plays.[7] He was not shy about riding his new teammates, particularly Ruth, who was playing first base in the early practices.

In the team's first exhibition game against Brooklyn, Evers hit a double, stole a base and turned a double play. Ruth played a flawless first base and hit two home runs as Boston won, 11–1.[8] A week later, Ruth hit a grand slam that was the longest home run anyone there had ever seen, and Evers handled eight chances without an error as the Red Sox again defeated Brooklyn.[9] The team then departed Hot Springs and began a barnstorming trip, playing against the Dodgers through Arkansas, Texas, Louisiana, Tennessee and Alabama. On March 30, Evers was the middle man on three double plays.[10] The next day he reached base twice as the Red Sox defeated Brooklyn for the fourth time in five games. Afterward he posed with Dick Hoblitzell, Everett Scott and Stuffy McInnis for a *Boston Globe* photograph of what was expected to be the Red Sox starting infield.[11]

But playing well, and playing well for someone nearly thirty-seven years old, are two entirely different things. The Red Sox were not prepared to rely on Evers as their second baseman and openly sought other options. At one point they traded for lightly-regarded Cincinnati Reds infielder Dave Shean, who was only two years younger than Evers and had spent all but one of the past six seasons in the minor leagues.

On the way to Dallas, Evers developed a 102-degree fever; Shean started in his place and scored the winning run in the sixteenth inning.[12] Then, in Austin, Shean collected five hits in five at bats.[13] Evers finally appeared in a game after a week's absence, playing the first six innings of a thirteen-inning contest, singling and turning his sixth double play in seven games.

The Red Sox were in Mobile, Alabama, the next day, and Evers was assisting Barrow in running the team from the bench. With two runners on base in the eleventh inning, Dutch Leonard wanted to pitch to Brooklyn's Hi Myers, but Evers signaled for an intentional walk to load the bases. Leonard then walked the batter after that to force in a run and at the end of the inning angrily confronted Evers, threatening violence. Refusing to take the blame, Evers pointed to Barrow and said, "There's the man who said to walk him."[14]

Evers did not participate in the team's final exhibition in Birmingham, but expected to be in the lineup on Opening Day. He made a quick detour home, intending to rejoin the Red Sox on the eve of the April 15 opener, and told friends he felt "fit as a fiddle" and expected to take part in the majority of Boston's games.[15]

But the Red Sox had other plans. Sunday's newspaper listed Dave Shean as the probable starting second baseman and carried a story about Jersey City of the International League wanting Evers as player-manager.[16] Asked to return to Boston a day early, Evers met for an hour with Barrow and was told that his services were no longer needed. He sat in the stands in street clothes during the opener, with former Red Sox star Heine Wagner coaching in his place.[17] When asked why he was not in uniform, he simply shrugged his shoulders. After the game, he caught a train for Troy.

There was speculation that the incident with Leonard had been the final straw; that Evers had rubbed his teammates the wrong way with his constant badgering and they had finally had enough. Others speculated that the Red Sox had decided Evers would not be happy as a full-time coach and therefore prove disruptive by wanting to play every day—something they felt he could not do anymore. Evers claimed to not understand why he was let go, but insisted he had an ironclad contract and would be paid regardless.[18]

Whatever the reason, Johnny Evers's playing career appeared to be at an end.

Evers hoped to latch on elsewhere; he reached out to the Yankees, at the same time betraying his bitterness toward the Red Sox, stating in no uncertain terms: "I don't think I deserve the kind of treatment that was accorded me in Boston."[19] The Yankees were set with newly acquired Del Pratt, so Evers met with Jersey City team president David Driscoll, who offered him the same salary he had been promised by the Red Sox.[20] But Evers was not interested in the minor leagues. With no big league contract forthcoming, he accepted an offer from the Knights of Columbus, a Catholic organization dedicated to charitable service, to serve as supervisor of athletics for the troops in Europe. He declared, "I was never more enthusiastic about anything in my life."[21]

He staged a "farewell game" in Troy on June 16, playing third base in a benefit contest. Demonstrating that he retained his flair for the dramatic, he thrilled the crowd with a game-winning two-run double in the eighth.[22] He then packed up his old Chicago Cubs uniform and prepared to board a steamer for France. The Knights hosted a grand sendoff from the steps of the New York Public Library, just down the street from their headquarters, and Evers expressed his desire to get as near the front lines as possible.[23]

By all accounts Evers did an outstanding job in Europe and returned to a hero's welcome in December, hitting the winter banquet circuit armed with stories about meeting with White Sox catcher Joe Jenkins under shelling at Verdun, and of other major leaguers he visited over there, including Hank Gowdy and Grover Cleveland Alexander.[24]

Not sure what he wanted to do next, Evers lent his efforts to promoting a bill that would legalize Sunday baseball in New York State.[25] Once Governor Al Smith signed the legislation, Evers met with the Troy City Council, which passed an ordinance allowing Sunday baseball—as long as the games began after two o'clock in the afternoon.[26]

Evers celebrated his successful lobbying efforts by forming an eight-team semi-professional league—an echo of his "Cheer-Ups" days and a resurrection of sorts of the old New York State League, which had folded when the country moved to a war footing.[27] The games would be played on weekends, with Evers running the team in Troy; he even planned to play some and convinced his brother Joe, who had played several years in the minors—and one game for John McGraw and the Giants in 1913—to suit up at shortstop.[28] Evers threw himself into the task of running his team and, as promised, appeared in several early season games, even turning a double play with his brother in one of them.[29]

But playing only increased his desire for major league competition. Late that summer, old friend Pat Moran called asking for help. Dismissed by the Phillies, Moran had taken over the Cincinnati Reds in 1919 when Christy Mathewson, ill with tuberculosis, was too sick to continue. Moran asked Evers to instill some of his fighting spirit into the Reds, and he jumped at the chance.

After being released by the Boston Red Sox in April 1918, Evers accepted an offer from the Knights of Columbus to act as supervisor of athletics to the allied troops in France. It was an assignment he would talk about the rest of his life. (San Francisco History Center, San Francisco Public Library.)

Then, after Cincinnati clinched the National League pennant, Moran asked him to scout their World Series opponents, the Chicago White Sox.[30]

Mathewson crossed paths with Evers prior to the World Series and, aware of his working for the Reds, asked him how he thought the Series would go. "Great," replied Evers. "I never saw a ball club so confident. They are as sure as we were before the series with the Athletics in 1914. And they'll ride some of those Chicago players ragged before they get through."[31]

The Reds won, of course—not without a little help from their infamous opponents who would become known as the "Black Sox," a revelation that remained in the future. Meanwhile, Evers gloried in Cincinnati's upset victory—and another besting of Eddie Collins, who was playing second base for Chicago. Upon returning home after the Series he told friends, "Gosh, it seemed like old times to be back in a World Series again."[32] In late October, Pat Moran traveled to Troy to visit Evers for a few days and attend a banquet held in his honor as a World Series champion and triumphant ex–New York State League player. Moran thanked those in attendance, singling out his friend and former teammate for his contribution to the World Series victory: "Johnny Evers is the greatest little man in baseball," Moran gushed. "Johnny had a very prominent part in my winning the World Series. I cannot understand how a man of so many brains does not have a big league club of his own. I would like to see Johnny back in the big show again."[33]

There were rumors that Pittsburgh owner Barney Dreyfuss had Evers on his short list of potential managers for the Pirates. Christy Mathewson, writing for the *New York Times*, said he considered Miller Huggins more likely to land the job, but also felt Evers would be a great choice. "I believe Johnny would make a better manager now than he did when he took over the Cubs [in 1913]," wrote Mathewson. "Personally, I think Johnny Evers is one of the finest little fellows ever developed in baseball. He is square and smart. He is a fighter all the way and even tried to enlist at the beginning of the war in spite of his size, weight, and a boiling attack of neuritis. I don't think Dreyfuss could pick a better man."[34]

But in the end, Dreyfuss hired his old catcher, George Gibson. Huggins remained with the New York Yankees and Evers remained unemployed. Wanting very much to return to the major leagues but lacking an opportunity to do so, Evers updated a Spalding Company instructional series, titled *How To Play Second Base*, and entertained an offer to become head baseball coach at Boston College—reaching a verbal agreement in early May 1920 that reportedly made him the highest paid coach in college baseball.[35] Two days after that announcement, Boston College officials were shocked to open the morning newspaper and read that the New York Giants had hired Evers as assistant manager to John McGraw.[36] The initial reaction from Boston College officials was one of disbelief, but it was true. Evers wired his regrets and reported to the Polo Grounds.[37]

While labeling Evers "ever the assassin of Giant rallies and Giant hopes," Dan Daniel of the *New York Herald* conceded, "Evers is just the man the Giants need to put ginger into them, to lift them out of their mental doldrums...."[38] For Evers, the decision was simple. "I want to get back into professional baseball," he explained.[39]

It seemed an odd pairing, John McGraw and his longtime nemesis—the man who had cost him a pennant in 1908. Yet there was a certain symmetry to it: a pair of Irishmen from upstate New York who played the game the same way—giving no quarter and taking no prisoners. And so it was that Johnny Evers donned the uniform of his favorite team from boyhood—the team that had replaced Troy in the National League so many years before—and sat chatting on the bench with Larry Doyle and Christy Mathewson. Speculation arose almost immediately that Evers was fated to be McGraw's eventual successor, supplanting Mathewson, who remained on the Giants coaching staff but whose health was too compromised by tuberculosis to consider managing again.

When Evers joined the Giants in Cincinnati, they sat in last place with a record of 6–11. Within a week, McGraw was serving a five-day suspension after disputes with umpires in both Pittsburgh and Chicago, and Evers was running the team.[40] He again took charge in August when McGraw faced legal entanglements stemming from his involvement in a mysterious New York nightclub brawl that left one of his actor friends with a fractured skull.[41]

Johnny Evers shocked everyone in May 1920 when he accepted an offer from his old nemesis John McGraw to serve as a coach for the New York Giants, but as is apparent from the look on his face, he was delighted to be back in a major league uniform after more than two years away from the game. Called on to run the club during John McGraw's frequent suspensions, he impressed everyone with his performance. (San Francisco History Center, San Francisco Public Library.)

Evers retained some of his old-time fire—Bill Klem chased him off the coaching lines when he came to the defense of outfielder Ross Youngs in a game against Brooklyn, and then ordered him from the bench to the clubhouse when he continued haranguing the umpire.[42] (Evers had promised McGraw he would not get thrown out of any games and had to do some fast talking to explain himself to the Giants manager.) But for the most part, Evers maintained his composure and made a positive contribution to the Giants. On the Fourth of July, New York was in seventh place. Two weeks later, the Giants were in fifth. By the beginning of August they were in third. Even with McGraw absent for stretches, due to continuing legal problems, and Evers running the club for a good portion of the final two months of the season, the Giants did not miss a beat. When the season ended on the third of October, New York sat in second, behind only the Brooklyn Dodgers; Evers's third-place-or-better magic remained intact.

After the season, Evers agreed to take a team consisting mostly of Giants players to Cuba for a winter barnstorming trip. Suddenly his plans were changed; the Chicago Cubs wanted him to be their manager again.

Chewing gum king William Wrigley had assumed control of the Cubs from Charles Weeghman when the ex–Federal League owner ran into financial problems. Two years removed from a World Series appearance—in which they lost to the Red Sox team with whom Evers had spent spring training—the Cubs had slipped into the second division under Fred Mitchell, and Wrigley was ready to make a change. He recognized that with the White Sox imploding due to the Black Sox scandal, he had a window of opportunity—the Cubs had devolved into the number-two team in a two-team baseball town. The White Sox regularly drew two hundred thousand more than their northside rivals; Wrigley thought Johnny Evers's name recognition might close the gap.

Impressed with the way Evers had served New York, Wrigley asked team president Bill Veeck, Sr., to obtain permission from the Giants to inquire about Evers's becoming Cubs manager in 1921. Veeck visited Evers in Jacksonville, Florida, where he was getting the Giants in shape for their trip to Havana; it was not a hard sell.[43] Evers formally signed a contract in December for $10,000, with bonuses of $1,000 for each position the Cubs finished above fourth place. He was ecstatic, explaining to reporters that it would be difficult for them to understand how much it meant for him to return to the Cubs.[44]

To Evers, baseball still revolved around speed, defense and strategy aimed at keeping the opponent off-balance. He set about remaking his roster into one that was much younger. Thirty-eight-year-old outfielder Dode Paskert was one of the first to go, claimed on waivers by the Cincinnati Reds.[45] To no one's surprise, Evers released Fred Merkle, who subsequently signed to play under former Braves manager George Stallings with Rochester in the International League.[46]

Infielder Buck Herzog and pitcher Claude Hendrix were also cut loose; both had remained under a cloud of suspicion that they had fixed a Cubs game in 1920. It was not clear that Herzog was directly involved, and he was allowed to play several more years, but only in the minor leagues. Hendrix announced his retirement and never again played professional baseball.[47]

Evers welcomed his pitchers and catchers, led by the great Grover Cleveland Alexander, to spring training on Wrigley-owned Catalina Island, where they worked out for a week before heading to Pasadena to meet the rest of the team. Wrigley was on hand to greet his new manager, who posed for photographs with eleven-year-old John Jr., clad in a Troy uniform. The young Evers had just become baseball's youngest owner; his father had purchased a one-third interest in the Albany Senators of the Eastern League and turned it over to his son.[48] A trio of ex–Miracle Braves teammates were on hand—Oscar Dugey as a coach, and pitcher Lefty Tyler and third baseman Charlie Deal on the active roster. Tyler had pitched the Cubs to the National League pennant with a 19–8 record in 1918, but arm problems, supposedly traced to bad teeth, had curtailed his effectiveness even after most of his bridgework had been removed.[49] Training camp itself was relatively uneventful, at least much more so than for Chicago's other team, which in March had seven of its players receive lifetime bans from Commissioner Landis for their roles in throwing the 1919 World Series. (An eighth, Chick Gandil, had already retired.)

With his old team training practically in his backyard, Frank Chance attended several exhibition games and advised Evers on potential roster cuts before the team departed Southern California.[50] The Cubs were enjoying one of their best exhibition seasons in recent memory, and an enthusiastic Evers told the *Chicago Tribune*, "I don't know where we will finish, but I know this team is going to fight. The Cubs will give the fans the best they have."[51]

The Cubs played in Sacramento, Oakland and San Francisco before heading home; on April 2, the Pacific Coast League's San Francisco Seals staged "Johnny Evers Day" at Recreation Park. Evers had promised to play, and he did, drawing a walk in the top of the first. He then went from first to third on a single before being caught in a rundown between third and home, at which point he decided he'd had enough and contented himself to sit on the bench for the rest of the afternoon.[52]

Twenty thousand were on hand to embrace Johnny Evers on Opening Day in Chicago. Longtime Cubs fan Commissioner Landis was photographed shaking hands with Evers, as yet another round in an endless chorus of "When Johnny Comes Marching Home" played in the background.[53] The Cubs played

Chicago Cubs owner William Wrigley welcomes Johnny Evers to Catalina Island and spring training as manager of the Cubs in March 1921. Evers was thrilled about being back with his old team, but the joy would be short-lived. (Cleveland Public Library Digital Gallery.)

a solid game behind Grover Cleveland Alexander to take the opener, and began the season promisingly, winning six of their first eight.

Evers behaved himself—he was not thrown out of a game until May 31; he had disagreed with Bob Emslie's call at first base and came close to ejection for reminding Emslie that Hank O'Day had made the famous Merkle call even though Emslie was the base umpire, implying a display of cowardice on Emslie's part. After a warning, Evers continued to argue and got the heave-ho.[54]

By that point Evers had grown frustrated, as the Cubs had lost seven of eight and fallen to sixth place. Alexander, who had won twenty-seven games in 1920, did not have the same zip on his fastball, and Hippo Vaughn, enduring marital discord that had led to his being stabbed by his father-in-law during the off-season, was plagued either by a sore arm or a sore head and was completely ineffective after seven consecutive seasons of seventeen or more victories.

On July 9, Vaughn surrendered consecutive home runs, the first a grand slam and the second to pitcher Phil Douglas, at which point a disgusted Evers removed him from the game.[55] Vaughn, whose record was 3–11 with an earned run average above six runs per game, promptly disappeared and was suspended. "I've got to take this stand," explained Evers.[56] Vaughn, whose career had been resurrected by Evers during his first stint as Cubs manager, did not pitch again that season, or ever again in the major leagues.

By the end of July, the Cubs had become hopeless and there were rumors of dissension among players. Lefty Tyler was released after winning only three games and Oscar Dugey was fired.[57] Wrigley was not used to losing; after conferring with Bill Veeck, he decided it was time for Evers to go. Rumors began to circulate when Evers missed a couple of games due to illness. On August 4, the Cubs announced catcher Bill Killefer was taking over as manager and Evers was out.[58] For the first time, the Evers magic failed—previously it had held true even when he barely touched a team; the Boston Red Sox had won the World Series in 1918 after he played for them in spring training, and the Cincinnati Reds had triumphed the next year when he scouted for them.

But Evers's failure with the Cubs did continue a pattern that persisted throughout his life. When there was a strong authority figure present to blunt his obsessive personality—Frank Chance with the Cubs, George Stallings with the Braves, John McGraw with the Giants—Evers was successful. But he was not able to repeat that success on his own—he never developed the ability to motivate other than the way he motivated himself. McGraw, as bombastic as he could be, calibrated his reactions to different players in response to the best way to motivate them. After Fred Merkle made his mistake in 1908, John McGraw was publicly sympathetic and offered him a raise; Merkle responded with a half-dozen solid seasons for the Giants. It is not apparent that Evers possessed that same kind of insight—as a result, he tended to wear out his welcome as a leader.

The Cubs' record stood at 41–55 when Evers was shunted aside—they played even worse following his dismissal, losing thirty-one of forty-four games before capturing ten of their final thirteen to finish with a seventh-place record of 64–89.

Evers was not unemployed for long; John McGraw hired him to scout the Yankees in preparation for the 1921 World Series, which the Giants would win from their cross-town rivals five games to three, coming back after dropping the first two contests.

Shortly after that, Charles Comiskey, always a fan of Evers, hired him as an assistant to Chicago manager Kid Gleason. The White Sox were still attempting to recover from the "Black Sox" scandal and Comiskey hoped Evers would put some fight into the team while drawing some attendance from Cubs fans across town.

"I know I've been here before," admitted Evers, "but I never get tired of coming back." The venerable Cap Anson, only days before his death, sat beside Evers at a baseball dinner and nodded in agreement. "That's the way it is with a lot of people," said Anson. "I came here a hundred years ago and I'm here for the finish." Sportswriter Al Spink summed up an article about the gathering by writing, "That [Evers] has an army of friends in Chicago who do not forget the faithful service he did for the Chicago Cubs when they were nearly always invincible and who will rally around him on his new stamping ground goes without saying."[59]

Evers signed a contract as both a coach and player, with an eye to manning the infield in case of emergency; that emergency came in Cleveland on April 27, 1922, when Eddie Collins had to sit due to a swollen wrist following a collision the day before with Cleveland's Les Nunamaker. In his first-ever American League appearance, the forty-year-old Evers batted seventh and played the entire game against the Indians, drawing a pair of walks and handling six chances without an error; it was said there were two others he "once might have had, but they were hard chances." Every time he made a play he shook his head and laughed, likely out of a sense of relief. He even turned a double play and was credited with a run batted in when he drew one of his walks with the bases loaded. The game ended in a 6–6 tie, with Evers reaching base twice in five at bats.[60] Collins would miss no other games that season, and Evers happily returned to the bench.[61]

The White Sox played better than many had expected. After languishing deep in the second division until mid–June, they caught fire and spent all of July in third place. They lost their final four games of the season to fall to a record of 77–77, the defeat on the season's final day dropping them out of the first division to fifth place.

Evers had surprised everyone—it had been openly predicted that he would clash with Eddie Collins, whom he had so mercilessly subjected to verbal abuse during the 1914 World Series, and that American League umpires would not put up with his "nagging tactics."[62] But he made it through the entire season without being ejected and the Sox enjoyed their best season since 1919.

Evers surprised everyone again when he decided not to return for the 1923 season, providing no explanation.[63] That February he received a call from John McGraw, who urged him to meet with Judge Emil Fuchs, who was purchasing the Boston Braves. At that meeting, Fuchs assured Evers that if he could raise $150,000, he could buy into the Braves and become team president. Evers replied that he could not raise that kind of money, but recommended that Fuchs contact Christy Mathewson.[64] Fuchs did partner with Mathewson and purchased the franchise; Mathewson became team president.

There had been rumors Evers would be appointed to the New York Boxing Commission by governor Al Smith, or that he would take another major league coaching position with a team on the East Coast. But Evers remained in Troy the entire year.

Meanwhile the White Sox plummeted to seventh place in 1923 and Kid Gleason resigned immediately after the team defeated the Cubs in the City Series.[65] Ten days later came a big surprise—the man replacing Gleason as White Sox manager for 1924 was none other than Frank Chance, and he wanted his old teammate on the bench with him. Johnny Evers and the legendary Peerless Leader were about to be reunited in Chicago.

CHAPTER THIRTEEN

The Human Dynamo
That Needs a Minder

While Johnny Evers sat out the 1923 season, Frank Chance had made a comeback, as manager of the Boston Red Sox. Evers had spoken to Chance at the 1922 World Series, where his old boss was openly lobbying for a return to the major leagues. Red Sox owner Harry Frazee, barely holding on after selling his best players, including Babe Ruth, was looking for someone to draw fans—at a reasonable price. Chance, who after an eight-year absence could hardly afford to be picky, fit the bill.[1]

The forty-six-year-old and his Red Sox helped the Yankees open their brand-new stadium on April 18, 1923; Babe Ruth vanquished Boston with a home run in front of a crowd of more than seventy-four thousand.[2] Unfortunately that loss would prove the highlight of the season for the Red Sox; they dropped their first four games and never reached the break-even mark. At times it became ugly. They lost a game to Cleveland in early June by a score of 17–4. A month later they lost to the Indians, 27–3.[3] The franchise was sold in August to a group led by former St. Louis Browns general manager Bob Quinn, a transaction that left Chance uncertain about his future. Facing the possibility of an end to his tenure, Chance had one task he wanted to complete.

On the afternoon of September 10, 1923, Johnny Evers left his home in Troy and boarded a train bound for Yankee Stadium. This was to be an important occasion; for the first time in more than a decade, there would be a reunion of baseball's most famous infield.[4] As Evers settled into the familiar lurching and jolting routine of rail travel—something he had experienced so often it was almost a comfort to him—he could not help but relive the greatest moments of his life, moments truly understood only by the two men he was going to meet. While he had seen Frank Chance and Joe Tinker individually on several occasions over the years, this would be the first time all three would be together since Charles Murphy had fired Chance eleven years earlier.

While Evers's train chugged along the Hudson River toward New York City, Joe Tinker was already on hand, attending a game between the Red Sox and the Yankees. The incomparable Ruth hit his thirty-fifth home run of the year that day—a rare inside-the-park shot that caromed off Red Sox outfielder Joe Harris's leg—to lead New York to an easy 9–1 victory over Boston.[5]

A totally delighted Evers was on hand at Yankee Stadium the following afternoon, swapping stories with his former teammates and waving off reporters' requests for the three to stage an exhibition during infield practice. "I wouldn't be able to walk for a week," he laughed, "and you can see Tinker has a waist line like a prosperous alderman."[6]

Tinker, Evers and Chance at their reunion in New York City in September 1923. It was the first time in more than a decade the three men had been together in the same room. Chance would live for only another year. (Reproduced from the original held by the Department of Special Collections of the Hesburgh Libraries of the University of Notre Dame.)

That evening, Tinker, Evers and Chance easily fell back into the old days, swapping tall tales and recalling victories, always large, and even larger in the retelling. In a photograph taken of the occasion, the three men are seated left to right as Franklin Adams had placed them in his famous poem; a relaxed Evers is leaning back in his chair, a twinkle in his eye and familiar black cigar clutched between his fingers—a man truly in his element. It was the tonic that Johnny Evers needed. He knew he wanted to get back into major league baseball.

Frank Chance was let go by the Red Sox at the conclusion of the 1923 season, but he was not ready to return to California. Charles Comiskey thought Chance had done an excellent job for Boston under trying circumstances and was interested in bringing one of Chicago's great baseball names to the South Side. By the end of October the two men had struck a deal for Chance to manage the White Sox.[7]

No one thought the White Sox a contender in 1924, but Comiskey thought he had hired the man to rebuild the team. Chance was not certain which players he wanted to trade or keep—there were rumors that Eddie Collins, the team's most valuable property, was on the block since he had not been named manager and might be offered that position by another team. There *was* one man Chance knew he wanted beside him in the dugout, and that man was Johnny Evers.[8] During the winter meetings in December, Evers agreed to serve as Chance's assistant.[9]

Despite his rugged appearance, Chance was never in the best of health and contracted the flu, complicated by asthma, shortly thereafter; when he could not shake its effects, he returned to the warmer climate of California to recover. He was in fact seriously ill—there were rumors he was suffering from cancer, tuberculosis or even congestive heart failure. Uncertain of his ability to withstand the rigors of travel and the pressures of leading two dozen men on a daily basis, Chance wired his resignation to Charles Comiskey. Comiskey would not hear of it, insisting that Chance instead take a leave of absence and spend time regaining his health. In the meantime, the White Sox owner put the team under the control of Johnny Evers and Ed Walsh.[10]

Once the White Sox reported to Florida for spring training, there were repeated rumors of Chance's imminent arrival, almost always followed by conflicting messages that he was never coming back. Looking to end the confusion, a reporter visited Chance at his home in Los Angeles in early March and the Peerless Leader insisted he was "raring to go."[11]

But it would be another month before Chance returned to Chicago. On April 12, only three days before the start of the 1924 season, it was announced he would manage the team at Comiskey Park in its final two exhibition games against the New York Giants. The White Sox won the first, with Chance directing the team from the bench in civilian clothes.[12] He was in uniform the next day as a crowd of more than thirty-four thousand officially welcomed him back to the Windy City. The White Sox lost to the Giants, 9–3, and an excited Evers, clearly reliving his old days, earned an ejection.[13] Chance was back, but he was not well. At the insistence of his wife, he visited a doctor who advised him to return to Los Angeles immediately or run the risk of permanent damage to his health. Chance gave Charles Comiskey the news and requested that Evers take his place. Comiskey told Chance that Evers would serve as interim manager, leaving the job open for Chance when his health recovered.[14] Chance told reporters that he did not believe he would be able to return until the 1925 season.[15]

For the second time in his life, Johnny Evers was succeeding Frank Chance as manager in Chicago.

After dropping the season opener to the St. Louis Browns, the White Sox reeled off four wins in a row at home. On the first of May, they carried a respectable record of 8–6 despite rumors of dissension, fueled no doubt by a one-hundred-dollar fine Evers imposed on pitcher Mike Cvengros after he walked off the mound during a 16–7 loss; Evers doubled the fine after becoming convinced that Cvengros had been lazily lobbing the ball to home plate.[16] Evers was trying to manage the team as Chance would have—with a zero tolerance for challenge to his authority. But once again he was doing so without another ally possessing sufficient clout to blunt his aggressiveness.

Evers was forced to take a leave of absence on May 16, with the White Sox sporting a still decent 11–11 record, to have his appendix removed.[17] The Sox had already been hit hard by injuries—pitcher Urban Faber had been operated on for bone chips in his elbow, as had Charlie Robertson, and shortstop Hervey McClellan underwent abdominal surgery for what was eventually diagnosed as liver cancer.[18] Now Chicago had lost its second manager of the season due to illness. Eddie Collins was put in charge of the team during Evers's convalescence—serving as an interim-interim manager.[19]

Evers missed a month, finally able to leave Troy on June 13 to rejoin the White Sox, insisting he was feeling fine and anxious to "get back into the harness."[20] He was officially back in charge on June 19 at St. Louis, with the team only one game below .500, still playing much better than conventional wisdom, or Charles Comiskey, had expected. And the White Sox continued to play solid, if unspectacular, baseball over the next month, sporting a record of 44–44 after the first game of a July 22 double-header. But it was all downhill from there.

More suspensions were handed out—pitcher Ted Blankenship was sent home in July after he was pulled from a game and threatened to attack Evers.[21] He was reinstated later in the season, but the episode reinforced the notion that the players did not like their interim manager. The fact that the popular Eddie Collins—who many Sox fans would have preferred run the team—remained on the roster, only made it that much more difficult for Evers. At one point Evers was forced to deny rumors that he and Collins were at odds: "Stories that we are not working together are without the slightest foundation," he insisted. "Collins not only is a fine chap personally, but also a wonderful ballplayer yet."[22]

The White Sox disintegrated, losing forty-three of sixty-five games to drop from the middle of the pack to last place. By that time Frank Chance was gone, having passed away in Los Angeles on September 15, 1924, at the age of forty-eight, succumbing to a combination of congestive heart and renal failure exacerbated by a severe asthmatic condition.[23]

After the 1924 City Series against the Cubs, which the White Sox won in six games, Evers led his team to Europe for a long-planned series of exhibitions against John McGraw and the New York Giants. Evers looked forward to the excursion, on which he would be accompanied by Helen and John Jr., who would celebrate his fifteenth birthday while they were across the Atlantic. He also expected to be back for another season as White Sox manager.[24] On Saturday, October 11, Evers and his family were given a rousing send-off at the train station as they embarked on the six-week tour of Europe.[25] Evers was in an effusive mood—he can be seen in newsreels wearing his White Sox uniform and pointing to the camera. The highlight of the trip was a game played in London attended by twenty-four thousand people, including King George V and his eventual successors, the Prince of Wales and the Duke of York. Although the tour was a financial failure, reportedly ending twenty thousand dollars in the red, Evers was happy because the Sox had split the sixteen games against McGraw's National League champions.

After the finale, a ten-inning affair in Paris, Evers returned to Troy and was visited by veteran major leaguer Nick Altrock, in town to address an athletic banquet sponsored by the local YMCA. The two joined Les Mann on the dais and Evers addressed the issue of his competitive nature, saying, "It's all right to say, 'Be a good loser,' but I'd like to see one. It's like a painted face; it don't reach very deep."[26]

A week later, Evers attended the winter meeting in New York and met with Charles Comiskey; he left at the end of the week without a contract.[27] The reason was that Comiskey did not want Evers as manager. He preferred Eddie

Following the 1924 season, the Chicago White Sox joined the New York Giants for an exhibition tour of Europe. Here, Evers and several of his players meet George V, King of the United Kingdom and the British Dominions, and Emperor of India (in the photograph, the king is mislabeled "King Edward"). Depicted in the photograph are (L to R) pitcher Charlie Robertson, outfielder Johnny Mostil, outfielder Bibb Falk, Dave Bancroft (who was player-manager of the Boston Braves but played for the White Sox on the tour), Evers and King George. (Reproduced from the original held by the Department of Special Collections of the Hesburgh Libraries of the University of Notre Dame.)

Collins, and in fact had wanted Collins as manager when Chance left for Los Angeles, but had bowed to the Peerless Leader's wishes. With Chance's passing, Comiskey was no longer beholden to anyone and chose his star second baseman.[28]

Johnny Evers went to work once again for John McGraw, as a spring training infield coach and scout for the 1925 season.[29] It was the third time McGraw had hired Evers, but this time his duties were ill-defined and he soon left. In the spring of 1926, Evers wrote to Jack Hendricks, manager of the Cincinnati Reds, about the possibility of a coaching job.[30] No offer was forthcoming, and Evers slowly drifted away from the game over the next couple of years. His marriage drifted as well. Sometime in 1926, Evers moved out of Lakewood Place and set up shop in Albany, where in September he opened a sporting goods store in the Hotel Kenmore Building on North Pearl Street.[31] According to friends interviewed at the time of Helen's filing for alimony two years later, she and John Jr. remained at Lakewood Place during this time.[32]

During the next couple of years, Evers busied himself with his store and played the role of baseball ambassador on every possible occasion, sometimes lapsing into the worn-out pastime of railing against how the game had changed. A man who had spent years cultivating the press, he was raked over the coals in a 1925 *Sporting News* editorial, which took him to task for saying, "Baseball has changed a lot in the last three or four years, and I cannot be convinced that it has changed for the better."

The "Baseball Bible" sniffed, "Where would Johnny Evers be today and what would he be doing if it were not for baseball? Johnny Evers never was a constructive force in baseball. At his best, no one can claim that for him." The editorial went on to say that Solly Hofman was more deserving for credit than Evers when it came to the famous Merkle play.[33]

Evers continued attending the World Series, declaring the 1925 Pirates to be one of the greatest teams he had ever seen and a dynasty in the making. He attended one regular season game in 1927, at Yankee Stadium, and was directed to a box where he was seated next to Fred Merkle. Evers later revealed that they had a nice chat and did not mention the famous play of two decades earlier that had forever connected them.

Evers attended the winter meetings each year, and shortly after returning from one of his trips wistfully remarked about wanting to make a comeback. "I'm trying to get accustomed to being a businessman," he told Joe Vila of the *New York Sun*, "but sometimes it's pretty hard, especially when there is a World Series coming on or I read in the paper that a league meeting is to be held. Then I put an assistant in charge of the shop and hurry off to join the gang."

He also related a story of sitting in the grandstand at the Polo Grounds, unrecognized by fans who were talking about the famous Tinker to Evers to Chance infield. One of the men in the group said he liked Tinker and Chance, but did not think much of Evers, declaring his opinion that Tinker had made Evers look good and that Evers was a "crab" who was more interested in fighting than playing ball. Evers claimed that when the fan turned to him to ask his opinion he ducked the issue by truthfully admitting, "I never saw Evers play."[34]

He attempted to keep his hand in the game, running a semi-professional team, the Evers All-Stars, which played at Saratoga during racing season. There was even a race horse named Manager Evers, owned and trained by Frank J. Kearns.[35]

Then on November 7, 1928, the Boston Braves surprised the baseball world by trading superstar second baseman/manager Rogers Hornsby and his forty-two-thousand-dollar salary to the Chicago Cubs. Reasoning that they had lost more than one hundred games with Hornsby—and could certainly do so without him—the Braves exchanged their star for five players and cash, reportedly two hundred thousand dollars. What was just as surprising, if not more so, was that Braves owner Emil Fuchs declared he would succeed Hornsby as the team's manager—or more exactly as "managing director," a title that raised eyebrows because of its lack of specificity or precedence. To counter his lack of experience in baseball as a player, coach or manager on any level, Fuchs announced that his bench assistant would be Johnny Evers.[36]

Implicit in the announcement was the unmistakable message that, as valued as Evers's baseball mind was, he needed a "minder" on the bench. *Boston Globe* sportswriter James O'Leary implied as much when he wrote of Evers's hiring: "There is no question as to [Evers's] unusual knowledge of the game in all its angles; that he is resourceful and aggressive. That he is a human dynamo ... he is a fighter who will give all that is in him. In the heat of battle he has, in times gone by, been on occasion too impetuous. He believes he has corrected this fault. With Judge Fuchs on the bench the latter will act as a stabilizer as well as moral support. If after working for a season under the new arrangement it is found Johnny does not need the support of these auxiliaries, Judge Fuchs will probably be quite willing to withdraw, and allow him to continue on 'his own.'"[37]

Evers insisted he was completely satisfied with the arrangement, saying, "I am more than glad to get back into the game, and I am particularly glad to return to Boston."[38] But it had to be galling for it to be considered that he needed "a minder," especially in light of his quarter-century experience while being asked to assist a man with none. Fuchs insisted that his involvement was temporary—that he was looking for an ideal manager. "It may be that Evers will be the man," insisted Fuchs. But his words lacked conviction.[39] With an equal lack of conviction, Evers insisted that Fuchs could be a great success, pointing out that Frank Selee, with the very same franchise, had no experience when he developed a juggernaut that dominated the National League in the 1890s.[40] It could be that Evers thought he would prove himself to Fuchs—that was certainly the opinion of some observers; Harold Burr wrote in the *Brooklyn Daily Eagle* that he thought Evers would be sole manager by May 1, once Fuchs tired of the job.[41]

But Evers also knew this could be his last chance at a big league job—he had not tasted any real success since assisting John McGraw in New York in 1920, a lifetime ago in major league baseball. And he had to admit it felt great being in a major league uniform again.

There was also the matter of the marriage of Johnny and Helen Evers—since they were Catholic, there would be no divorce. John Jr. had enrolled at Georgetown University and was showing promise as a ballplayer, although he was more interested in studying law. His parents had been living separately for three years, despite repeated interventions by friends of both aimed at reconciliation. Helen Evers filed for legal separation in December 1928; the suit claimed abandonment on the part of her husband.[42] Evers was shaken, although the news was certainly not unexpected—Helen had previously filed for legal separation in January 1926, and had been receiving thirty dollars per week for the previous six months.

"I have nothing to say about it," declared Evers when asked about the situation. "I hope it is all for the best. I'm afraid it may trouble our son, but I hope not. Jack's interests are my chief concern."[43] Evers did not contest the proceeding.

On his way to spring training in Florida, Evers stopped in Boston to speak at a St. Alphonsus Athletic Association dinner, and then spent a couple of days in Washington to look in on his son after receiving a note from a physician that John Jr. had been treated for an ankle injury. "I wrote to him saying that I preferred to get information about such things first-handed, but on the whole, I was not very much displeased, for it is certain he was doing something. I broke both legs and I know I did not break them doing nothing."[44]

Helen was granted legal separation in April 1929, pending final arrangements for alimony, and the couple sold the handsome Lakewood Place home that Johnny Evers had purchased with the bonus he had received for signing with the Boston Braves fifteen years earlier.[45]

Evers and Boston Braves owner Emil Fuchs in 1929. After Fuchs traded player-manager Rogers Hornsby to the Chicago Cubs, he decided to manage the Braves himself and asked Evers to serve as assistant manager. The experiment would prove unsuccessful. (National Baseball Hall of Fame Library—Cooperstown, New York.)

When Evers arrived in Florida there were a couple of familiar faces there to greet him—Hank Gowdy and Rabbit Maranville. His Miracle Braves teammates had been acquired during the winter meetings, Maranville in a cash deal from the St. Louis Cardinals and Gowdy as a coach.[46] The thirty-seven-year-old Maranville could still play; he had been the starting shortstop for St. Louis, and one of its few effective performers in the just-completed World Series against the Yankees—his first such appearance since 1914. When Maranville reported, he and Evers acted as if long-lost brothers.[47]

Evers once again proclaimed himself entirely satisfied about the arrangement with Judge Fuchs. "I would not have it different and, so far as I am concerned, I wish it to be permanent," he insisted. He seemed in good spirits, even allowing himself to be photographed riding in a wheelbarrow pushed by Hank Gowdy and Bill Cronin.[48]

Following two days of postponements due to extremely frigid weather, the Braves opened their 1929 season on April 18 at Braves Field with a decidedly inartistic 13–12 victory over Brooklyn. The Braves led 11–4 after five innings and held on despite three Dodgers home runs; centerfielder Earl Clark crashed into the fence in the fifth inning in an unsuccessful attempt to catch a fly ball and was knocked out cold for several minutes. George Sisler collected three hits and Maranville two as four thousand brave souls were on hand, half of whom left early.[49]

The Braves got off to an excellent start, winning their first three games, and on May 7 sat in first place with a record of 9–4. They were also drawing decent crowds—thirty-five thousand against Pittsburgh on a Sunday, twenty-five thousand a week later against Cincinnati, and thirty thousand for a Saturday double-header against New York. It was against the Giants that Evers earned his first ejection of the season, when John McGraw caught him batting his players out of order. Evers argued so strenuously that he also earned three days' suspension, although because of rainouts he did not actually miss any games.[50]

The Braves soon came down to earth. Three of their everyday starters, George Sisler, George Harper and Rabbit Maranville, were either thirty-six or thirty-seven years old. Their starting pitching was not good, they had no speed, were bad defensively and had no promising young players. By the first of June, the Braves were in seventh place and Judge Fuchs was pleading with Evers to take over as bench manager while he tended to the front office and sought new talent. Evers, undoubtedly recognizing he would be left managing a sinking ship, declined to do so.[51]

Judge Fuchs had counted on having baseball's best minds surrounding him—Johnny Evers, George Sisler, Hank Gowdy and Rabbit Maranville—and felt he could do better than Hornsby. But as Dave Egan of the *Boston*

Globe put it, "All the heavy thinking in the world will not put a batter on first base if he insists on striking out, and not even intense mental concentration will cause a hostile batter to strike out if he insists on flailing the ball over the fence."[52] The Braves lacked the talent to compete.

But Evers did not stop competing, even as he grew more frustrated at the realization that what could be his last shot with a major league team was slipping away.

He even put on his glove and got out there himself. On July 5, roughly two weeks shy of his forty-eighth birthday, he played all ten innings of an exhibition game against the Portland Mariners of the New England League, collecting two hits in six at bats, driving in a run and handling four chances without an error.[53] In Cincinnati, he engaged in bench-jockeying of such ferocity that Reds manager Charlie Dressen had to be forcibly restrained from rushing across the diamond and throttling him during a game the last-place Reds won, 14–2.[54]

The Braves soon supplanted the Reds in the National League basement, taking up residence on August 20, where they remained—a reverse "Miracle Braves" season, as it were. In the season's final game Boston used twenty players against the Giants, including thirty-nine-year-old Hank Gowdy, who a couple of months earlier had played his first major league game in four years, surprising everyone by lining out four hits in four at bats and throwing out the only runner who attempted to steal.[55] But Gowdy would only play one inning this day, neither batting nor accepting a chance in the field.

In the bottom of the ninth, the Braves inserted their twentieth player of the game—forty-eight-year-old Johnny Evers. He trotted out to second base and took his warm-ups to a tremendous ovation. It would be nice to say he turned one last double play against his longtime rivals, but instead his final inning as a major league player consisted of one ground ball hit in his direction, which bounced through his legs for an error.[56] The Giants won, 9–4—the score coincidentally matching the Braves' high water won-loss mark for the season—and while not losing 100 games as they had the year before, Boston still finished in last place. Meanwhile, Rogers Hornsby, freed from the pressures of managing, starred on the Chicago Cubs' first pennant-winner since 1918.[57]

The next day, Judge Fuchs announced he was stepping down as manager and would replace himself with Bill McKechnie, who had led the Pittsburgh Pirates to a World Series title in 1925 and the St. Louis Cardinals to a National League pennant in 1928. McKechnie was given a four-year contract.[58] Johnny Evers agreed to remain as a full-time scout for the Braves.[59] He would never again sit in a major league dugout.

CHAPTER FOURTEEN

Albany, Alabama Pitts
and One Last Reunion

After serving as quasi-manager of the Boston Braves in 1929, Johnny Evers bounced around for the next five years. Officially he was a scout for the Braves—and unofficially an advisor of sorts—frequently traveling to Boston from parts unknown to provide opinions about players or to discuss the team's state of affairs. Whenever scouting on the road, he would often put on his old uniform and work out. His brother Joe remained in Albany, operating the sporting goods store.

By that time John Jr. was studying law at Georgetown University and serving as team captain of the school's baseball team; Evers made sure to attend as many Hoyas games as he could.[1] He evolved into an elder statesman of sorts, participating in the occasional Old-Timer's game and promoting baseball at every opportunity, almost always for free, making appearances and delivering speeches that advised kids to practice every day, stay in top physical condition, and lay off umpires. He was always generous with his time, whether for a cause or simply to spend an hour or two with someone wanting to talk about baseball. David Duval of the *Schenectady Union Star* said, "We don't know of a better way to pass the time than with a bowl full of pretzels and 3.2 [beer] and listen to Evers."[2]

He served as president of the "Oldtime Ballplayers Group" in Troy—essentially an excuse for gray-haired men to relive past glories, some real, many exaggerated or even the product of pure imagination.[3] He refereed charity wrestling matches for the benefit of the unemployed and became a crack bowler, playing on the Elks team that won the state championship.[4] While on a scouting trip to the West Coast he stopped to place flowers on Frank Chance's grave. And he intermittently received unwanted notice in the press for his battles over alimony, including losing a request in 1934 to lower his payments from $1,020 per year.[5]

Evers continued suffering personal tragedies—his father's last living brother, Michael, died in January 1930. Two months later, close friend Charles Stack, who had helped Evers write his *Spalding Guide* series on playing second base, passed away following a stroke.[6] His forty-three-year-old brother Thomas died suddenly while on a camping trip in the summer of 1932.[7] A teenage niece died from pneumonia in 1933.[8]

Life on the road, even for one as accustomed to it as Johnny Evers, is a lonely existence. Anxious to root in one spot, as well as return to baseball in a more direct capacity, in 1935 he accepted the position of general manager of the International League Albany Senators, a perennial also-ran fresh from one of their rare contending seasons.[9] Evers retained recently hired former Dodgers and Pirates pitcher Al Mamaux as manager, and recruited Hack Wilson, the former Cubs slugger released in September 1934 by the Philadelphia Phillies, to replace Jake Powell, a young star sold to the Washington Senators. Wilson was pretty much finished as a ballplayer—the consequence of his bulky physique combined with prodigious drinking habits—but he remained a drawing card, something desperately needed with the Great Depression continuing to hammer the country into submission.

Evers arranged for the Boston Braves to visit Albany for an exhibition game on April 22—the Braves were wildly popular that spring thanks to their recent signing of forty-year-old Babe Ruth and the comeback of shortstop Rabbit Maranville, who had missed the entire 1934 season with a broken leg. Ruth played five innings at first base, smashing two long doubles and drawing a walk, while Maranville laced a pair of singles and made a leaping catch of a line drive. Hack Wilson managed to land flat on his back, unintentionally executing an awkward somersault after tripping on Ruth's leg while running out a ground ball.[10]

But the exhibition with the Braves, while successful, was a singular event. As always, Evers was a fighter looking for an edge—if not to win, to at least remain competitive. He would find another drawing card that summer in a most unexpected place, and as a result, he would once again find himself briefly in the national spotlight.

Twenty-five-year-old Edwin Pitts, imaginatively nicknamed "Alabama" in honor of the state of his birth, was a star two-sport athlete—an extraordinary halfback as well as an outfielder of some promise. He had starred in exhibition games against the New York Giants and received tryout offers from professional football teams.[11] There was one hitch—Alabama Pitts was an inmate at New York's Sing Sing Prison.

Pitts had received a prison sentence of eight to sixteen years for his involvement in a string of robberies, but was fortunate to be incarcerated under Lewis Lawes, a warden of national renown whose reputation was built on his staunch belief in the rehabilitation of prisoners. Pitts became a poster boy for Lawes's theories, even toiling unsupervised outside the prison walls, tending the warden's yard. Sport was a cornerstone of Lawes's program, and to that end he employed top coaches whose charge was to field teams capable of playing exhibitions against professionals. Pitts gained notoriety for his athletic prowess, and Lawes, conscious of Pitts's potential to boost the prison reform movement, cut his sentence by one-third, making him eligible for release in June 1935.

Sensing an opportunity, Albany Senators owner Joe Cambria dispatched Evers to sign Pitts before his release from prison. Evers did so, unprepared for the resulting firestorm. The International League refused to honor the contract of the convicted felon, and on June 4, William Bramham, head of the National Association of Minor Professional Baseball Leagues, supported that decision, informing the Senators that having Pitts on their roster would be detrimental to professional baseball.[12]

Two days later Pitts bid farewell to prison and Warden Lawes, who had already fired off a telegram to Bramham urging him to reconsider his decision. Pitts departed Sing Sing, his mother at his side as he walked through the prison's iron gates on a misty June morning, wearing a brand-new suit with thirty dollars tucked in the pocket. Once outside, he haltingly addressed newspapermen gathered for the occasion. As camera bulbs flashed, he remarked, "I'm sorry about this objection to my playing baseball." He then vowed that if allowed to play, "I will never do anything to make anyone regret giving me this opportunity."

Public opinion was solidly on the side of Pitts, and Bramham's decision especially angered the citizens of Albany; nearly one hundred of them were on hand when the ballplayer arrived with Johnny Evers later that day. Pitts exclaimed that he was "rarin' to go" and hoped Judge Bramham would "change his mind." Evers then escorted Pitts to the State Parole Board office so he could officially report his presence. Meanwhile, Bramham explained that his decision was a matter of "policy" and that any appeal would have to be made to Commissioner Landis.[13]

Pitts traveled to Syracuse to meet what he hoped would be his future teammates. He dined with Al Mamaux and attended that night's game, seated in a box on the third base side with Red Sox scout Bibb Falk and the retired Syracuse chief of police.[14] Meanwhile, his competitive juices flowing, Evers appealed to Warren Giles, chairman of the executive committee of the Association—at the same time promising to file a protest to Commissioner Landis, his old fan, should Giles and the executive committee rule against Albany and Pitts. St. Louis Cardinals stars Dizzy Dean and Pepper Martin lent their names to the cause, as did Phillies manager Jimmy Wilson. New York state assemblyman Arthur Swartz asked, "What harm can Pitts do to baseball?"[15]

But Giles and the committee seemed reluctant to reverse Bramham's ruling. The parties gathered to hear the final decision, and when Giles stated that ex-convicts could not play professional baseball, Evers leapt to his feet and declared that he would quit the game "unless this wrong is righted." Pointing to Pitts, he shouted, "I have been connected with baseball for thirty-three years and I played the game squarely and by the rules. Baseball is a game of sentiment, a game which appeals to the heart. This decision tramples on sentiment and stabs fair play in the heart." He immediately declared his intention to petition New York Governor Herbert Lehman for a pardon of Pitts.[16]

Giles's decision only made the ex-convict more popular. Pitts appeared at the June Night Festival in Lansingburgh, an annual fundraiser for St. Augustine's Catholic Church, and was introduced by Evers to a cheering crowd of four thousand, many of whom were last-minute attendees of the festival after learning Pitts would be there.[17] The Sing Sing athlete submitted to national radio interviews regarding his situation, and evangelist Billy Sunday joined the chorus of those insisting Pitts be given a chance. Pitts and Evers traveled to New York to await Landis's decision and attended a game between the Cardinals and Giants at the Polo Grounds—a bored Cherry Lawes, the warden's teenage daughter, sat next to Pitts, directly behind Evers and her father.[18]

On June 18, Commissioner Landis stepped in. Based on the pleas in support of the player, and Landis's concern that keeping Pitts from playing could interfere with his rehabilitation, Sing Sing's most famous alumnus would be allowed to suit up for Albany. But Landis also required that Pitts sign a new contract restricting his participation to regular season games so the Senators could not exploit his notoriety through the scheduling of extra exhibition contests.

Pitts was effusive in his appreciation for Evers and Lawes: "They have been great. They stuck with me from the start of this thing and I'm glad to have the chance to show they were right." Evers was ecstatic, declaring that Landis's ruling "gave me the greatest thrill in my thirty-three years in baseball."

Evers said that Pitts's debut would come in the team's next day game. "I don't feel that he should make his start in a night game under the lights," he said. "It would be too much of a handicap to ask until he has a chance to get used to things."[19]

Thursday, June 20, was Johnny Evers Night at Hawkins Stadium in

Johnny Evers, wearing a Cubs uniform, gives pointers to new Albany Senators out-fielder and ex–Sing Sing inmate Edwin "Alabama" Pitts (right) as manager Al Mamaux looks on. (Reproduced from the original held by the Department of Special Collections of the Hesburgh Libraries of the University of Notre Dame.)

Albany as the Senators hosted minor league legend Ike Boone and the Toronto Maple Leafs.[20] Evers was presented a chime clock during a pre-game ceremony emceed by Warden Lawes. Albany Mayor John Boyd Thacher II also took to the microphone and noted that when Evers set out to do something, "he stuck with it until it was accomplished."[21]

Pitts made his debut that Sunday, wearing uniform number seven, in a double-header against Syracuse that drew nearly eight thousand people, as well as press from all over the country. And he performed surprisingly well despite his long layoff amid the distractions of the previous month; batting leadoff and playing centerfield, Pitts collected two hits in five at bats in the first game, and was hitless in three times in the nightcap.

Afterward, he received a hearty slap on the back from Evers after exclaiming, "I'm more confident than ever that I can make a go of it in the International League."[22] Pitts had shown enough that the Senators sold Hack Wilson to the Portland Beavers, although Wilson never reported and his baseball career came to an end.[23]

While Pitts initially displayed excellent speed and defense, he struggled with both injuries and International League pitching, hitting only .233 in 114 at bats. He was clearly not the second coming of Ty Cobb, and one cannot escape the impression that he *was* being exploited to some extent—Evers and Mamaux guaranteed he would remain with Albany all season no matter how he played, even after he requested to be sent to a lower league.[24] His old warden, whose book, *20,000 Years in Sing Sing*, had been made into a Hollywood movie starring Spencer Tracy, wrote a script about Pitts for Warner Brothers titled *The Comeback*; Hollywood columnist Louella Parsons suggested Jimmy Cagney for the lead role.[25]

Pitts's career quickly fizzled—he was a good lower-level minor league player, but nothing more. He spent the next baseball season in the New York–Pennsylvania League, and then bounced around the lower minors for a few years. By the end of the decade he was married, had a daughter and was employed in a North Carolina textile mill, playing baseball on weekends. But his end would not be a happy one.

On June 6, 1941, Pitts and several teammates visited a roadhouse to celebrate after one of their games. An argument ensued after Pitts attempted to cut in on a dancing couple and he was stabbed; he died in the hospital the next morning. Edwin "Alabama" Pitts was thirty-one years old.[26]

After reaching the playoffs a year earlier, the Albany Senators were clearly overmatched in 1935—one of the reasons they had signed Alabama Pitts. After the team finished deep in the cellar with a record of 49–104, Evers resigned as general manager, publicly giving no reason but rumored to be frustrated by his lack of authority over the team.[27] The franchise would continue for one more year before being replaced by Jersey City; a new team representing Albany was fielded in the New York-Pennsylvania League beginning in 1937.

Not long after leaving the Senators, Evers declared bankruptcy at the Federal Court in Utica.[28] To help make ends meet he accepted the position of supervisor of Albany's Bleecker Stadium, overseeing the city's amateur sports

program, and kept himself busy at the sporting goods store—which he had
sold to his brother Joe—located between the Elks Lodge and the De Witt
Clinton Hotel.[29] Evers greeted everyone who stopped by, happily talking
baseball by the hour and occasionally bringing out the famous Merkle ball,
the holy baseball relic that he had inscribed and dutifully preserved to commemorate the event that had made him famous. He spent every evening at the
Elks Lodge talking baseball. After a serious bout with pneumonia, he regained
his strength and soon weighed one-ninety, giving the appearance of a prosperous banker or city councilman.

All the while, he insisted he was ready and anxious to return to baseball
when the opportunity presented itself.[30]

During the summer of 1937, Evers joined Hack Wilson as a guest sports-
caster for several Cubs and White Sox games. The two were well-received,
and Evers surprised veteran reporters with his calm demeanor. "The Evers of
today," claimed columnist Charles Young, "is not the Human Crab of his playing days. The Evers of today is a dignified gentleman, bespectacled, looking as
if, at any moment, he might arise to address the Rotary Club in the subject of
what to do about the membership drive."[31]

The Cubs honored Frank Chance that summer and invited several of his
former teammates to mark the occasion, including Johnny Evers and Joe Tinker. The team commissioned a plaque honoring Chance, which was to be permanently displayed at Wrigley Field. Tinker was recovering from heart and
kidney problems that had put him at death's door earlier that year—at the
same time Evers was battling pneumonia—but to the delight of fans, he and
Evers donned Cubs uniforms and threw the ball around the infield before the
game. Afterward, they were photographed while holding Chance's plaque.[32]
The two, who earlier that week had attended the Joe Louis-James Braddock
championship fight, assured everyone that their feud was long dead and buried.

Evers kept up with the game, always ready and willing to talk to the press.
Arch Murray of the *New York Post* visited him in December 1937 in his office
at the sporting goods store, where he puffed away on cigars and declared that
the young centerfielder of the New York Yankees, Joe DiMaggio, could become
the equal of Ty Cobb and Honus Wagner. He also said that Giants left-hander
Carl Hubbell—who had just completed his fifth straight twenty-win season
while leading the National League in strikeouts—was losing his stuff. "He'll
be lucky if he goes over fifteen wins," predicted Evers.[33] (Hubbell would win
only thirteen games in 1938, and no more than eleven in any season after that.)

Evers appeared on the popular radio quiz show *Information Please*, and
one of the guest panelists was Franklin P. Adams. The two had never met;

In 1939, Johnny Evers (left) reunited with his old Miracle Braves teammate Rabbit Maranville when Maranville was named manager of the Albany Senators of the Eastern League. (National Baseball Hall of Fame Library, Cooperstown, New York.)

after being introduced, Evers thanked Adams for his famous verse. "I owe you a debt of lasting gratitude for keeping my name before the public all these years," he said. "I'd have been forgotten long ago if it wasn't for 'Baseball's Sad Lexicon.'"[34]

Johnny Evers took one more shot at baseball, returning to the Albany Senators in 1939 as vice-president; he insisted on a salary of one dollar per year and was adamant about paying his way into every ballgame. He also successfully lobbied team president Tom McCaffrey to name his old friend Rabbit Maranville as manager.[35]

Maranville, whose twenty-three-year major league career ended in 1935, had most recently managed Montreal of the International League. The pairing was extremely popular in Albany, seen as a reunion of one of the great double-play combinations in baseball history.

But Evers would spend quite a bit of time away from the Senators that summer, seemingly not interested in the team's fate. On May 27, he traveled to Cooperstown to assist in the unveiling of a bust of Christy Mathewson. After being photographed beside the sculpture along with Mathewson's widow, he threw out the first pitch for a game staged in honor of the pitching great at Doubleday Field between Bucknell University, Mathewson's alma mater, and St. Lawrence.[36]

Two weeks later, thousands of baseball fans descended upon upstate New York to attend the "Cavalcade of Baseball," a celebration of the sport's supposed one hundredth birthday, held at the brand-new museum dedicated to the sport—the National Baseball Hall of Fame. The eleven living inductees were in attendance, although Ty Cobb was late and therefore absent from the now iconic photograph taken to mark the occasion.[37] Evers was among the retired players in attendance and was advanced, along with Bill Terry, Pie Traynor and Rabbit Maranville, as among those most likely to eventually join those immortals in bronze.[38]

Evers then traveled to Boston to help celebrate the twenty-fifth anniversary of the Miracle Braves and the centennial of baseball in New England. He announced his intention to play in the Old-Timer's Day ballgame, insisting, "I shall be there, even if all I can do is sell peanuts."[39]

Although introduced with the rest of the players, he did not play. But he was among two hundred former players who gathered at the Hotel Statler afterward to form the Association of Retired Major League Baseball Players, which was designed to aid ex-players in financial need. Evers was elected to the Board of Governors, along with Walter Johnson, Kitty Bransfield, Joe Wood and Bill Carrigan.[40]

Then it was back to Albany, where the Senators hosted an exhibition game against the Brooklyn Dodgers. Rabbit Maranville and Dodgers manager Leo Durocher played a couple of innings at shortstop for both teams, to the delight of the five thousand fans in attendance.[41]

The forty-seven-year-old Maranville remained in excellent condition, playing a handful of regular season games for the Senators, and the team enjoyed a successful campaign, defeating Elmira in the first round of the play-offs before losing to Scranton in the Governor's Cup final in five games.[42] But

Albany secured a working agreement with a different major league club after the season and Maranville was let go.

🄼 🄼 🄼

Johnny Evers suffered his first stroke in 1940. It slowed him somewhat and ended his active involvement with the Albany Senators. Based on his volatile on-field temperament and history of breakdowns, it might have been predicted that Evers would depart this mortal coil in a final meltdown of some sort or another, but instead his physical decline was steady and inevitable, against which he would predictably wage a noble and impressive battle. In August 1942, while reminiscing with friends late into the evening at the Albany Elks Club, he suffered a serious stroke that paralyzed his right arm and leg and left him without the ability to speak.[43] Able to return home after spending several weeks in the hospital, he spent the next year and a half gamely battling back and painstakingly learned to speak again, although he remained confined to his bed much of the time. Inundated with letters and postcards wishing

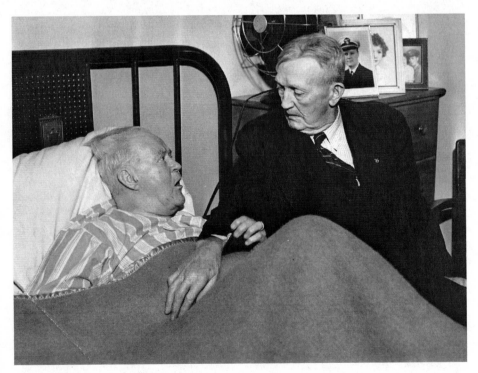

Evers spent most of the final half-dozen years of his life confined to bed. In 1944, Cy Young dropped by Albany to visit the ailing ballplayer. (Sporting News/Rogers Photograph Archive.)

him well, he remained upbeat and deeply interested in baseball—even though he could only do so as an armchair analyst—with Notre Dame football and boxing next in line for his attention.[44]

In 1943 he consented to an interview with James J. Murphy as he sat propped up in a chair, positioned near a window from which he could see his sporting goods store.[45] He maintained a fifty-pound scrapbook that he added to daily, most often the result of someone inquiring about the Merkle play. He corresponded with friends and fans, as well as his son, John Jr., who was serving in the South Pacific.[46] While he was unable to participate in the February 1944 Hot Stove League meeting at the Albany Elks Lodge as he had in past years, two months later he resumed his duties as keynote speaker for the Albany Senators kickoff dinner via a microphone set up in his bedroom.[47]

On May 21, 1944, after twenty months either in the hospital or confined to his home under the watchful eye of a live-in caretaker, Johnny Evers fulfilled his boast that he "would be out to see the boys in action again." The occasion was an Eastern League game between the Albany Senators and the Elmira Pioneers; in true Evers fashion, he chose to attend a double-header, witnessing the action from his automobile.

After complimenting the Senators, who swept the double-header, Evers expressed satisfaction about being in public again. "I had a swell time and met many of my old friends," he said. "And I certainly enjoyed those two games."[48]

Evers continued interacting with the public, clearly delighted that summer to present a trophy to members of the winning team in the junior CYO baseball tournament, carefully arranged in an overstuffed chair and smiling widely for the local newspaper photographer.[49]

Evers also enjoyed visits from major leaguers passing through Albany, often as guests of the Senators. Cy Young stopped by to visit the ailing Cubs great. "Evers was a great ballplayer," said the seventy-eight-year-old Young, "and a great man for the game. I'm looking forward to talking to him."[50] They spent a half hour discussing players past and present and agreed that baseball would boom after the war.[51]

Evers welcomed these interludes and was eager to talk about baseball for hours. He listened regularly to Brooklyn Dodgers games, but not because he was a Dodgers fan: "That's the only ball broadcast I can get on this radio," he explained.[52]

And like his father a half-century before, a virtually bedridden Evers would occasionally rally his strength and sneak out to the ballpark to watch baseball games—roughly ten times in 1946 alone—enjoying the sunshine and the crack of the bat, taking comfort in what he knew best and undoubtedly reflecting on his father, sitting on the hill outside the ballpark in Troy watching him play so many years ago.

CHAPTER FIFTEEN

Which Is As It Should Be

Following Evers's stroke in August 1942, efforts intensified to see him elected to the Baseball Hall of Fame. He had finished seventh in the voting that year and the sporting press of upstate New York began to aggressively push his candidacy while he could still appreciate it; columnist Jack McGrath first proposed Evers as a prime candidate in January 1943.[1] When he did not get in that year, McGrath enlisted Troy's mayor, John Ahern, to launch an official campaign in 1944.[2] The effort began to gather momentum—in 1945, Evers received 134 votes, finishing fourth in the balloting.[3]

During the first week of January 1946, Evers was announced as one of twenty-one semi-finalists for the Hall of Fame. From that list, a maximum of five names could be chosen by each eligible sportswriter, and to gain election a player had to appear on at least seventy-five percent of the ballots. Only then would he join the thirty-eight men previously enshrined. Frank Chance had come closest the year before, falling seven votes shy of the 186 required for election; no one had earned induction since Rogers Hornsby in 1942, and many writers complained that there was so little separating the top ten to twelve candidates that only voting for five made the seventy-five percent threshold almost impossible to attain.

Sure enough, none of the twenty-one achieved the required 197 votes—Frank Chance collected the most with 150. Evers finished second with 110. Miller Huggins, Ed Walsh and Rube Waddell rounded out the top five. Carl Hubbell, Lefty Grove, Dizzy Dean, Joe McGinnity and Mordecai Brown were among the also-rans, as were Joe Tinker and Rabbit Maranville, the shortstops who had played beside Evers for most of his career.[4]

The repeated failure to elect anyone created a backlash that stirred action; three months later the Hall of Fame Committee, a group akin to today's

Veteran's Committee, selected eleven players, including Joe Tinker, Johnny Evers and Frank Chance, to become members of the Hall of Fame.[5] Evers heard the news on the radio and was so excited he could not sleep. Instead, he hauled out his old scrapbooks and reminisced.

Evers was in bed when reporters called on him the next morning, and photos of an obviously crippled man clad in pajamas were published nationwide. Ignoring the obvious indignity, Evers granted an audience: "I'm tickled to pieces that they selected me. I feel fine ... great. That leaves me with no more worries. I wish Chance were alive to feel as happy about it as I do." He expressed his thrill at going in together with Chance and Tinker and then added, "Chance should have been there long ago. And I'd like to see them get Rabbit Maranville in there soon."[6]

Bill Corum of the *Journal American*, representing the New York City sportswriter contingent, said, "None of the recent selections to Baseball's Hall of Fame delighted us so much as that of Johnny Evers." While admitting that he and other New York City journalists had exclusively campaigned for Clark Griffith in the January balloting, thinking it likely only one player would be chosen, Corum reckoned, "Nobody ever more surely belonged in the Hall at Cooperstown than Evers. There may have been greater second basemen. But no gamer one ever, or will there ever be."

Fellow *Journal American* columnist Frank Graham reflected on Evers's competitive nature and how tortured he was to have to sit on the sidelines whenever he was ejected, admitting to beat writers, "I'd die a thousand deaths."

Graham concluded his column by writing, "All that was long ago and far away. Frank Chance is dead. And yet he and Evers and Tinker have, in a sense, been reunited in Cooperstown. Which is as it should be."[7]

Even as his health continued to falter, Evers remained current in the game following his Hall of Fame selection, publicly defending Ted Williams against criticism of his sub-par offensive production in the 1946 World Series.[8] He donated a trophy to be awarded to the Most Valuable Player in the Troy Amateur Baseball League and hoped to present it in person at the league's December banquet. He was unable to attend, however, and his brother Joe carried out the honors.[9] He was saddened by the January deaths of two more of his teammates, Johnny Kling and Jimmy Sheckard, and of news that Joe Tinker had lost a foot to diabetes. Meanwhile, despite remaining active mentally, Evers was growing ever weaker physically.

In the end, Johnny Evers was able to enjoy his selection to the Hall of Fame for slightly less than a full year; on March 25 he suffered a major cerebral hemorrhage at his home on State Street.[10] He fought hard, but each succeeding

Funeral Mass for Johnny Evers, held at St. Mary's Church in Troy on March 31, 1947. (Reproduced from the original held by the Department of Special Collections of the Hesburgh Libraries of the University of Notre Dame.)

hospital bulletin grew more pessimistic than the last. Evers drew his last breath at St. Peter's Hospital at 9:25 a.m. on Friday, March 28, 1947. "Dad passed away quietly," said John Evers, Jr., who was at his father's bedside.[11]

Franklin P. Adams heard the news a couple of hours later and pronounced himself "mighty much downcast to hear of the death of John J. Evers, a great hero of mine when I came to the home town of the Giants, whom I was an enemy of."[12]

After learning of his old teammate's death, Joe Tinker, contacted at his home in Orlando, Florida, where he was recovering from his amputation, said that baseball had lost one of its greatest players and praised Evers as "a fighter in everything he did."[13] Tinker had learned of Evers's poor health from a mutual friend and had penned a note of encouragement to his old teammate. It began, "Dear John, your friend Bill Bolte is here and I want to say hello old Pal and fight, John." He wrote about the days they had played together and good times they had enjoyed. Referring to the recent deaths of their teammates, he added,

"Just think of Sheckard and Kling, they are signed up with Chance already."
He closed by writing, "Well John, lots of good luck and thank the good God
we are still here. I hope I can see you someday, Your old sidekick, Joe Tinker."[14]

Evers's casket was borne from Compton Funeral Home in Albany by a
number of local dignitaries, including Troy mayor John Ahern, who had led
the campaign responsible for his ultimate induction into the Hall of Fame.
The procession crossed the Hudson River to Troy for a funeral mass at St.
Mary's Church, followed by Evers's burial in the family plot, underneath the
large marble monument bearing his last name, and next to his tiny daughter
Helen—the reason the marker, paid for by his "Miracle Braves" signing bonus,
had been erected back in 1914.[16]

Evers's Hall of Fame plaque was placed on an easel at Cooperstown and
draped in black for a thirty-day period of mourning—the plaque had not yet
been publicly displayed, awaiting his official induction later that year.[15] The
ceremony was held that July, prior to the annual Hall of Fame exhibition game
between the Boston Braves and New York Yankees.[17]

Joe Tinker died on July 27, 1948, on his sixty-eighth birthday, of com-
plications from diabetes. The last quarter-century of Tinker's life had been
tough. On Christmas Day 1923—only three months after the reunion in New
York with Evers and Chance—his wife, Ruby, who had long suffered from illness and depression, committed suicide by gunshot. He married again in 1926,
but his second wife also preceded him in death, in 1934. He married for a
third and final time in 1942.

After his playing days, Tinker managed and/or owned minor league
teams in Columbus, Orlando and Jersey City. He was an excellent businessman
and became rich during the 1920s—some say he was a millionaire—thanks to
real estate investments tied to the Florida land boom, especially in central
Florida. But he then went bust when the land boom did the same. He helped
run a baseball school in Orlando, Florida, and a successful billiard hall, but
never recovered financially. Tinker nearly died in both 1936 and 1944 due to
heart and kidney ailments complicated by the flu, but recovered each time,
and battled diabetes for much of the latter part of his life, losing a leg to the
disease a year and a half before his death. He was buried in Orlando, beside
his first wife Ruby.

Johnny Evers's trusted brother Joe continued to run the sporting goods
store in Albany before dying of liver failure in January 1949 at the age of fifty-
five.[18] The family then incorporated the business, with Johnny Evers, Jr., in
charge, until selling it in 1954 to local sports figure Pete Horan and Joe Evers's
son, Joe Jr.[19]

That same year, sixty-one-year-old Rabbit Maranville died of a heart attack at his home in New York, where he had been serving as head of the city's sandlot baseball program for youth. He was buried in Springfield, Massachusetts.[20] Two weeks later, Maranville was elected to the Baseball Hall of Fame, along with Bill Dickey and Bill Terry; the ballots had been mailed out the same day he died.[21]

Mordecai Brown returned to the Chicago Cubs after his two years in the Federal League and ended his big league career in 1916, appropriately enough with a game against Christy Mathewson. It would be the final time either man pitched in the majors.[22] Brown died in 1948, a year before he joined Tinker, Evers and Chance in the Hall of Fame. Frank Selee also was eventually enshrined, in 1999. Hank O'Day was inducted in 2013.

Johnny's wife Helen remained estranged from the family for the rest of her life; she died in an Albany nursing home in January 1974. Although family members had thought she and Johnny divorced, they had not; after a half-century apart, the couple was finally reunited when she was buried beside Johnny and their daughter in the family plot in Troy. Her maiden name on the monument is listed incorrectly as "Fitzgibbons."

John Jr. died in Florida in 1980 at the age of seventy. He and his wife had no children, so there are no living direct descendants of Johnny Evers.[23]

Fred Merkle made his last public appearance at an Old-Timer's game in St. Petersburg, Florida, in January 1956, six weeks before his death. Driving across the state from his Daytona Beach home, he chose not to be in uniform that day, but did ride in the motor parade to the ballpark and spent an enjoyable day talking about the "Glory Days" with old teammates and opponents such as Tommy Leach, Heine Groh and Edd Roush.[24]

However, enjoyable moments proved far too infrequent for Fred Merkle. He was a member of six teams that went to the World Series, but all of them lost.[25] Despite a solid major league career that spanned two decades, he became infamous for a simple mistake made when he was nineteen years old. Nearly a half-century later, he lamented that it was the only thing for which he was remembered; it was a burden he never carried easily. He died in his sleep at the age of sixty-seven—some teammates attributed his demise to a broken heart.

In 1991, John T. Evers, great-grand-nephew of Johnny Evers, was researching his family history while unpacking boxes in the family sporting goods store during a break from his studies at Siena College. He and his father came across an old cardboard box in the back of a filing cabinet drawer. "It was like a scene out of *Raiders of the Lost Ark*," he remembered. "The top of the box said 'Historic Baseballs' or something like that. Inside I found an old brown baseball that had written across it 'Merkle, Sept. 23, 1908' in faded black lettering."[26]

John Evers took the artifact home and sat it on his desk for a couple of years, until it was taken to auction for what turned out to be a futile attempt to save the family store, which had fallen on hard times. The ball was sold by Christie's for $27,500 to actor Charlie Sheen. It was re-sold a couple of more times before eventually ending up in the possession of television commentator Keith Olbermann. In an interview with *Sports Illustrated* writer Tim Layden, a great-nephew of Evers, Olbermann labeled the ball "almost a spirit-filled object. It took a little of the souls of everyone who touched it."[27]

The day after the 1951 reunion at the Hotel Somerset in Boston, the surviving members of the Miracle Braves headed to the ballpark to relive their glory days. The Harvard Band led a march to the grounds, followed by members of the armed forces and three thousand Little League ballplayers. Finally came the guests of honor, riding in vintage 1914 automobiles, large poster boards mounted on each car to identify the occupants.

Twelve players in Braves uniforms and the son of the team's famous manager posed in the dugout for a commemorative photograph; after they were introduced, a large seventy-fifth anniversary emblem was unveiled on the pitcher's mound.[28]

The surviving Miracle Braves then trotted out, one by one, to take their positions on the field. Charlie Deal covered second base for Johnny Evers, while Red Smith positioned himself at third. Les Mann, Paul Strand and Herb Moran took spots in the outfield. Pitchers Lefty Tyler, Bill James and Dick Crutcher walked to the mound while Hank Gowdy and Bert Whaling grabbed their catcher's mitts and walked to home plate.

Rabbit Maranville, who had missed the parade to the ballpark because of a previous commitment, was the last to take the field, and the crowd applauded as he scooped up grounders and fired perfect strikes to Butch Schmidt at first base with an agility that belied his having recently turned sixty. The crowd cheered when it was announced he would demonstrate his famous basket catch. Hank Gowdy tossed the ball high in the air toward Maranville, who cupped his hands at his waist and let the ball plop into his glove before playfully twisting his cap sideways, as had been his usual custom.[29] Maranville's only complaint was that he was just getting warmed up when the proceedings were halted so the regular game could begin.

Over the next few years, each of the Miracle Braves passed on, just as

Johnny Evers had. The thinning ranks of the survivors was remembered on the fiftieth anniversary in 1964—Bill James was still around at that point, as were Paul Strand, Charlie Deal, Red Smith and a couple of others.[30] But the group gradually faded away—the last member, Jack Martin, died in 1980; he was also one of the last who could claim a memory of Johnny Evers as a lightning-quick, razor-tongued whirling dervish at the middle of the diamond.

There are no highlight reels of Johnny Evers, the man who refused to lose. The man who battled hardships off the field as ferociously as he fought opponents on it. He will have to live in our imagination as "The Kid from the Collar City." "The Trojan." "Iron Jawn." "The Crab." Always young, always fighting, often exasperating, but always entertaining. Always seeking an edge to win a game and giving the last ounce of everything he had for the game he loved.

Which is as it should be.

Notes

Chapter One

1. *Boston Globe*, June 1, 1951.
2. *Boston Globe*, January 24, 1950.
3. *New York Tribune*, August 26, 1869. There were whispers that Troy's exit was staged because of wagering on the game. The Red Stockings went undefeated in 1869, finally losing their first game on June 14, 1870, to the Brooklyn Atlantics. The team had played against other professional and semi-professional teams from Boston to San Francisco. The Red Stockings disbanded after the 1870 season and the core of the team became the Boston Red Stockings—today's Atlanta Braves, via Boston and Milwaukee.
4. Lipman "Lip" Pike was one of the first professional baseball players and one of its first slugging stars. Reportedly a devastating bad ball hitter, he played from the mid–1860s to well into the 1870s, and stories of his hitting feats lasted long after his career ended. After he retired, he became prominent in Tammany Hall politics and owned a haberdashery. Pike played his last game for New York in 1887, a one-game farewell performance. He died in 1893 of heart disease at the age of 48. Steve Bellan played four years for Troy, two in the National Association. A native of Cuba, Bellan was a star athlete at Fordham, and following a year with New York in 1873 (after Troy folded), he returned to Cuba and was heavily involved in the development of the game on the island. He died in Havana in 1932 (*Brooklyn Daily Eagle*, October 10, October 11, and October 12, 1893; *New York Herald*, October 11, 1893).
5. Those banned along with Craver were star pitcher Jim Devlin, outfielder George Hall and utility infielder Al Nichols. Although it was never proven that Craver threw games, he had previously been dismissed by the Chicago White Stockings for gambling in 1870. He was the only player who refused to cooperate with the National League's investigation. His baseball career over, Craver returned to Troy, where he became a police officer. When Craver died in Troy of heart trouble in June 1901, no mention was made either of his playing for Louisville or the scandal that ended his career (*Troy Northern Budget*, June 23, 1901).
6. *Troy Record*, August 28, 2001. Kelly learned the game after his father's death, and the family moved again to Paterson, New Jersey. He was the game's highest paid player, won two National League batting titles, led the league in doubles and runs scored three times, and retired with a lifetime batting average of .308.
7. *Spalding's Official Baseball Guide, 1883*; *Sports Illustrated*, July 2, 1990. New York and Philadelphia had been charter members of the National League, but were dropped after the inaugural season of 1876 when the teams refused to finish the schedule after falling out of contention. Troy and Worcester were also promised annual exhibition games featuring major league teams. The San Francisco Giants have in recent years acknowledged their roots in both New York and Troy—after winning the 2010 World Series, the Giants arranged to have the trophy displayed in Troy for several days in recognition of their ties to the city.
8. Tom Evers played one game in 1882 for the Baltimore Orioles of the major league American Association at age thirty, and 109 of

112 games for Washington of the Union Association two years later. He led the league in errors, but also finished second in putouts and assists. Second base is widely considered the most difficult baseball position for a left-handed thrower. The Union Association was a vanity league of sorts founded by Henry Lucas, the son of a St. Louis real estate tycoon. When Lucas's team ran away with the pennant thanks to a 94–19 record, the league folded. Lucas moved his team to the National League and finished last in 1885, with a record of 36–72. A year after that he was out of baseball.

9. *Troy Northern Budget*, August 24, 1902.

10. *Albany Evening Journal*, October 14, 1914.

11. *Sporting Life*, January 2, 1915; *Troy Record*, March 29, 1947.

12. *Baseball Magazine*, February 1915.

13. *Baseball Magazine*, September 1911.

14. John J. Evers and Hugh S. Fullerton, *Touching Second: The Science of Baseball* (Chicago: Reilly & Britton, 1910; reprint, Jefferson, NC: McFarland, 2004).

15. *Baseball Magazine*, September 1911. (Emphasis on "my" in italics added by the author.)

16. *New York Sun*, November 22, 1914; *Troy Record*, November 10, 2010; United States Census, 1900.

17. *New York Tribune*, January 24, 1915; *Milwaukee Sentinel*, July 6, 1947.

18. *Amsterdam Evening Recorder*, March 27, 1902. The *Recorder* noted, "Jack Evers of Troy, well known in Amsterdam as a baseball and football player, has joined the New York league team for a trial. He is a very clever youngster and his Amsterdam friends are sure that he will be able to make good in such fast company."

19. *New York Herald*, January 22, 1911.

20. *Amsterdam Evening Reporter*, May 10, 1902.

21. *Troy Northern Budget*, May 11, 1902.

22. *New York Tribune*, January 24, 1915.

23. *Syracuse Evening Telegram*, June 6, 1902; *Sporting Life*, June 14, 1902.

24. *Auburn Daily Bulletin*, June 7, 1902; *Sporting Life*, June 21, 1902.

25. *Auburn Bulletin*, July 15, 1902; *Sporting Life*, July 26, 1902.

26. Wiltse indicated after the season that he wanted to give up pitching in favor of becoming a first baseman. He changed his mind and won twenty-one games for Troy in 1903.

27. *Sporting Life*, July 12, 1902.

28. *Utica Herald Dispatch*, July 17, 1902.

29. *New York Tribune*, January 24, 1915.

30. Bierbauer had one hit in seven at bats. He was hitless in the second game he played

and booted two of his four chances in the field. When he made another error on the first ball hit to him in his third game with the team, he was pulled from the lineup. Legend has it that Bierbauer is responsible for the nickname of the Pittsburgh Pirates. He jumped Philadelphia for the Players League in 1890. After that league folded, most players went back to their original teams. However, Pittsburgh's National League team signed Bierbauer to a contract, which Bierbauer's old team labeled an act of "piracy." The nickname stuck (*Gloversville (N.Y.) Daily Leader*, August 1, 1902; *Sporting Life*, August 9 and August 16, 1902).

31. *New York Tribune*, January 24, 1915.

32. *Troy Northern Budget*, August 24 and August 31, 1902.

33. *Chicago Tribune*, August 30, 1902. It was repeatedly claimed over the years that the Cubs never actually paid for Evers.

34. *New York Sun*, November 22, 1914.

Chapter Two

1. *Sporting News*, October 11, October 18, October 25 and October 30, 1886. What is often labeled as "The First World Series" began as a challenge to Al Spalding from Chris von der Ahe, president of the American Association champion St. Louis Browns, for a championship series between the Browns and Spalding's NL champions from Chicago. The two men agreed to a series of six games, three to be held in each city. St. Louis won four of the six games to capture the "championship."

2. The fence did not slope out to centerfield. Rather, it ended abruptly, making the deepest part of the park a separate rectangle. Ed Delahanty of the Philadelphia Phillies hit four home runs in a July 1896 game at West Side Grounds—the final two were inside-the-park shots that went over Bill Lange's head in center. Delahanty added a triple and two doubles the next day (*Chicago Tribune*, July 14 and July 15, 1896).

3. *Chicago Tribune*, February 1 and February 2, 1898. Even though he had hit .285 in 114 games, Anson accepted it was time to retire as a player and agreed to manage the New York Giants. Spalding almost did not have to release Anson. The two were traveling back from Europe in December 1897 on a German steamship, the *Saale*, when it was hit by a rogue wave that nearly washed the legendary ballplayer overboard. Anson managed to survive by clinging to the door pull of a bulkhead.

4. *Chicago Tribune*, October 16 and October 17, 1899; *San Francisco Chronicle*, April 17, 1900.

5. Spalding and his partner, John Walsh, retained ownership in West Side Grounds and rented it to the Cubs. In May, Hart bought out Walsh and several other stockholders, including Cap Anson, and assumed total control of the franchise (*Sporting Life*, May 31, 1902).

6. *Sporting Life*, May 16, 1903.

7. *Chicago Tribune*, August 31, 1902.

8. The Braves had thirteen straight winning seasons prior to Bergen's deed; they would have only one winning season in the thirteen years afterward. Marty Bergen was widely regarded as the best catcher in the major leagues and a key reason for Boston's pennants in 1897 and 1898. Unfortunately, he was also mentally disturbed—dangerously so. In late April 1899, one of Bergen's sons died of diphtheria; he barely arrived in time for the burial, and the incident initiated a severe downward spiral. He abandoned the team for a brief time in September, and after the season, the Beaneaters reluctantly began making arrangements to trade him to the New York Giants. In an incident that evoked memories of Lizzie Borden's maniacal deed a few years earlier in a town not too far from Bergen's home, the Beaneaters catcher rose early in the morning on January 19, 1900, and readied a fire to warm the house. After gathering wood, he suddenly grabbed his ax and went berserk. Rushing into the bedroom, he bashed in his wife's head with the blunt end of the weapon, and then chased his screaming children until he caught and killed both of them. Bergen then grabbed a straight razor and slashed his throat so violently that he nearly decapitated himself. Teammate Billy Hamilton and Philadelphia Athletics manager Connie Mack—who lived nearby—were the only baseball figures to attend the funeral (*Boston Globe*, April 26, April 28, September 27, October 10 and October 20, 1899, and January 20 and January 21, 1900; *Sporting Life*, December 9 and December 30, 1899; *Sports Illustrated*, June 4, 2001).

9. One of the best demonstrations of the difficulty in relying on players was typified by outfielder Davy Jones, who had been purchased by Chicago from Rockford of the I.I.I. (Indiana, Illinois, Iowa) League on September 11, 1901, but jumped the team for the American League four days later without appearing in a game for Chicago. A few weeks into the 1902 season, Jones grew disenchanted with Browns manager Jimmy McAleer and jumped back to the Cubs. For all of his jumping contracts, Jones earned the nickname "Kangaroo" (*Milwaukee Journal*, September 14, 1901; *Sporting Life*, February 22, 1902).

10. *Boston Globe*, July 15, 1894. Lowe's record performance came on May 30, 1894, against Cincinnati at Congress Street Grounds, where Boston played while their home field was being rebuilt after being destroyed by fire. Two of Lowe's home runs came in one inning. The game was the second of a double-header—Lowe was hitless in six at bats in the first game (*Boston Globe*, May 31, 1894).

11. *Chicago Tribune*, March 27, 1902.

12. *The Sporting News*, March 22, 1934.

13. *Chicago Tribune*, September 2, 1902.

14. *Sporting Life*, May 26, 1917.

15. *Boston Globe*, January 4, 1917.

16. *Sporting Life*, September 20, 1902.

17. *Chicago Tribune*, September 16, 1902.

18. *St. Louis Republic*, October 5 and October 6, 1902.

19. *Sporting Life*, October 18, 1902.

20. *Sporting Life*, October 25, 1902.

21. *Chicago Tribune*, January 12, 1903.

22. *Sporting Life*, October 11, 1902.

23. *Chicago Tribune*, March 8, 1903.

24. *Chicago Tribune*, March 12, 1902.

25. *Chicago Tribune*, March 13, 1903.

26. *Sporting Life*, March 14, 1903.

27. *Sporting Life*, April 18, 1903.

28. *Chicago Tribune*, March 14, 1903.

29. *Baseball Magazine*, April 1914. A note in *Sporting Life* said that Selee considered Evers "a comer" (*Sporting Life*, April 18, 1903).

30. *Kansas City Star*, April 13, 1903; *Chicago Tribune*, April 13 and April 14, 1903.

31. *Sporting News*, March 28, 1903.

32. *Chicago Tribune*, April 11 and April 15, 1903.

33. *Chicago Tribune*, April 17, 1903.

34. *Chicago Tribune*, April 18, 1903.

35. *Chicago Tribune*, April 19, 1903.

36. *Chicago Tribune*, April 22, 1903. Evers also played shortstop in an exhibition game on April 20 against the University of Illinois. He made one error in that game (*Chicago Tribune*, April 21, 1903).

37. *Chicago Tribune*, May 4, 1903.

38. *Chicago Tribune*, June 14, 1903.

39. *Chicago Tribune*, June 29, 1903.

40. *Chicago Tribune*, July 8, 1903.

41. *Chicago Tribune*, July 9, 1903.

42. *Chicago Tribune*, July 10, 1903. The other nominee for captain was Doc Casey.

43. *Chicago Tribune*, July 12, 1903.

44. *Sporting Life*, July 18, 1903. Lowe signed to manage Denver in the Western League while he recuperated and planned a comeback in 1904 (*Sporting Life*, August 8, 1903).

45. *Sporting Life*, August 1, 1903.

46. *Sporting Life*, September 19, 1903.

47. *Sporting Life*, November 21, 1903.

Chapter Three

1. *Sporting Life*, October 22, 1904.
2. *Chicago Tribune*, December 13, 1903; *St. Louis Republic*, December 13, 1903. The teams also swapped catchers, with rookie Larry McLean going to St. Louis and thirty-one-year-old Jack O'Neill coming to the Cubs.
3. Evers and Fullerton, *Touching Second*.
4. *Sporting Life*, March 5, 1904.
5. *Sporting Life*, April 9, 1903.
6. *Pittsburgh Press*, October 4, 1907; John J. Evers, *How To Play Second Base* (New York: Spalding's Athletic Library, 1920).
7. Chance had a bad ankle, Kling a split finger and O'Neill's toe was nearly severed by a spiking in one of the team's last exhibition games, in Omaha. On April 19, the Cubs resorted to using twenty-nine-year-old Tom Stanton, a local player from St. Louis who had played in the Texas League a few years earlier. The Cardinals stole nine bases off him. Casey volunteered to catch the next game and Stanton never played again. After bad defense at third cost the team a couple of games, Selee moved Casey back to his normal position and employed Fred Holmes, who had caught once for the Giants in 1903. But Holmes also was victimized by base stealers and released after one game, at which point Johnny Kling returned to the lineup (*Chicago Tribune*, April 20, 1904; *Sporting Life*, April 23 and May 14, 1904).
8. *Chicago Tribune*; May 1, May 2, May 4 and May 5, 1904. The triple play came after Frank Chance had unsuccessfully bunted at two pitches. He then hit a line drive that was caught, and two Cubs runners were caught off base as well. Chance spent the entire morning before the next game working on his bunting.
9. *Chicago Tribune*, May 21, 1904. Three days later, Mathewson and Weimer again dueled, this time for eleven innings in a game finally called because of darkness with the score tied, 1–1. The Cubs loaded the bases with one out in the ninth, but Evers grounded back to Mathewson, who got a force play at the plate, and Jack O'Neill popped out to end the inning. Evers made a great play to keep the Giants from scoring in the seventh—with a runner on third, New York's Frank Bowerman hit a pop-up behind first base, and Evers made a long run to catch it. He then whirled and made a perfect throw to home plate to catch the runner from third, who had tagged up in an attempt to score (*Chicago Tribune*, May 24, 1904).
10. *Chicago Tribune*, June 5, 1904.
11. *Chicago Tribune*, June 11, 1904.
12. *Chicago Tribune*, June 12, 1904.
13. *Chicago Tribune*, June 14, 1904. Evers collected the only other hit off Mathewson. Mordecai Brown earned the win.
14. *Chicago Tribune*, June 15, 1904.
15. *Pittsburgh Press*, July 5, 1904.
16. *Chicago Tribune*, July 27, 1904. Miller Huggins had made a great fielding play on a line shot hit by Joe Tinker, knocking the ball down, but his throw was dropped by the first baseman. Nevertheless, umpire August Moran called Tinker out and the Cubs stormed the field. Chance shoved Moran, which earned him an ejection, further inciting the crowd. After fifteen minutes of arguing, Moran threatened forfeit and the game finally resumed. Glass bottles were thrown onto the field several times during the game, and Moran had to be escorted away by police. Moran afterward claimed he had called Tinker out after he left the base and was tagged—but the Cubs countered he had only left the base after being told by Moran he was out. James Hart called Moran incompetent and declared he would not allow him to umpire at West Side Grounds again, even if that meant forfeiting every game.
17. *Sporting Life*, September 3 and September 10, 1904.
18. *Chicago Tribune*, April 23, 1905.
19. *Chicago Tribune*, June 14, 1905.
20. *Chicago Tribune*, June 25, 1905.
21. *Chicago Tribune*, August 25, 1905; *Sporting Life*, September 9, 1905. Both teams scored a run in the thirteenth inning. It was so hot that after the fifteenth inning Reulbach had to be sponged down and fanned with towels so he could return to the mound. Tully Sparks pitched a complete game for the Phillies, allowing nineteen hits. Reulbach allowed thirteen.
22. *Chicago Tribune*, July 22, 1905.
23. *Chicago Tribune*, July 6, 1905.
24. *Chicago Tribune*, July 30, 1905.
25. *Chicago Tribune*, July 1, 1905.
26. *Sporting Life*, July 15, 1905.
27. *Chicago Tribune*, July 29, 1905.
28. *Sporting Life*, August 12 and August 19, 1905. The plan was for Selee to summer in Colorado and winter in New Mexico.
29. The total raised was $3,640.25. Selee was paid $640.25 immediately and provided with $125 per month for twenty-four months (*Sporting Life*, October 28, 1905).
30. *Chicago Tribune*, July 16, 1905.
31. *Chicago Tribune*, July 30, 1905. Charles Taft, who like Murphy was from Ohio, had married into money—his wife was the sole heir of her late father, industrialist David Sinton.
32. *Chicago Tribune*, September 23, September 24 and September 25, 1905. Roger Bresnahan was ejected in the fifth inning of the first

game over a called strike three. After Sam Mertes was kicked out in the eighth, McGraw took his place. Joe Tinker was also ejected for arguing after he came off the base receiving a wide throw.

33. *Chicago Tribune*, October 9, 1905; *St. Louis Republic*, October 9, 1905.

34. *Sporting Life*, September 30, 1905.

Chapter Four

1. *Chicago Tribune*, October 17, 1905; *Sporting Life*, October 28, 1905.

2. *Sporting Life*, October 28, 1905. The best-of-seven series had been won by the Cubs in five games and generated more than $26,000 in revenue, which was spilt between the two teams.

3. There were also rumors that Selee was interested in managing the St. Louis Cardinals. Instead he managed the Western League team in Pueblo, Colorado, where he was living (*Chicago Tribune*, December 14, 1905).

4. *Sporting Life*, October 21, 1905.

5. *New York Times*, October 26, 1919.

6. *Sporting Life*, April 7, 1906.

7. *Sporting Life*, October 13, 1906. Evers earned only one ejection all season, along with Chance, for insulting an umpire from the bench on April 16. That same day, Joe Tinker got into a fistfight with a Reds fan as the Cubs left the ballpark in Cincinnati (*Chicago Tribune*, April 17, 1906).

8. *Chicago Tribune*, October 21, 1905. The Cubs also acquired outfielder Jimmy Sebring, who had hit the first home run in World Series history off Cy Young as a twenty-one-year-old with the Pittsburgh Pirates. Sebring was playing for the outlaws in Williamsport of the Tri-State League and would never appear in a Cubs uniform.

9. *Chicago Tribune*, December 16, 1905.

10. *Chicago Tribune*, April 13, 1906.

11. *Chicago Tribune*, April 14, 1906.

12. *Chicago Tribune*, April 26, 1906.

13. *Chicago Tribune*, May 8, 1906.

14. *Chicago Tribune*, May 21, 1906.

15. *Chicago Tribune*, May 22 and May 23, 1906.

16. *Chicago Tribune*, May 25, 1906.

17. *Los Angeles Times*, September 22, 1912.

18. *Chicago Tribune*, June 2, 1906.

19. *Sporting Life*, June 16, 1906.

20. *Sporting Life*, June 2, 1906; *Chicago Tribune*, June 7, 1906. There have been stories over the years asserting that Chance had acquired Harper in order to destroy his career—supposedly because Harper had beaned Chance one too many times. That seems doubtful. Harper did hit Chance three times in one game

in 1904, but he was nearly cut by Cincinnati in spring training in 1906 and had a reputation as one who would avoid work if he could still draw a paycheck. He suffered the two injuries, and after the season, the *Sporting Life* reported that he had reported to Chicago "in poor shape." After his hand was injured, he "did not attempt to get back in the game." Instead, it was said he had been satisfied to pull his salary while running his shoe shop. In addition, his obituary in *The Sporting News* states that his career ended when he could not reach agreement with the Cubs on a contract—if he had been blackballed by Chance, it was not mentioned. Harper was loaned to Columbus of the American Association for the 1907 season so he could get back into shape, but he showed no inclination to do so and was returned to the Cubs, who released him (*Sporting Life*, October 13 and December 1, 1906, June 1, 1907; *The Sporting News*, October 11, 1950). Rob Neyer published an excellent analysis of the Chance-Harper story in his book, *Rob Neyer's Big Book of Baseball Legends* (New York: Touchstone, 2008).

21. *Chicago Tribune*, June 7, 1906. Giants fans grew so disgusted that one threw a lemon at Roger Bresnahan, who was playing centerfield. Bresnahan insisted that the fan be arrested.

22. *Chicago Tribune*, June 8, 1906. The Cubs were worried that rain would stop the game after the first inning. When the Giants began delaying tactics, Chance ordered his men to swing at the first pitch. Jimmy Slagle and Jimmy Sheckard both deliberately got themselves tagged out after collecting hits in the fourth inning. The Cubs scored nineteen runs and also left twelve men on base.

23. *Chicago Tribune*, June 25, 1906.

24. *Albany Knickerbocker News*, February 12, 1947.

25. *Chicago Tribune*, July 3, 1906.

26. *The Sporting News*, January 7 and January 14, 1905.

27. *Chicago Tribune*, October 10, 1906; *The Sporting News*, October 13, 1906; *Sporting Life*, October 13, 1906.

28. *Chicago Tribune*, October 11, 1906.

29. *Baseball Magazine*, November 1912.

30. *Chicago Tribune*, October 12, 1906.

31. *Chicago Tribune*, October 13, 1906.

32. *Chicago Tribune*, October 14, 1906.

33. *Chicago Tribune*, October 15, 1906.

34. Ibid.

Chapter Five

1. *Sporting Life*, October 27 and December 29, 1906.

2. Indoor baseball was not dissimilar to

softball played today except the game was staged in a gymnasium. The diamond was smaller and the pitcher generally threw underhanded. The ball was usually a little larger than a regulation baseball and not quite as hard. The game was most popular as a winter activity in the East, especially before basketball gained in popularity.

3. *Sporting Life*, December 29, 1906. Henry Mathewson had made his major league debut on September 28, 1906, against the St. Louis Cardinals, pitching an inning in relief of his brother. He made one start, on October 5 against Boston. Even though he allowed only five hits, he lost, 7–1, largely because he issued fourteen bases on balls. His final major league appearance came on May 4, 1907, when he again pitched an inning, against Brooklyn, this time in relief of Hooks Wiltse. Mathewson succumbed to tuberculosis in July 1917. Another Mathewson brother, Nicholas, committed suicide in 1909 at age nineteen. He had played on an indoor baseball team run by Christy (*Sporting Life*, January 23, 1909).

4. *Fresno Morning Republican*, November 5, 1906. Once the major league season ended it was common practice for big league players to barnstorm, play semi-pro or winter ball, or sign with a team that was still playing its season, such as the Pacific Coast or California State Leagues. Frank Chance played in the Pacific Coast League in 1904 and the California State League in 1905 after the end of the Cubs season.

5. *Sporting Life*, March 9, 1907.

6. *Sporting Life*, April 27, 1907.

7. *Sporting Life*, March 23, 1907.

8. *Chicago Tribune*, April 12, 1907.

9. *Brooklyn Daily Eagle*, July 21, 1929.

10. *Chicago Tribune*, May 22, 1907; *New York Sun*, May 22, 1907. Bresnahan was suspended by McGraw for a week after he tried to blame Art Devlin for one of his errors after the game, resulting in a heated argument between the two. When McGraw intervened, Bresnahan turned on McGraw (*Sporting Life*, June 1, 1907).

11. *Chicago Tribune*, July 9, 1907. Chance was suspended for a week (*Chicago Tribune*, July 10, 1907; *Sporting Life*, July 27, 1907).

12. *Sporting Life*, August 24, 1907.

13. *Sporting Life*, August 24, 1907; *Chicago Tribune*, August 25, 1907.

14. *Chicago Tribune*, August 13 and August 14, 1907.

15. *New York World Telegram*, December 9, 1936.

16. *Chicago Tribune*, August 22, 1907. Frank Chance had left the team for a few days for a scouting trip and to recover from the flu. Jimmy Sheckard ran the team while Chance was ab-

sent, as he had when Chance was suspended for the incident in Brooklyn. Taylor pitched the entire game in the 12–4 loss. Taylor's final appearance for the Cubs was an inning in relief of Chick Fraser against the St. Louis Cardinals on September 2 (*Chicago Tribune*, September 3, 1907).

17. *Sporting Life*, September 28, 1907.

18. *Brooklyn Daily Eagle*, June 15 and June 16, 1907; *Chicago Tribune*, June 15, 1907.

19. *Chicago Tribune*, September 1, 1907.

20. *Chicago Tribune*, August 12, 1907.

21. *Chicago Tribune*, September 9, 1907. Three Pirates were also kicked out of the same game.

22. *Chicago Tribune*, September 24, 1907. Del Howard started the triple play by catching a line drive with runners at first and second. He touched first for the second out and then threw to Tinker covering second for the final out. It was then realized that Howard could have run over to second and easily completed an unassisted triple play.

23. *Chicago Tribune*, October 6, 1907.

24. *Sporting Life*, October 12, 1907.

25. *Chicago Tribune*, October 12, 1907.

26. *Chicago Tribune*, October 13, 1907.

27. *Chicago Tribune*, October 14, 1907.

28. *Chicago Tribune*, October 18, 1907.

29. *Chicago Tribune*, October 18, October 20 and October 21, 1907.

30. *Troy Record*, October 21, 1907; *Sporting Life*, November 2, 1907.

31. *Sporting Life*, September 28, 1907.

Chapter Six

1. *Sporting Life*, January 25 and May 2, 1908. Dovey also investigated the possibility of acquiring Tommy Leach from Pittsburgh, but settled for ex–Cincinnati Reds star Joe Kelley, drafting him from Toronto of the International League.

2. *Sporting Life*, February 1, 1908. W.A. Phelon called Kling the "Oliver Twist" of baseball—he always asked for more.

3. *Sporting Life*, February 29, 1908.

4. *Sporting News*, April 2, 1908.

5. *Sporting Life*, February 15 and April 4, 1908. Chance had to be fitted with blunt spikes and umpire Hank O'Day said Chance would not be allowed to wear them in a game. Chance abandoned the custom shoes for a looser fitting one on his sore foot (*Sporting Life*, April 11 and April 25, 1908).

6. *Sporting Life*, May 23, 1908.

7. *Chicago Tribune*, April 15, 1908.

8. *Chicago Tribune*, April 23, 1908.

9. *Chicago Tribune*, May 4, 1908.

10. *Pittsburgh Press*, May 7, 1908.

11. *Chicago Tribune*, May 7, 1908; *Pittsburgh Press*, May 7, 1908.

12. *Chicago Tribune*, May 10, 1908; *Pittsburgh Press*, May 10, 1908.

13. *Chicago Tribune*, May 13, 1908.

14. *Chicago Tribune*, May 16, 1908.

15. *Chicago Tribune*, May 22, 1908.

16. *Sporting Life*, June 6, 1908.

17. *Chicago Tribune*, June 3, 1908. Sheckard turned his ankle sliding into third but the Cubs were allowed to use newly acquired back-up catcher Doc Marshall as a courtesy runner. Sheckard returned to the game when the Cubs took the field in the top of the next inning (*Chicago Tribune*, June 2, 1908).

18. *Sporting Life*, August 1, 1908. Three decades later, Jimmy Sheckard publicly stuck to the story of the exploding ammonia bottle, mentioning neither Zimmerman nor their fight. By that time, Sheckard was loading milk cans onto trucks for a dairy in Lancaster, Pennsylvania, after having been wiped out financially in the stock market crash of 1929 (*The Sporting News*, March 7, 1940).

19. *Chicago Tribune*, June 5, 1908.

20. *New York Globe*, July 24, 1908. For a brief time, Sheckard wore glasses with smoked lenses to protect his eyes.

21. *Auburn Citizen*, June 27, 1908.

22. *Sporting Life*, August 1, 1908.

23. *Chicago Tribune*, July 18, 1908. In order to score, Tinker had to run past Heine Zimmerman, who was coaching third base for Chicago and tried to hold him at third. Zimmerman had lost sight of the ball and grabbed Tinker as he rounded the bag. Tinker, however, knew where the ball was and broke free of Zimmerman's grasp to cross the plate. Tinker had only two hits in forty-six at bats off Mathewson during the 1904 and 1905 seasons. Mathewson was quoted as saying, "[Tinker's] weakness was a low curve on the outside, and I fed him low curves so often that I had him looking like an invalid every time he came to the plate." Then, according to Mathewson, Tinker took to using a longer bat and setting up his stance a little further from the plate. After making that adjustment, Tinker hit Mathewson regularly, with averages of .364 or better for five of the next six seasons—his best was .556 (ten for eighteen) in 1911 (Arthur R. Ahrens, "Tinker vs. Matty: A Study In Rivalry," *Baseball Research Journal* 3, 1974).

24. *Chicago Tribune*, July 19, 1908. Chicago trailed, 3–0, going to the bottom of the eighth. Tinker hit a two-run double off Hooks Wiltse, scoring Pat Moran and Johnny Evers, to win the game in the ninth.

25. *Chicago Tribune*, July 28, 1908. As in Chicago, the players' benches in Brooklyn were sunken below the level of the playing field. Evers was banished for riding Rigler from the bench. He was already angry at Rigler for calling him out for missing third base while attempting to score during the first game.

26. *Sporting Life*, August 15, 1908.

27. *Chicago Tribune*, August 11, 1908. Overall pitched well despite receiving news that his wife was seriously ill. As he prepared to leave for California after the game, he received another telegram letting him know his wife was recovering, so he decided to remain with the team.

28. *Pittsburgh Press*, September 5, 1908; *Chicago Tribune*, September 5, 1908; *Sporting Life*, September 12, 1908. Gill had played most of the season with Grand Rapids of the Central League, whose player-manager was Bobby Lowe. Gill had also been involved in a controversy in his first major league game, against New York on August 26. Gill hit a smash to Giants third baseman Art Devlin, who could not handle it. The ball then caromed off Pirates base runner Tommy Leach and Hank O'Day called Leach out, which was an incorrect ruling. The Pirates successfully argued for a reversal of the call, which upset the Giants. During the confrontation with O'Day, both Gill and Honus Wagner advanced an extra base, further infuriating the Giants (*Pittsburgh Press*, August 27, 1908; *Chicago Tribune*, August 27, 1908).

29. *New York Herald*, September 19, 1908.

30. *Chicago Tribune*, September 19, 1908.

31. Evers and Fullerton, *Touching Second*.

32. *Sporting Life*, August 22, 1908.

33. *Sporting Life*, July 18, 1908.

34. The Giants had a record of 87–50, Chicago was 90–53 and Pittsburgh was 88–54. The Cubs trailed the Giants by six percentage points.

35. *New York Times*, September 24, 1908.

36. *New York Journal American*, March 28, 1947.

37. *The Sporting News*, April 9, 1947. The article represented Joe Tinker's reminiscence, printed in the wake of Evers's death. To this point in the narrative, he and Evers's versions mesh pretty well.

38. *Chicago Tribune*, September 24, 1908; *New York Evening Telegram*, September 23, 1908; *New York Sun*, September 24, 1908; *New York Herald*, September 24, 1908; *New York Evening World*, September 24, 1908; Report of umpire Hank O'Day to National League president Harry G. Pulliam, September 23, 1908.

39. *New York Times*, September 24, 1908.

40. Lawrence Ritter, *The Glory of Their Times* (New York: Macmillan, 1966).

41. *Brooklyn Daily Eagle*, September 27, 1908. Reulbach was masterful in the first game of the twin bill, allowing only five hits. He struck out seven and walked only one in an easy 5–0 victory. The Cubs star was even better in the second game, allowing only four hits, three of them to Harry Lumley, and pitching a second shutout for a 3–0 victory. After allowing a first-inning single, Reulbach did not allow another hit until the seventh, and did not allow an extra base hit all day. Prone to fits of erratic control, Ed Reulbach nevertheless remains among the most underrated pitchers of the twentieth century. Six-foot-one and two hundred pounds, Reulbach was an imposing presence on the mound—hiding his pitches with a high leg kick and big wind-up. When he had his curve going he was almost impossible to hit. He had no set pitching philosophy, opting instead to study hitters and pitch to them accordingly. He won seventeen straight games over the 1906 and 1907 seasons. In 1909 he would fashion a fourteen-game winning streak, allowing only fourteen runs in those games and an average of just over four hits per game. He led the National League in winning percentage three seasons in a row. He once pitched a twenty-inning complete-game victory and threw forty-four consecutive scoreless innings at one point in 1908.

42. *Chicago Tribune*, October 1, 1908; *Buffalo Evening News*, March 23, 1925.

43. *Chicago Tribune*, October 5, 1908.

44. *Chicago Tribune*, October 9, 1908.

45. *Baseball Magazine*, November 1908.

46. In *Touching Second*, Hugh Fullerton and Johnny Evers placed this event in the 1907 World Series with Jimmy Slagle as the victim, but it happened in the opening game of the 1908 Series, with Hofman in center.

47. *Chicago Tribune*, October 11, 1908.

48. *Chicago Tribune*, October 12, 1908.

49. *Chicago Tribune*, October 13, 1908.

50. *Chicago Tribune*, October 14, 1908. This story was often told by Evers as being a tag out of Cobb in 1907 World Series, but Cobb was never picked off at second base in the World Series. Crawford was caught off second during this game, so this is the likely source of the story, especially if combined with Cobb's attempt to steal second.

51. *Chicago Tribune*, October 15, 1908.

52. *Chicago Tribune*, October 17, 1908. Frank Chance added $100 to the pot so that Semmens, Kroh and Durbin could receive $500 apiece.

53. *Chicago Tribune*, October 19, 1908.

Chapter Seven

1. *Chicago Tribune*, January 13, 1909. Evers had announced his engagement to Helen Fitzgibbon the previous October, shortly after his arrival in Troy for yet another hero's welcome following the 1908 season (*Sporting Life*, October 26, 1908).

2. *Sporting Life*, February 6, 1909.

3. *Troy Northern Budget*, January 17, 1909; *Sporting Life*, January 30, 1909.

4. *Sporting Life*, February 6, 1909.

5. *Troy Times*, March 27, 1909. The offer was for two weeks of appearances of ten minutes' duration each evening.

6. *Chicago Tribune*, February 7, 1909; *Sporting Life*, February 13, 1909. There was an intense baseball war being waged between the Pacific Coast League and the upstart California State League, which was operating as an outlaw. There were rumors that the outlaws had offered Chance $25,000 to throw his lot in with them. Harry Pulliam stepped in and spoke to Chance, to the irritation of Charles Murphy, who charged Pulliam with interfering with negotiations.

7. *Troy Times*, March 8, 1909.

8. *Troy Northern Budget*, March 14, 1909.

9. *Chicago Tribune*, January 5, 1909.

10. *Chicago Tribune*, March 21 and March 22, 1909.

11. *Sporting Life*, March 5, 1910.

12. *Chicago Tribune*, April 29, 1909.

13. *Chicago Tribune*, April 30, 1909.

14. *Chicago Tribune*, May 3, 1909. The Cubs were also missing Johnny Kling—in one inning the Pirates stole six bases, with Honus Wagner stealing second, third and home off Pat Moran and Ed Reulbach. Reulbach said Moran was not to blame, insisting, "That was my fault, not his. I was pitching rotten ball, and I wasn't even guarding my bases. They were half way down the line before I even thought about them, and Pat had no chance to get them" (*Sporting Life*, May 29, 1909).

15. *Chicago Tribune*, May 4, 1909.

16. *Chicago Tribune*, May 5, 1909.

17. *Chicago Tribune*, May 6, 1909. The previous day's game could have been protested by Pittsburgh had they lost.

18. *Chicago Tribune*, May 8, 1909; *Sporting Life*, May 15, 1908. The National Commission was attempting to curtail the practice of players holding out in contract disputes, even though Evers's case did not really fit into that category. He had really been granted a leave of absence, but the Cubs had failed to formally file that notice.

19. *Chicago Tribune*, July 1, 1909; *Pittsburgh*

Press, June 29 and June 30, 1909. A major streetcar strike was settled the morning before the first game at Forbes Field.

20. *Boston Evening Transcript*, July 6, 1909; *Sporting Life*, July 24, 1909. One of Selee's Boston stars, Herman Long, was also dying of tuberculosis in Denver, and would succumb in September (*Sporting Life*, September 25, 1909).

21. *Sporting Life*, August 7, 1909. The bullet tore through Pulliam's skull, dislodging his eyes from their sockets, but did not kill him immediately. It was speculated that Pulliam had been on the floor for a couple of hours before he was discovered after he had struggled to call the hotel's front desk. He lived until the next morning, briefly regaining consciousness a couple of times.

22. *Sporting Life*, September 25, 1909.

23. *Chicago Tribune*, October 7, 1909. Harry Steinfeldt was the only regular in the lineup for the season's final game.

24. *Sporting Life*, October 30, 1909. John Jr. was born October 17, 1909, the day before Evers returned.

25. *Sporting Life*, December 11, 1909.

26. *Sporting Life*, December 25, 1909.

27. *Chicago Tribune*, May 3, 1910. Taft said he attended the game specifically to see Wagner play.

28. *Sporting Life*, April 16, 1910; *Chicago Tribune*, May 5, 1910.

29. *Chicago Tribune*, May 10, 1910.

30. *Sporting Life*, August 1, 1908.

31. *Sporting Life*, May 28, 1910.

32. *Baseball Magazine*, September 1913.

33. *Baseball Magazine*, September 1913.

34. *Sports Illustrated*, December 3, 2012.

35. Tim Layden, "Tinker to Evers to Me," *Baseball Magazine*, February 1915.

36. *Chicago Tribune*, June 2, 1910. Evers would later claim he missed five weeks, but he was only absent from the lineup from May 22 through May 31. A number of books and articles place the accident in 1911, but that is incorrect (*Baseball Magazine*, September 1913).

37. *Chicago Tribune*, June 3, 1910.

38. *Chicago Tribune*, June 5, 1910.

39. *Chicago Tribune*, June 7 and June 8, 1910.

40. *Pittsburgh Press*, June 26, 1910. Barney Dreyfuss was so angry about Evers's behavior that he pressured new league president John Heydler to punish Evers, but Heydler refused (*Sporting Life*, July 16, 1910).

41. Evers would strike out only eighteen times during the entire 1910 season.

42. *Chicago Tribune*, July 7, 1910.

43. The poem was supposedly written as Adams was either on his way to the Polo Grounds

or on his way out the door and was requested to add another eight lines to his column. The final game played between the Cubs and Giants before the poem was published was on July 11 at West Side Grounds, and the contest featured a "Tinker to Evers to Chance" double play. Ironically, there had been an attempt earlier in the inning for an "Evers to Tinker to Chance" twin killing, but Tinker threw the ball wildly against the stands behind first base after forcing the Giants runner at second. There was no game played by either the Cubs or Giants on July 12 (*Chicago Tribune*, July 12, 1910).

44. *Chicago Tribune*, July 15, 1910.

45. Tim Wiles, director of research at the Baseball Hall of Fame, discovered no fewer than twenty-nine such poems printed during the 1910 season, all seemingly in response to Adams's poem.

46. *Chicago Tribune*, July 20 and July 28, 1910. Evers was ejected for arguing when Bill Klem ruled that Johnny Kling had left third base early on a short fly ball.

47. *Sporting Life*, August 13, 1910.

48. *Chicago Tribune*, August 14, August 28, August 29 and September 11, 1910. In the August 27 game, Evers fielded a line shot that grazed pitcher Lew Richie's mitt, spearing the ball on the fly over the second base bag and then stepping on the base to retire Al Bridwell, who had taken off for third. Evers then noticed Red Murray was halfway to home plate and began running toward third to complete what he thought would be an unassisted triple play (which it would not have been, since Richie got a glove on the line drive before Evers caught it). Murray woke up and ran back toward third, so Evers threw the ball to Heine Zimmerman to complete the triple play.

49. *Chicago Tribune*, September 23, 1910; *New York Sun*, September 23, 1910. Interestingly, Evers's hometown newspaper, the *Troy Daily Times*, did not mention the incident at all in its article about the game.

50. *Chicago Tribune*, October 2 and October 3, 1910; *Cincinnati Enquirer*, October 2, 1910.

51. *Chicago Tribune*, October 3, 1910.

52. *Chicago Tribune*, October 3 and October 4, 1910.

53. *Chicago Tribune*, October 6, 1910.

54. *Chicago Tribune*, October 9, 1910.

55. *Chicago Tribune*, October 10, 1910.

56. *Chicago Tribune*, October 11, 1910

57. *Chicago Tribune*, October 16, 1910.

58. *Baseball Magazine*, September 1913; *Chicago Tribune*, December 21, 1910.

59. *Sporting Life*, November 5, 1910.

60. *Sporting Life*, November 12, 1910.

61. *Chicago Tribune*, December 6, 1910.
62. *Brooklyn Daily Eagle*, December 25, 1910.
63. *New York Herald*, January 22, 1911.
64. *Chicago Tribune*, April 27, 1911.
65. *Chicago Tribune*, April 29, 1911.
66. *Chicago Tribune*, May 5, 1911.
67. *Chicago Tribune*, May 6, 1911.
68. *Chicago Tribune*, May 7, 1911.
69. *Sporting Life*, May 20 and May 27, 1911.
70. *Pittsburgh Press*, May 26, 1911.
71. *Baseball Magazine*, September 1913.
72. *Chicago Tribune*, June 12, 1911.
73. *Sporting Life*, August 12, 1911.
74. *Chicago Tribune*, August 6, 1911; *Sporting Life*, August 12, 1911.
75. *Chicago Tribune*, August 7, 1911.
76. *Chicago Tribune*, August 8, 1911.
77. *Chicago Tribune*, August 22, 1911.
78. *Sporting Life*, September 16, 1911.
79. *Chicago Tribune*, September 9, 1911.
80. *Chicago Tribune*, September 16 and September 17, 1911.

Chapter Eight

1. *Sporting Life*, February 3, 1912.
2. *Sporting Life*, January 6, 1912.
3. *Chicago Tribune*, July 2, 1911. Chance had returned to the lineup after a long absence only the day before. His return had been against doctor's orders; at one point he tripped reaching for a grounder in practice and had to be helped to the clubhouse suffering from concussion-like symptoms.
4. *Sporting Life*, January 13, 1912.
5. *Syracuse Herald*, February 2, 1912; *Chicago Tribune*, February 2, 1912; *Troy Daily Times*, February 3, 1912. Doyle, yet another New York State League product recommended by Evers, hit .282 for the Cubs after moving into the lineup when Evers suffered his nervous breakdown and Heine Zimmerman was shifted to second base. Evers traveled to Syracuse to attend Doyle's funeral.
6. *Chicago Tribune*, April 12, April 13 and April 14, 1912.
7. *Chicago Tribune*, April 17 and April 18, 1912.
8. *Chicago Tribune*, May 7, 1912. A month later, Jimmy Sheckard and Johnny Evers pulled off a play that enraged Kling. With runners at first and second, a Braves batter lifted a fly ball to Sheckard, who raced under it, only to let it drop. The Braves runners held, thinking the ball would be caught, and Sheckard fired the ball to Evers, who was standing near second base. Evers tagged the runner at second and then touched the bag to force out the runner who had remained at first. Kling argued with

enough persistence to earn an ejection (*Chicago Tribune*, June 5, 1912).
9. *Sporting Life*, May 25, 1912.
10. *Chicago Tribune*, May 31, 1912; *Pittsburgh Press*, May 31, 1912. Chance had wanted Leifield for some time and hoped he would prove an able replacement for Jack Pfiester.
11. *Chicago Tribune*, July 9, 1912.
12. *Chicago Tribune*, July 16, 1912. Brown would not start another game that season.
13. *Chicago Tribune*, July 12, 1912. National League president Thomas Lynch was in attendance, and Evers accused Rigler of showing off for his boss. After allowing Evers "plenty of time to express in fiery language his opinion of umps in general and Rigler in particular," Rigler took out his pocket watch as a warning that Evers had better get moving to the clubhouse, which he finally did.
14. *Chicago Tribune*, July 22 and July 23, 1912.
15. *Chicago Tribune*, August 13, 1912.
16. *Chicago Tribune*, August 18, 1912.
17. *Chicago Tribune*, September 4, 1912; *Pittsburgh Press*, September 4, 1912. The *Pittsburgh Press* declared, "If there is one unpopular player in Pittsburgh, the individual is Johnny Evers." During the game, Solly Hofman made his first-ever appearance against the Cubs, playing centerfield and collecting one hit in four at bats.
18. *Chicago Tribune*, September 9, 1912; *Sporting Life*, September 21, 1912.
19. *Chicago Tribune*, September 11, 1912.
20. *Chicago Tribune*, September 18, 1912. Before he was wheeled into the operating room, Chance signed a letter lifting a season-ending suspension he had given Frank Schulte.
21. *Sporting Life*, September 28, 1912. In the same game, Heine Zimmerman caught a foul ball between home and third and catcher Jimmy Archer bumped into him. Zimmerman responded by angrily spiking the ball into the ground.
22. *Chicago Tribune*, September 29, 1912.
23. *Chicago Tribune*, September 29 and September 30, 1912. Chance admitted that Charles Murphy had asked him on August 15 whether he wanted to manage the Cubs in 1913, and that he had replied, "I'd rather not." Murphy then told Chance he'd like to see him return, if he could. Chance insisted he was feeling much better after his operation and was ready to run the team again. Chance had also been angered by Murphy's insistence on a no-drinking policy for the Cubs; Chance felt Murphy was implying that the Cubs had failed to win the pennant because he had lost control of his players (*Sporting Life*, October 5, 1912).
24. *Chicago Tribune*, October 24, 1912. Chance, who was making roughly $10,000 per

year, said he'd be willing to sign a contract for as little as $1,200.

25. *Chicago Tribune*, October 13, 1912.

26. *Chicago Tribune*, October 23, 1912.

27. *Chicago Tribune*, October 24, 1912.

28. *Chicago Tribune*, October 25, 1912; *Sporting Life*, November 2, 1912.

29. *Chicago Tribune*, October 27, 1912.

30. *Chicago Tribune*, October 31, 1912.

31. *Sporting Life*, November 9, 1912.

32. *Sporting Life*, November 9, 1912.

33. *Chicago Tribune*, November 10, 1912. The Reds only claimed Chance as insurance in case they failed to work out a deal with Murphy for Tinker.

34. *Chicago Tribune*, November 15, 1912. O'Day had recently been fired as manager of the Cincinnati Reds.

35. *Chicago Tribune*, December 12, 1912.

Chapter Nine

1. *New York Sun*, November 30, 1912.

2. *Sporting Life*, March 22, 1913.

3. *Chicago Tribune*, December 12, 1912.

4. *Sporting Life*, February 15, 1913.

5. *Chicago Tribune*, January 7, 1913; *Sporting Life*, January 18, 1913.

6. *Sporting Life*, February 1, 1913.

7. *Sporting Life*, February 22, 1913.

8. *Chicago Tribune*, April 5, 1913; *Sporting Life*, April 12, 1913. Evers and Murphy claimed that Semmens already had a verbal agreement with Tinker at higher pay, and was looking for any excuse to leave the Cubs.

9. *Chicago Tribune*, April 11, 1913.

10. *Chicago Tribune*, April 13, 1913.

11. *Chicago Tribune*, April 18, 1913.

12. *Chicago Tribune*, April 21, 1913. Redlands Field was renamed Crosley Field in 1934 and remained home to the Cincinnati Reds until 1970.

13. *Chicago Tribune*, April 22, 1913. Both Evers and Roger Bresnahan were chased from the game in the eleventh inning for becoming too boisterous in their complaints to the umpires.

14. *Chicago Tribune*, April 23, 1913. Evers was batting sixth in the lineup and removed himself for pitcher Bert Humphries. Tommy Leach had pinch-hit for the pitcher, so Evers left him in the game and removed leadoff hitter Otis Clymer. He then put in Art Phelan to bat leadoff and play second base. The situation became so confusing that the umpires had to ask the official scorer a couple of times who was supposed to be at bat.

15. *Chicago Tribune*, April 24, 1913. Evers tried to have the game called at the end of the eighth with the Cubs leading, 5–3—the teams had agreed to end the game no later than five o'clock so the Reds could catch a train for their road trip. The eighth inning ended at eight minutes to five, but Evers was unable to persuade the umpires to dispense with the ninth inning.

16. *Chicago Tribune*, April 30, 1913.

17. *Chicago Tribune*, May 2, 1913. Tinker would continue collecting old Cubs teammates as the season wore on. The same day Brown pitched for the Reds for the first time, it was announced that Johnny Kling had agreed to terms with Cincinnati. Later that summer, Tinker also acquired Jimmy Sheckard from St. Louis.

18. *Chicago Tribune*, May 4, 1913.

19. *Chicago Tribune*, May 11, 1913.

20. *Chicago Tribune*, May 13, 1913.

21. *Chicago Tribune*, May 14, 1913.

22. *Chicago Tribune*, June 14, June 15 and June 16, 1913. There had also been rumors Zimmerman had feigned illness in order to get out of playing.

23. *Chicago Tribune*, June 18, 1913.

24. *Chicago Tribune*, June 19, 1913.

25. *Chicago Tribune*, June 20, 1913.

26. *Chicago Tribune*, June 21 and June 22, 1913.

27. *Chicago Tribune*, July 3, 1913.

28. *Chicago Tribune*, July 4, 1913.

29. *Chicago Tribune*, July 4, 1913. Tinker was so shaken by Semmens's death that he turned the team over to Marty Berghammer for the game against the Cubs.

30. *Baseball Magazine*, September 1913.

31. *Sporting Life*, July 19, 1913.

32. *Chicago Tribune*, July 7, 1913.

33. *Chicago Tribune*, July 12, 1913.

34. *Chicago Tribune*, July 30, 1913.

35. *Chicago Tribune*, August 24, 1913.

36. *Chicago Tribune*, August 22, 1913.

37. *Chicago Tribune*, August 7, 1913.

38. *Sporting Life*, August 2, 1913.

39. *Sporting Life*, August 30, 1913.

40. Vaughn would become a star, winning twenty or more games five times for the Cubs between 1914 and 1919.

41. *Sporting Life*, October 25, 1913.

42. *Sporting Life*, December 6, 1913.

Chapter Ten

1. *Chicago Tribune*, December 21, 1913.

2. *Chicago Tribune*, February 11, 1914.

3. *Chicago Tribune*, February 11, 1914.

4. *Chicago Tribune*, February 12, 1914.

5. *Sporting Life*, February 7, 1914.

6. *Boston Globe*, February 11, 1914.

7. *Brooklyn Daily Eagle*, February 11, 1914.

8. *Boston Globe*, February 12, 1914.

9. *Chicago Tribune*, February 13 and February 15, 1914. The owners probably had a reason to feel Evers might be willing to jump—he

had been one of the "All-Stars" recruited for a post-season trip to Australia in 1910 that Toledo, Ohio promoter Daniel Fletcher turned into an effort to launch a third baseball league composed of the game's best players. All players signing up for the tour also signed a contract with Fletcher's new league, Evers among them. At the end of the day, Fletcher's dreams got ahead of his reality and the idea folded before it really got started. Evers kept the $500 bonus he had received for the Australia trip, even though after he broke his leg, he could not have participated (*Sporting Life*, October 8 and October 22, 1910). See also David Pietrusza, *Major Leagues: The Formation, Sometimes Absorption and Mostly Inevitable Demise of 18 Professional Baseball Organizations* (Jefferson, NC: McFarland, 1991).

10. *Baseball Magazine*, April 1914.
11. *Chicago Tribune*, February 22, 1914.
12. *Boston Globe*, March 11, 1914.
13. *Boston Globe*, May 26, 1888.
14. *Boston Globe*, May 16 and July 15, 1894.
15. *Boston Globe*, January 17, 1915. If Stallings did come into possession of a two-dollar bill, he would tear off the corners in order to eliminate the jinx. He also insisted that all scraps of paper be picked up and all bats be lined up neatly in a row, and he banned yellow signs, or anything else yellow, at the ballpark.
16. *Sporting Life*, November 7, 1914.
17. Walter "Rabbit" Maranville, *Run, Rabbit, Run* (Cleveland, OH: Society for American Baseball Research, 1991).
18. *Boston Globe*, March 14, March 15 and March 16, 1914.
19. *Boston Globe*, March 27, 1914.
20. The swastika symbol was used by American Indian tribes and other cultures as a good-luck charm prior to its adoption by the German Nazi Party in 1921. The research into the Braves' caps began with discovery of Rabbit Maranville and Johnny Evers wearing them in photographs from the George Bain collection in the Library of Congress. Baseball researcher Tom Sheiber analyzed the photographs to determine when and where they were taken. It was his conclusion that the photographs were taken at Ebbets Field on Opening Day 1914. This would certainly jibe with the superstitious nature of George Stallings.
21. *Boston Globe*, April 15, 1914.
22. *Boston Globe*, April 20, 1914. Ruth allowed two runs in his three innings pitched and struck out two batters.
23. *Chicago Tribune*, May 12, 1914.
24. *Boston Globe*, May 22, 1914; *Chicago Tribune*, May 22, 1914.

25. *Chicago Tribune*, May 23, 1914.
26. *Boston Globe*, December 27, 1914.
27. Maranville, *Run Rabbit Run*.
28. *Boston Globe*, June 13, 1914.
29. *Boston Globe*, June 20 and June 21, 1914. It was the third home run Hess had hit in the past two seasons, and the fifth of his career, an impressive number for a pitcher in the dead ball era. Hess, who had batted .313 for the Braves in 1913, was used a dozen times as a pinch-hitter by Stallings in 1914.
30. *Boston Globe*, June 23, 1914.
31. *Boston Globe*, December 20, 1914.
32. *Boston Globe*, June 30, 1914.
33. *Boston Globe*, July 4, 1914.
34. *Boston Globe*, July 8, 1914.
35. *Boston Globe*, January 24, 1950. The same day the Braves were embarrassed by Buffalo, the Cincinnati Reds were no-hit by Dayton of the Class B Central League (*Boston Globe*, July 8, 1914).
36. *The Sporting News*, August 6, 1914. Weart was the first secretary of the Baseball Writers Association of America.
37. *Boston Globe*, July 29, 1914.
38. *The Sporting News*, August 13, 1914.
39. *Boston Globe*, August 5, 1914.
40. *Boston Globe*, August 7, 1914.
41. *Troy Daily Times*, August 7, 1914; *Boston Globe*, August 8, 1914; *The Sporting News*, August 13, 1914.
42. *New York Press*, August 9, 1914.
43. *Boston Globe*, August 9, 1914; *Sporting Life*, August 22, 1914.
44. *Boston Globe*, August 9, 1914.
45. *Boston Globe*, August 11, 1914.
46. *Boston Globe*, August 12, 1914.
47. *New York Times*, August 4, 1914; *The Sporting News*, August 13, 1914.
48. *New York Times*, August 16, 1914; *Boston Globe*, August 16, 1914.
49. *The Sporting News*, August 20, 1914.
50. *Chicago Tribune*, August 27, 1914. Tener fined Zimmerman and Evers one hundred dollars each and Maranville fifty dollars (*The Sporting News*, September 3, 1914).
51. *Boston Globe*, September 7, 1914.
52. *Boston Globe*, September 6, 1914.
53. *Boston Globe*, September 8, 1914; *New York Times*, September 8, 1914.
54. *Boston Globe*, September 9, 1914; *New York Times*, September 9, 1914.
55. *Boston Globe*, September 10, 1914.
56. *Troy Times*, September 18, 1914; *Boston Globe*, September 18, 1914.
57. *Boston Globe*, September 17, 1914.
58. *Boston Globe*, September 25, 1914.
59. *Boston Globe*, September 28, 1914.

60. *Chicago Tribune*, September 30, 1914.

61. *Boston Globe*, September 30, 1914. Boston's record after the game on July 15 was 33–43. They finished the season with a record of 94–59. They also had four tie games during this streak.

62. *Boston Globe*, October 7, 1914. Evers rode with Smith to the hospital in ex-teammate Ed Reulbach's automobile.

63. *New York Times*, October 7, 1914.

64. *Boston Globe*, October 7, 1914.

65. Evers garnered fifty votes to forty-four for Maranville. Interestingly enough, Evers received fewer votes from his teammates than did Maranville. Bill James finished third overall with thirty-three votes. Eddie Collins of the Philadelphia Athletics easily captured the American League MVP Award (*Boston Globe*, October 4, 1914).

66. *Chicago Tribune*, September 30, 1914. Chance made his prediction the night the Braves clinched the pennant, as he was boarding the train along with his wife for Los Angeles after having resigned as manager of the New York Yankees and announcing his retirement from baseball.

67. *The Sporting News*, October 15, 1914.

68. *Philadelphia Evening Ledger*, October 9, 1914.

69. *Philadelphia Evening Ledger*, October 9, 1914.

70. *Philadelphia Evening Ledger*, October 10, 1914; *New York Times*, October 10, 1914. The *New York Times* estimated that perhaps ten thousand were perched on rooftops ringing the stadium.

71. *Boston Globe*, January 17, 1915.

72. *New York Times*, October 10, 1914.

73. As a pitcher, Dinneen won three games in the 1903 World Series against the Pittsburgh Pirates. He would eventually serve as an American League umpire for twenty-nine seasons, officiating in eight World Series and the first major league All-Star Game in 1933.

74. *The Sporting News*, October 15, 1914.

75. *Boston Globe*, October 10, 1914. Rose Fitzgerald Kennedy, daughter of ex-mayor Fitzgerald, would become the mother of future President John Fitzgerald Kennedy. The Royal Rooters dated back to the 1890s and gained fame during the 1903 World Series when they began singing a mildly popular Broadway tune, "Tessie," to encourage the Red Sox after they had fallen behind the highly-favored Pittsburgh Pirates three games to one. As Boston rallied, eventually winning the Series five games to three, they kept it up and began changing some of the lyrics in the song to harass particular Pirates

players. The Rooters were led by saloon owner Michael "Nuf Ced" McGreevey, whose nickname reportedly was derived from his warning for arguments to end in his bar. His establishment, the 3rd Base Saloon, is thought by some to be the first "sports-themed" bar. In 2004, a Boston band, the Dropkick Murphys, recorded "Tessie" as their tribute to the Red Sox, who subsequently won their first World Series since 1918. The band's leader helped lead a successful effort to reopen McGreevey's saloon in 2008.

76. *New York Times*, October 10, 1914. There were also rumors that Mack was angry at Bender because he had supposedly been given a day off late in the season to scout the Braves and had blown off the assignment.

77. *Philadelphia Evening Ledger*, October 10, 1914.

78. *Philadelphia Evening Ledger*, October 10, 1914.

79. *Amsterdam (N.Y.) Daily Democrat and Recorder*, January 30, 1948.

80. *Philadelphia Evening Ledger*, October 10, 1914.

81. *Baseball Magazine*, February 1915.

82. *Philadelphia Evening Ledger*, October 13, 1914.

83. *Boston Globe*, January 17, 1915.

84. *Sporting Life*, October 24, 1914.

85. *New York Times*, October 14, 1914.

86. *Washington Post*, October 14, 1914. Jack Johnson was the first African American heavyweight in boxing history. Mack's reference compared Johnson's perceived smugness and lack of humility to the attitude of Stallings.

87. *Philadelphia Evening Ledger*, October 14, 1914.

88. *Boston Globe*, January 17, 1915.

Chapter Eleven

1. *Troy Daily Times*, October 19, 1914; *Auburn Citizen*, October 20, 1914; *Sporting Life*, October 24, 1914.

2. *Boot and Shoe Recorder*, November 7, 1914.

3. *Troy Daily Times*, October 20, 1914.

4. *Troy Daily Times*, October 21, 1914; *Sporting Life*, October 31, 1914.

5. *Sporting Life*, October 31, 1914.

6. *Baseball Magazine*, February 1915. Joe Evers was playing in the Tri-State League and had already appeared in his only game in the major leagues, as a pinch-runner for the New York Giants in 1913.

7. *Sporting Life*, December 5, 1914.

8. *New York Times*, December 12, December 15 and December 22, 1914; *New York Evening Telegram*, December 11, 1914; *Schenectady Gazette*, December 25, 1914; *Sporting Life*, January 2, 1915.

9. *Syracuse Post-Standard*, February 8, 1915.

10. To commemorate the Braves' victory over the Athletics, the National Commission issued an enamel button to each player. It was gold and decorated with a wreath around the edge, had a diamond in the middle, and bore the inscription, "World's Champions 1914." A pair of rings owned by Evers and Rabbit Maranville that appear to have been modeled on these buttons surfaced years later. Maranville's ring once resided in Barry Halper's famous baseball memorabilia collection. The Evers ring was auctioned by his family in 2011 and sold for $45,000. The origin of the jewelry is unclear, but today they are considered to be the first World Series rings (*Sporting Life*, January 9, 1915).

11. *Boston Globe*, December 25, 1914.

12. *Sporting Life*, April 3, 1915. Magee hit fifteen home runs for the Phillies in 1914 but only two for Boston in 1915.

13. *Brooklyn Daily Eagle*, April 18, 1915.

14. *Troy Times*, April 27, 1915. Evers was certain he had broken his ankle.

15. *Troy Daily Times*, June 4, 1915; *New York Times*, June 4, 1915. The Troy players struck when they were not paid, forcing the Trojans to forfeit three straight games. The league approached Evers, who agreed to take over the team, along with two local men who would run it.

16. *Troy Daily Times*, June 28, 1915.

17. *Boston Globe*, June 28, 1915.

18. *New York Times*, June 29, 1915; *Boston Globe*, June 29, 1915.

19. *New York Times*, June 30, 1915.

20. *Sporting Life*, July 24, 1915.

21. *Chicago Tribune*, July 23, 1915; *Sporting Life*, July 31, 1915.

22. *Brooklyn Daily Eagle*, July 28, 1915; *New York Times,* July 28, 1915; *Boston Globe*, July 28, 1915.

23. *Sporting Life*, August 14, 1915.

24. *New York Times*, August 8, 1915; *Sporting Life*, August 14, 1915.

25. *Boston Globe*, August 18 and August 19, 1915; *Sporting Life*, August 28, 1915.

26. *Brooklyn Daily Eagle*, September 3, 1915; *Boston Globe*, September 4, 1915. Evers was replaced by Eddie Fitzpatrick, and he too was ejected before the inning was over. As Fitzpatrick was replaced by Dick Egan, Butch Schmidt got into it with Byron and was sent packing as well. Gaffney blamed Evers for the incident.

27. *Chicago Tribune*, September 14, 1915.

28. The St. Louis Browns of the American League also merged with their Federal League counterpart.

29. *Sporting Life*, January 15, January 29 and

February 12, 1916. Gaffney retained control of Braves Field. Haughton had won national collegiate football championships at Harvard in 1910, 1912 and 1913. His career record as a college coach was 97–17–6 and he was inducted into the College Football Hall of Fame in 1951.

30. *Sporting Life*, March 11, 1916.

31. *Boston Globe*, May 19, 1916. Evers complained that Reds pitcher Pete Schneider was throwing an emery ball. After Bill Klem refused to remove the ball from play, Evers yelled to teammate Ed Reulbach that he should use it too.

32. *Sporting Life*, July 15, 1916. It was only Evers's second ejection of the year.

33. *The Sporting News*, October 6, 1948.

34. *Chicago Tribune*, July 26, 1916.

35. *Sporting Life*, August 12, 1916.

36. *Boston Globe*, August 4 and August 5, 1916.

37. *Boston Globe*, August 7, 1916.

38. *Boston Globe*, August 23, 1916; *Sporting Life*, September 2, 1916. Evers claimed he had been yelling something to teammate Ed Konetchy that the umpire misinterpreted as being aimed at him.

39. *Sporting Life*, September 16, 1916.

40. *Boston Globe*, December 18, 1916.

41. *Sporting Life*, October 21, 1916. There were also rumors that the Cubs wanted Frank Chance, who had made a comeback as manager of the pennant-winning Los Angeles Angels of the Pacific Coast League.

42. *Sporting Life*, December 23, 1916.

43. *Troy Times*, February 10, 1917; *Sporting Life*, February 24, 1917.

44. *Schenectady Gazette*, March 24, 1917.

45. *Sporting Life*, March 24, 1917.

46. *Baseball Magazine*, September 1917.

47. *Boston Globe*, May 8, 1917. Stallings married the widow of Bud Sharpe, a former teammate and close friend who had died a year earlier at Stallings's plantation. Sharpe had retired from baseball due to ill health and Stallings hired him to run "The Meadows."

48. *Albany Knickerbocker News*, August 14, 1943.

49. *Boston Globe*, July 12, 1917.

50. *Philadelphia Evening Ledger*, July 12 and July 13, 1917; *Boston Globe*, July 13, 1917.

51. *Baseball Magazine*, September 1917.

52. *Chicago Tribune*, August 21, 1917; *Philadelphia Evening Ledger*, August 21, 1917.

Chapter Twelve

1. *Schenectady Gazette*, November 16, 1917. The Phillies asked waivers on Evers in November.

2. *Boston Globe*, February 14, 1918.

3. *Troy Daily Times*, February 14, 1918;

Syracuse Post Standard, February 15, 1918; *Binghamton Press*, February 28, 1918.

4. *Boston Globe*, February 22 and March 2, 1918.

5. *Boston Globe*, March 10, 1918.

6. *Boston Globe*, March 25, 1918.

7. *Boston Globe*, March 13, March 14, March 15 and March 17, 1918; *Troy Daily Times*, August 5, 1920.

8. *Boston Globe*, March 18, 1918.

9. *Boston Globe*, March 25, 1918.

10. *Boston Globe*, March 31, 1918.

11. *Boston Globe*, April 1, 1918.

12. *Boston Globe*, April 2 and April 3, 1918; *Brooklyn Daily Standard Union*. April 3, 1918.

13. *Boston Globe*, April 5, 1918.

14. *Brooklyn Daily Standard Union*, April 9, 1918; *New York Sun*, April 9, 1918; *Boston Globe*, April 9, 1918.

15. *Boston Globe*, April 13, 1918; *Troy Daily Times*, April 13, 1918. Evers hit .211 in seven exhibition games and handled twenty-six chances without committing an error.

16. *Boston Globe*, April 14, 1918.

17. *Boston Globe*, April 15 and April 16, 1918; *Troy Daily Times*, April 16, 1918.

18. *Albany Evening Journal*, May 9, 1918. The Red Sox went on to win the World Series against the Cubs that September, the last they would capture for eighty-four years.

19. *New York World*, May 9, 1918.

20. *Boston Globe*, May 8, 1918.

21. *New York Tribune*, June 4, 1918; *New York Sun*, June 4, 1918; *Troy Times*, June 4, 1918.

22. *Troy Daily Times*, June 17, 1918. About his performance, it was said "he covered so much ground that he left no doubt in the minds of spectators that he is fully capable of major league activity" (*New York World*, July 1, 1918).

23. *New York Herald*, July 28, 1918.

24. *Troy Daily Times*, December 19, 1918.

25. *Boston Globe*, March 5, 1919. Evers went to Albany along with New York Yankees part-owner Colonel Tillingham Huston to speak before the state legislature.

26. *Troy Daily Times*, May 1 and May 15, 1919.

27. *Troy Times*, April 19, 1919; *Schenectady Gazette*, April 25, 1919.

28. *Schenectady Gazette*, April 25, 1919. Joe appeared as a pinch-runner for the Giants against the Phillies and was caught on an attempted double steal (*New York Times*, April 25, 1913).

29. *Troy Times*, May 14, May 19, May 25 and May 31, 1919.

30. *Troy Daily Times*, September 26, 1919.

31. *Boston Globe*, October 19, 1919.

32. *Troy Daily Times*, October 13, 1919.

Evers returned home in time to see his semiprofessional team capture the final game of its championship series before a crowd of five thousand. Babe Ruth had played an exhibition a day earlier at Center Island Park and drew only two thousand.

33. *Troy Times*, October 13, 1919.

34. *New York Times*, October 26, 1919.

35. *Boston Globe*, April 29 and May 7, 1920.

36. *New York Times*, May 9, 1920; *Boston Globe*, May 9, 1920.

37. *Boston Globe*, May 10 and May 11, 1920. Evers's telegram read, "Sorry, but you can realize what a great opportunity this is for me and the only one that would make me change my plans. Best of good luck to yourself and the team. J.J. Evers." He was paid $1,000 per month by the Giants (John J. Evers player file, National Baseball Hall of Fame Museum and Library).

38. *New York Herald*, May 11, 1920.

39. *New York Evening Telegram*, May 9, 1920.

40. *New York Evening Telegram*, May 19, 1920.

41. *New York Times*, August 9, 1920.

42. *Brooklyn Standard Union*, August 15, 1920. Evers earned a suspension and Youngs a $50 fine (*Brooklyn Standard Union*, August 17, 1920).

43. *Chicago Tribune*, October 29, 1920; *New York Times*, October 29, 1920.

44. *The Sporting News*, December 9, 1920. The Cubs also reserved his services for 1922 and 1923 at $12,500 per year (John J. Evers player file, National Baseball Hall of Fame Museum and Library).

45. *Chicago Tribune*, January 11, 1921.

46. *Chicago Tribune*, January 25, 1921. Stallings resigned at the end of the 1920 season after suffering through four straight losing seasons. He was replaced by his former top coach, Fred Mitchell, who had recently been replaced by Johnny Evers as manager of the Cubs. Stallings then joined with Braves business manager Walter Hapgood to purchase the Rochester franchise in the International League, with Stallings becoming manager (*Boston Globe*, November 7 and December 1, 1920; *Rochester Democrat Chronicle*, December 6, 1920).

47. *Chicago Tribune*, January 26 and February 8, 1921. Herzog was accused of conspiring to throw a game on August 31, 1920, along with Hendrix, who was supposed to pitch the game in question. Cubs manager Fred Mitchell got wind of the plot and substituted Grover Cleveland Alexander instead. During questioning about that incident, Herzog revealed his knowledge of the 1919 World Series fix, which was being investigated by a Chicago grand jury. Herzog proclaimed his innocence but told what he knew about the Black Sox. Hendrix

did not pitch again for the Cubs that season, although he continued to travel with them.

48. *New York Times*, January 28, 1921.

49. *Brooklyn Daily Eagle*, January 13, 1921.

50. *Chicago Tribune*, March 23, 1921.

51. *Chicago Tribune*, March 28, 1921.

52. *San Francisco Chronicle*, April 2 and April 3, 1921; *San Francisco Examiner*, April 3, 1921; *Chicago Tribune*, August 3, 1921. Evers had promised to play five innings. He had also participated in the team's first intra-squad exhibition game on Catalina because no other position players had yet reported. He played shortstop and made an error on the first ball hit to him (*Chicago Tribune*, March 5, 1921).

53. *Chicago Tribune*, April 14, 1921.

54. *Chicago Tribune*, June 1, 1921.

55. *Chicago Tribune*, July 10, 1921.

56. *Chicago Tribune*, July 11, 1921.

57. *Chicago Tribune*, July 27, 1921. Tyler caught on with the Rochester Colts of the International League, which were run by his old Braves manager, George Stallings. Tyler, who had appeared in only ten games for the Cubs before his release, made his debut for Rochester on August 8, and won four of five decisions, but never recovered his form and never again appeared in the major leagues (*Rochester Democrat and Chronicle*, August 9, 1921).

58. *Chicago Tribune*, August 4 and August 5, 1921.

59. *Auburn (N.Y.) Citizen*, April 14, 1922.

60. *Chicago Tribune*, April 28, 1922.

61. Evers did play second base in an exhibition game in Erie, Pennsylvania, on July 5, collecting a hit and turning a double play. He also appeared briefly in the second game of the postseason Chicago City Series, playing the eighth inning at third base after starter Eddie Mulligan committed two errors in the seventh during a 10–3 loss (*Chicago Tribune*, July 6 and October 6, 1922).

62. *Chicago Tribune*, December 19, 1922.

63. *Syracuse Journal*, March 2, 1923.

64. *Geneva (N.Y.) Daily Times*, March 7, 1923.

65. *Chicago Tribune*, October 17, 1923.

Chapter Thirteen

1. *Boston Globe*, October 14, 1922, and December 12, 1922. Frazee at first denied that Chance was signed, or was becoming part owner. He also had to deny that a syndicate from Toronto was buying the franchise and moving it to Canada (*Boston Globe*, October 20, November 24 and December 7, 1922).

2. *Boston Globe*, April 19, 1923.

3. *Boston Globe*, July 8, 1923. They also lost to the Yankees on September 28 by a score of 24–4 (*Boston Globe*, September 29, 1923).

4. *Troy Times*, September 10, 1923.

5. *New York Times*, September 11, 1923.

6. *New York Times*, September 12, 1923.

7. *Chicago Tribune*, October 27 and October 28, 1923; *The Sporting News*, November 1, 1923.

8. *Chicago Tribune*, December 8, 1923.

9. *Chicago Tribune*, December 12, 1923.

10. *The Sporting News*, February 21 and February 28, 1924.

11. *The Sporting News*, March 6, 1924.

12. *New York Times*, April 13, 1924. Chance was further delayed in late March to have seven teeth extracted (*Troy Times*, April 1, 1924).

13. *New York Times*, April 14, 1924.

14. *The Sporting News*, April 24, 1924.

15. *The Sporting News*, April 24, 1924.

16. *The Sporting News*, May 8, 1924.

17. *Boston Globe*, May 16, May 18 and May 19, 1924. Helen Evers at first denied that her husband needed an operation. The couple's son had undergone the same procedure only five months earlier (*Troy Times*, January 14, 1924).

18. McClellan would come back late in the season after it was said he would be out all year, but the cancer returned the next year and he died in November 1925.

19. *Boston Globe*, May 20, 1924.

20. *Troy Times*, June 14, 1924.

21. *Binghamton (N.Y.) Times*, July 7, 1924.

22. *New York Sun*, July 9, 1924.

23. *Los Angeles Times*, September 16 and September 19, 1924. Some sources list Frank Chance's birthdate as September 9, 1876, while others list him as being born in 1877. On his World War I draft registration card, Chance lists 1876 as his birth year.

24. *Troy Times*, October 9, 1924.

25. *Troy Times*, October 13, 1924.

26. *Troy Times*, December 4 and December 5, 1924.

27. *Auburn (N.Y.) Citizen*, December 12, 1924.

28. *The Sporting News*, December 18, 1924.

29. *Troy Times*, February 17, 1925.

30. Letter from John Evers to Jack Hendricks, March 5, 1926, John J. Evers player file, National Baseball Hall of Fame.

31. *Troy Times*, September 22, 1926.

32. *Amsterdam (N.Y.) Evening Recorder*, December 21, 1928.

33. *Sporting News*, August 27, 1925.

34. *New York Sun*, December 17, 1927.

35. *Brooklyn Daily Eagle*, July 24, 1929.

36. *Boston Globe*, November 8, 1928.

37. *Boston Globe*, November 9, 1928.

38. *Schenectady Gazette*, November 9, 1928.

39. *Boston Globe*, November 10, 1928.

40. *Boston Globe*, November 14, 1928.

41. *Brooklyn Daily Eagle*, November 10, 1928.
42. *Brooklyn Daily Star*, December 21, 1928.
43. *Amsterdam (N.Y.) Evening Recorder*, December 21, 1928.
44. *Boston Globe*, February 13, 1929.
45. *Troy Times*, April 4, 1929.
46. *Boston Globe*, December 9, 1928.
47. *Boston Globe*, March 4, 1929.
48. *Boston Globe*, February 13 and February 27, 1929.
49. *Boston Globe*, April 19, 1929.
50. *Boston Globe*, May 19, May 20 and May 22, 1929. Joe Dugan and Earl Clark were flip-flopped in the batting order that day, but had missed that fact and batted in their usual turn. They were caught the second time they had done so, after Dugan singled, and McGraw found a reason to nullify the resulting base hit.
51. *Boston Globe*, June 1, 1929. Maranville said he was offered the job after Evers declined, but that he too turned it down.
52. *Boston Globe*, June 13, 1929.
53. *Boston Globe*, July 6, 1929.
54. *Boston Globe*, July 26, 1929.
55. *Boston Globe*, August 19, 1929.
56. *Boston Globe*, October 7, 1929. That same day, fifty-three-year-old Nick Altrock stroked a single as a pinch-hitter for the Washington Senators against the Boston Red Sox.
57. The thirty-three-year-old Hornsby had his last great season for the Cubs in 1929, hitting .380 with thirty-nine home runs, 156 runs scored and 149 runs batted in. He was named the National League's Most Valuable Player. Leg and foot injuries began taking their toll the next season, limiting him to 274 games over the next eight seasons.
58. *Boston Globe*, October 8, 1929.
59. *Boston Globe*, December 12, 1929.

Chapter Fourteen

1. *Brooklyn Daily Eagle*, June 21, 1931.
2. *Schenectady Union Star*, December 7, 1933.
3. *Troy Times*, April 8, 1931.
4. *Gloversville (N.Y.) Morning Herald*, January 14, 1932; *Troy Daily Times*, August 5, 1920.
5. *Schenectady Gazette*, February 28, 1934. Helen Evers claimed her husband had not kept his payments up to date, having paid only $250 over the previous year. The judge rejected Evers's claim that he had no source of income and ordered that the previous judgment remain intact.
6. *Troy Times*, April 19, 1930. Stack was born in Troy and worked for the local newspaper before taking a position with the Associated Press. He was forty-two years old at his death.
7. *Troy Times*, August 27, 1932.

8. *Troy Times*, January 20, 1933. The niece was the daughter of Johnny's brother, Edward.
9. *Albany Evening News*, January 31, 1935.
10. *Boston Globe*, April 23, 1935. Boston won 10–4. It was Ruth's seventh in-season appearance in Albany since 1928; he'd homered twice in one game in each of his three previous appearances. During the game, the Senators received word that utility infielder Malcolm Pickett, who had been hospitalized five days earlier with an undisclosed illness, had died. Pickett, in his first season with Albany, had married just before spring training (*Schenectady Gazette*, June 19, 1930; July 31, 1931; and April 24, 1934; *Rochester Democrat Chronicle*, April 23, 1935).
11. *New York Sun*, September 26, 1933. Pitts's performance against the Giants was somewhat over-hyped—he did drive in two runs, but those came off a fellow prisoner the Giants allowed to pitch the final two innings of the game.
12. *Brooklyn Daily Eagle*, June 5, 1935.
13. *New York Sun*, June 6, 1935; Associated Press Wirephoto, June 6, 1935.
14. *Syracuse Journal*, June 8, 1935.
15. *Troy Times Record*, June 7, 1935.
16. *Rochester Democrat*, June 11, 1935. Lehman was one of three brothers who founded the Lehman Brothers investment firm.
17. *Troy Times Record*, June 15, 1935.
18. Associated Press Wirephoto, June 18, 1935.
19. *Amsterdam (N.Y.) Daily Democrat and Recorder*, June 18, 1935.
20. *Troy Times Record*, June 20, 1935.
21. *Troy Times Record*, June 21, 1935.
22. *Troy Times Record*, June 24, 1935; *Gloversville and Johnstown (N.Y.) Morning Herald*, June 24, 1935.
23. *Brooklyn Daily Eagle*, June 29, 1935. Wilson had gotten off to a fast start at the plate for Albany, leading the International League in hitting at one point, but had slumped to a .263 batting average at the time of his sale.
24. *The Sporting News*, July 25, 1935. In early August, Pitts was hitting .217 when Joe Cambria declared that he would return as a regular in 1936 and receive a substantial raise in salary. Evers said, "I think the boy has exceeded expectations thus far. He has proved he can take it on the ball field. It is also possible he will develop into a better hitter" (*Amsterdam (N.Y.) Daily Democrat and Recorder*, August 3, 1935).
25. *Syracuse Journal*, July 22, 1935.
26. Pitts's funeral was attended by nearly five thousand people, with his textile mill baseball teammates serving as pall bearers.
27. *The Sporting News*, September 19, 1935.
28. *Amsterdam Evening Recorder*, January 16, 1936; *Utica Observer*, May 11, 1936. Evers

claimed more than ten thousand dollars in debts and no assets.

29. Bleecker Stadium is a sports complex built by the Works Progress Administration in the 1930s. More than three quarters of a million people attended various sporting events there in 1942. The stadium also hosted high school football games and the Albany Twilight League, an amateur baseball league that sent several players to the majors.

30. *Corning (N.Y.) Evening Leader*, August 14, 1936.

31. *Albany Evening News*, June 14, 1937.

32. *New York Sun*, June 29, 1937; *The Sporting News*, July 1, 1937.

33. *New York Post*, December 27, 1937.

34. Tim Wiles, "Reason for the Rhyme: Adams' 'Baseball's Sad Lexicon' Turns 100" (*Memories and Dreams* 32, Summer 2010). Adams had never met any of the three men he had immortalized in his verse. He asked columnist John Kieran to introduce him to Evers (*The Sporting News*, February 14, 1943).

35. *Albany Knickerbocker News*, December 8, 1938; *The Sporting News*, December 1, 1938.

36. *The Sporting News*, June 1, 1939; *Niagara Falls Gazette*, May 29, 1939.

37. The ten men in the photograph were Grover Cleveland Alexander, Eddie Collins, Walter Johnson, Napoleon Lajoie, Connie Mack, Babe Ruth, George Sisler, Tris Speaker, Honus Wagner and Cy Young.

38. *The Sporting News*, June 15, 1939.

39. *Boston Globe*, July 4, 1939.

40. *Boston Globe*, July 13, 1939.

41. *Albany Knickerbocker News*, July 11, 1939.

42. *Albany Knickerbocker News*, September 20, 1939. The playoffs pitted the top four teams at the end of the regular season in a two-round playoff. Maranville appeared in six regular-season games during the 1939 season, his first action since playing regularly for Elmira as player-manager in 1936. He collected only two hits in seventeen at bats.

43. *Albany Knickerbocker News*, August 25 and August 26, 1942.

44. *Troy Times Record*, January 12, 1943.

45. *Brooklyn Daily Eagle*, April 14, 1943.

46. *Troy Record*, January 15, 1944.

47. *Troy Times Record*, February 3 and February 8, 1943; *Troy Record*, April 24, 1944; *Albany Knickerbocker News*, April 26, 1944.

48. *Troy Record*, May 22, 1944.

49. *Troy Record*, June 21, 1944.

50. *Albany Knickerbocker News*, June 4, 1945.

51. *The Sporting News*, June 14, 1945.

52. *Albany Knickerbocker News*, April 24, 1946; *Gloversville (N.Y.) Leader Republican*, April 24, 1946.

Chapter Fifteen

1. *Troy Times Record*, January 16, 1943.

2. *Troy Record*, April 29, 1944.

3. *The Sporting News*, January 3, 1946.

4. *The Sporting News*, January 24, 1946.

5. *Boston Globe*, April 24, 1946.

6. *Albany Knickerbocker News*, April 24, 1946.

7. *Troy Times Record*, May 1, 1946.

8. *Troy Times Record*, November 9, 1946.

9. *Troy Times Record*, December 10 and December 11, 1946.

10. New York Department of Health, Certificate of Death, 13064–499.

11. *Troy Times Record*, March 28, 1947.

12. *New York Evening Post*, April 5, 1947.

13. *Gloversville (N.Y.) Morning Herald*, March 29, 1947.

14. Undated letter from Joe Tinker to Johnny Evers, 1947. Joyce Sports Research Collection, Hesburgh Libraries of Notre Dame.

15. *Troy Times*, March 29, 1947.

16. *Troy Times Record*, April 1, 1947.

17. *Troy Times Record*, July 22, 1947.

18. *Troy Times Record*, January 4, 1949.

19. *Albany Knickerbocker News*, January 29, 1949, and April 15, 1954.

20. *Boston Globe*, January 6, 1954.

21. *Boston Globe*, January 21, 1954.

22. *Chicago Tribune*, September 5, 1916. Mathewson had recently become manager of the Cincinnati Reds and was making his only pitching appearance for them. Mathewson won, 10–8, with both pitchers completing the game and allowing a combined thirty-four hits. Brown did pitch in the minor leagues through 1920.

23. Florida Death Records, 1877–1988.

24. *St. Petersburg Times*, January 15, 1956; *The Sporting News*, March 14, 1956.

25. Merkle played in the World Series for the New York Giants in 1911, 1912 and 1913, for Brooklyn in 1916 and for the Chicago Cubs in 1918. In addition, he appeared in one game near the end of the 1926 season for the New York Yankees.

26. *New York Daily News*, September 22, 1908.

27. Layden, "Tinker to Evers to Me."

28. *The Sporting News*, June 13, 1951. Those photographed in the dugout were Butch Schmidt, Bert Whaling, George Stallings, Jr., Les Mann, Red Smith, Dick Crutcher, Lefty Tyler, Herbie Moran, Charlie Deal, Paul Strand, Fred Mitchell, Hank Gowdy and Bill James.

29. *Boston Globe*, June 3, 1951.

30. *Baseball Digest*, October–November, 1964.

Bibliography

Archival Collections

Albany, New York, City Directories
Chicago, Illinois, City Directories
Cleveland Public Library Digital Collection
John J. Evers Collection, Hesburgh Libraries of the University of Notre Dame
Library of Congress—Prints & Photographs Collection
New York Passenger Lists
New York State Census, 1915, 1925
Player Files, National Baseball Hall of Fame and Library
San Francisco Historical Photograph Collection, San Francisco Public Library
Troy, New York, City Directories
United States Census, 1900, 1910, 1920, 1930, 1940

Articles

Ahrens, Arthur. "The Split Century." *Baseball Research Journal* 2, 1973.
___. "Tinker vs. Matty: A Study In Rivalry." *Baseball Research Journal* 3, 1974.
Amedio, Steve. "Hidden Treasure: One of Baseball's Most Important Artifacts Found in Albany." *Albany Sunday Gazette,* September 20, 1992.
Basenfelder, Donald. "Jimmy Sheckard, Once-Famous Outfielder of Cubs, at 61, Wrestles Ten-Gallon Milk Cans For His Living." *The Sporting News,* March 7, 1940.
Burr, Harold. "When McGraw and Evers Were Young Men, Rooters Heard Lots of Baseball." *Brooklyn Daily Eagle,* July 21, 1929.
Evans, Billy. "New Stories About Johnny Evers, Who Won a Pennant Single Handed." *Brooklyn Daily Eagle,* December 25, 1910.

Evers, John J. "My Latest Move in Major Company." *Baseball Magazine,* September 1917.
___. "Some Baseball Confessions by Johnny Evers, of the Braves." *New York Tribune,* January 24, 1915.
___. "When I Sat in the Bleachers." *Baseball Magazine,* September 1911.
Evers, John J., and George Stallings. "The Truth About John Evers' Historic Misplay." *Baseball Magazine,* February 1915.
Keetz, Frank. "Johnny Evers, the Find of the 1902 Season." *Baseball Research Journal* 12, 1983.
Lane, F.C. "The Gamest Player in Baseball." *Baseball Magazine,* September 1913.
Layden, Tim. "Tinker to Evers to Me." *Sports Illustrated,* December 3, 2012.
Lieb, Frederick. "'14 Braves Top '48 Team in Daring Deeds." *The Sporting News,* October 6, 1948.
Phelon, W.A. "Why The Braves Won and The Athletics Lost the Championship of the World." *Baseball Magazine,* December 1914.
Price, Bill. "Braves Field." *Baseball Research Journal* 7, 1978.
Reulbach, Edward. "Reminiscences of a World Series Pitcher." *Baseball Magazine,* November 1912.
Rothe, Emil. "History of the Chicago City Series." *Baseball Research Journal* 8, 1979.
Stack, C.P. "A Day With John Evers." *Baseball Magazine,* February 1915.
Wiles, Tim. "Reason for the Rhyme: Adams' 'Baseball's Sad Lexicon' Turns 100." *Memories and Dreams* 32 (Summer 2010).

Books

Achorn, Edward. *Fifty-Nine in '84: Old Hoss Radbourn, Barehanded Baseball, and the*

Greatest Season a Pitcher Ever Had. New York: Smithsonian, 2010.

Asinof, Eliot. *Eight Men Out: The Black Sox and the 1919 World Series.* New York: Holt Rinehart and Winston, 1963.

Bogen, Gil. *Tinker and Evers and Chance: A Triple Biography.* Jefferson, NC: McFarland, 2003.

Dewey, Donald, and Nicholas Acocella. *The Black Prince of Baseball: Hal Chase and the Mythology of the Game.* Wilmington, DE: Sports Media, 2004.

Evers, John J. *How to Play Second Base.* New York: American Sports, 1920.

Evers, John J., and Hugh S. Fullerton. *Touching Second: The Science of Baseball.* Chicago: Reilly & Britton, 1910; reprint, Jefferson, NC: McFarland, 2004.

Gershman, Michael. *Diamonds: The Evolution of the Ballpark.* New York: Houghton Mifflin, 1993.

Golenbock, Peter. *Wrigleyville: A Magical History Tour of the Chicago Cubs.* New York: St. Martin's Griffin, 1999.

Leventhal. Josh. *Take Me Out to the Ballpark: An Illustrated Tour of Baseball Parks Past and Present.* New York: Black Dog and Leventhal, 2006.

Macht, Norman L. *Connie Mack and the Early Years of Baseball.* Lincoln, NE: University of Nebraska Press, 2007.

Maranville, Walter "Rabbit." *Run, Rabbit, Run.* Cleveland, OH: Society for American Baseball Research, 1991.

Murphy, Cait. *Crazy '08: How a Cast of Cranks, Rogues, Boneheads and Magnates Created the Greatest Year in Baseball History.* New York: Smithsonian, 2008.

Nemec, David. *Major League Baseball Profiles, 1871–1900,* Volume 1: *The Ballplayers Who Built the Game.* Lincoln, NE: Bison Books, 2011.

___. *Major League Baseball Profiles, 1871–1900,* Volume 2: *The Hall of Famers and Memorable Personalities That Shaped the Game.* Lincoln, NE: Bison Books, 2011.

Neyer, Rob. *Rob Neyer's Big Book of Baseball Legends: The Truth, the Lies, and Everything Else.* New York: Touchstone, 2008.

Pietrusza, David. *Major Leagues: The Formation, Sometimes Absorption and Mostly Inevitable Demise of 18 Professional Baseball Organizations.* Jefferson, NC: McFarland, 1991.

Regalado, Samuel O. *Viva Baseball: Latin Major Leaguers and Their Special Hunger.* Champaign, IL: University of Illinois Press, 1998.

Ritter, Lawrence. *The Glory of Their Times: The Story of the Early Days of Baseball by the Men Who Played It.* New York: Macmillan, 1966.

Roberts, Randy, and Carson Cunningham. *Before The Curse: The Chicago Cubs Glory Years, 1870–1945.* Champaign, IL: University of Illinois Press, 2012.

Seymour, Harold, and Dorothy Seymour Mills. *Baseball: The Early Years.* New York: Oxford University Press, 1960.

___. *Baseball: The Golden Age.* New York: Oxford University Press, 1971.

Snelling, Dennis. *The Greatest Minor League: A History of the Pacific Coast League, 1903–1957.* Jefferson, NC: McFarland, 2012.

Vitti, Jim. *Cubs on Catalina: A Scrapbook Full of Memories About a 30-Year Love Affair Between One of Baseball's Classic Teams and California's Most Fanciful Isle.* Bay City, CA: Settefrati Press, 2003.

Weisberger, Bernard A. *When Chicago Ruled Baseball: The Cubs-White Sox World Series of 1906.* New York: William Morrow, 2007.

Wilson, Nick C. *Early Latino Ballplayers in the United States: Major, Minor and Negro Leagues, 1901–1949.* Jefferson, NC: McFarland, 2005.

Newspapers/Publications

Albany Knickerbocker
Amsterdam Evening Recorder
Baseball Digest
Baseball Magazine
Boston Evening Transcript
Boston Globe
Brooklyn Daily Eagle
Brooklyn Standard Union
Chicago Tribune
Los Angeles Herald
Los Angeles Times
New York Evening Tribune
New York Herald
New York Sun
New York Times
New York World
Philadelphia Evening Ledger
Pittsburgh Post-Gazette
Pittsburgh Press
Reach-Spalding Baseball Guides
Rochester Democrat
St. Louis Post-Dispatch
San Francisco Call
San Francisco Chronicle
San Francisco Examiner
Schenectady Gazette
Sporting Life
The Sporting News
Syracuse Journal
Troy Budget
Troy Times

Index

Numbers in *bold italics* indicate pages with photographs.